What people are saying about *Beyond Strategic Vision* . . .

"Success in a highly competitive world requires focus and direction. This book will benefit any organization. It provides a template for process-driven thinking which will create bottom-line results."—**Stuart Levine**, CEO, Stuart Levine & Associates LLC, coauthor, *The Leader in You*

"Hoshin planning has long been recognized as the premier tool in developing a competitive and successful organization. ***Beyond Strategic Vision*** develops a hands on practical approach to this process. The authors have meticulously collected tools they have seen work, tools which are woven into the Hoshin process in a way that hands the implementor the proper instrument at just the right time."—**Pete Weber**, VP, TQM Implementation, Aerojet General Co.

"Corporations need vision, but just having a vision is not enough. A vision needs to be translated into action, in a way that produces the desired results. Hoshin Planning is that way. Its message has been artfully and practically put into book-form by Ellen Domb and Michael Cowley. ***Beyond Strategic Vision*** represents far more than just knowledge. It is a step-by-step guide, based on the authors' experiences with some of the best organizations in the world. This is a MUST-READ and MUST-HAVE for those executives—and their corporate staffs—who want to make their strategic vision happen."—**James F. Kowalick**, President, Renaissance Leadership Institute

"Major organizational change requires constancy of purpose not only from year to year but throughout the organization. The authors present a clear, straight forward description of the Hoshin planning process, which will assist any organization in accomplishing this deployment and alignment requirement."—**Joseph W. Martinelli**, President (retired), Chevron Pipeline Company

"If you recognize the value of planning, or even just want to decide if it is worth your time, this book is a must read. In plain and practical language you will learn how to apply some basic and practical techniques that can be implemented in a straight forward manner to any size business."—**Bert Frydman**, Service Policy And Quality Vice President, Pacific Bell

Butterworth-Heinemann Business Books . . . for Transforming Business

Beyond Strategic Vision: Effective Corporate Action with Hoshin Planning
Michael Cowley and Ellen Domb, 0-7506-9843-8

Beyond Time Management: Business with Purpose
Robert A. Wright, 0-7506-9799-7

Breakdown of Hierarchy: Communicating in the Evolving Workplace, The
Eugene Marlow and Patricia O'Connor Wilson, 0-7056-9746-6

Business and the Feminine Principle: The Untapped Resource
Carol R. Frenier, 0-7506-9829-2

Cultivating Common Ground: Releasing the Power of Relationships at Work
Daniel S. Hanson, 0-7506-9832-2

Fifth Generation Management: Co-creating Through Virtual Enterprising, Dynamic Teaming, and Knowledge Networking, Revised Edition
Charles M. Savage, 0-7506-9701-6

Flight of the Phoenix: Soaring to Success in the 21st Century
John Whiteside and Sandra Egli, 0-7506-9798-9

Getting a Grip on Tomorrow: Your Guide to Survival and Success in the Changed World of Work
Mike Johnson, 0-7506-9758-X

Innovation Strategy for the Knowledge Economy: The Ken Awakening
Debra M. Amidon, 0-7506-9841-1

Intelligence Advantage: Organizing for Complexity, The
Michael D. McMaster, 0-7506-9792-X

Knowledge Evolution: Expanding Organizational Intelligence, The
Verna Allee, 0-7506-9842-X

Leadership in a Challenging World: A Sacred Journey
Barbara Shipka, 0-7506-9750-4

Beyond Strategic Vision

Beyond Strategic Vision

Effective Corporate Action with Hoshin Planning

Michael Cowley
and
Ellen Domb

Butterworth-Heinemann
Boston   Oxford   Johannesburg   Melbourne   New Delhi   Singapore

Butterworth-Heinemann

 A member of the Reed Elsevier group

Library of Congress Cataloging-in-Publication Data
Cowley, Michael, 1937–
    Beyond strategic vision: effective corporate action with Hoshin
planning / Michael Cowley and Ellen Domb.
      p.   cm.
    Includes bibliographical references and index.
    ISBN 0-7506-9843-8 (pbk. : alk. paper)
    1. Strategic planning.   I. Domb, Ellen.   II. Title.
HD 30.28.C697   1997
658.4'012—dc21   96-46662
                         CIP

British Library Cataloguing-in-Publication Data
A catalogue record for this book is available from the British Library.

The publisher offers special discounts on bulk orders of this book.
For information, please contact:
Manager of Special Sales
Butterworth–Heinemann
313 Washington Street
Newton, MA 02158–1626
Tel: 617-928-2500
Fax: 617-928-2620

For information on all Business Books available, contact our World Wide Web
home page at: http://www.bh.com/bb

10 9 8 7 6 5 4 3 2 1

Printed in the United States of America

Table of Contents

Acknowledgments

We are indebted to many of our clients, and to present and former colleagues, for help with this book and support during its creation:

David DeFeyter, Power City Electric

Maarten Kalisvaart, Jim Leising, and Lisa Zuegel, Hewlett-Packard

Special thanks to Craig Walter, former Director of Quality for the Hewlett-Packard Company, for introducing one of us (MC) to Hoshin Planning.

Claire and Bruce Pickering, The Silhouette Shop

Gerry Dillingham and Mike Maslak, CEO, North Island Federal Credit Union

Herb Moniz, City Manager, The City of San Ramon

Joe Schaeffer, Vice President, Business Development, Patelco Credit Union

James Davis, Owner, AutoExcellence

Rob Kessler, Superintendent, San Ramon Valley Unified School District

Our colleagues at GOAL/QPC: Casey Collett, Cha Nakui, Joe Colletti, Dave Ridgeway, Bill Montgomery, Bob King, Chris Dillon, Sue Tucker, Lisa Boivert, and Stan Marsh

And, finally, to our families, especially Bill Domb and Sharon Cowley, thanks for your patience and understanding.

Chapter 1

Introduction: What Is Planning and Why Do We Do It?

O ur reasons for writing this book are several:

- Both authors have been in the business of developing and using planning methods as part of their management jobs. We are experienced practitioners who can share best (and worst) planning methods and practices with our readers, from our own practical experience.
- For the last 5 years we have both been consultants in and facilitators of planning for a wide variety of clients. We have learned that effective planning at several levels is the common denominator for success in any effort to effect *change* in an organization. It is the primary *enabler* of the successful deployment of concepts like Total Quality Management (TQM) and Process Reengineering. Indeed, lack of integration of TQM and Reengineering with a sound business strategy has resulted in disappointment, or even failure, for these efforts in many companies.
- We also believe that planning is the most important activity that managers do. It is *how* they manage. Our observation is that Strategic and Operational planning are seen as obligatory, onerous activities. Our hope is that this book will change this perception to one in which managers see planning as their most powerful agent and mechanism for setting and meeting ambitious and exciting goals for the organization.
- Finally, we have both found that a specific planning system, Hoshin, is dramatically superior to any of the other systems we have encountered. In the course of our practical and consulting work, we have refined this system to a point where we feel it is appropriate to share it with a wider audience. Hoshin is a system that was developed in Japan in the 1960s

1

and is a derivative of Management By Objectives (MBO). Having recognized the power of this system, we have modified it to fit the culture of North American and European organizations.

This book is intended to be a "how-to" guide to the Hoshin method for executives, managers, and any other professionals who must plan as part of their normal job. A few comments and definitions regarding the purposes for planning in modern organizations are in order before we begin.

WHAT IS PLANNING?

The word "planning" evokes many different ideas in different people, so we need to be clear about what we mean in this book. Webster defines planning as follows:

> to devise a scheme for doing, making, or arranging.

Ackoff (1970) defines planning as:

> the design of a desired future and of effective ways of bringing it about.

In our own consulting work, we have used this definition:

> Planning consists of defining the important objectives an organization needs to achieve and determining *how* it plans to achieve them.

The word "planning" is sometimes used to describe the process of scheduling work through, say, a machine shop. We will not be covering that usage in our book, but will be focusing on what most people nowadays refer to as *Strategic Planning* and *Operational* or *Business Planning*.

THE HOSHIN PLANNING SYSTEM INCLUDES "DOING" AND "REVIEW"

While the forgoing definitions are a good starting point, our focus in this book will be on the use of Hoshin as a Planning System. This system includes the implementation, or the *doing*, of what is planned, as well as the review of what is done. The entire process is "closed loop," that is, one where corrections to the plan can be applied based on the outcomes.

This definition is probably different from most readers' conception of planning, in which it is perhaps more common to imagine that *doing* the plan is a separate issue from *developing* the plan. It is our opinion that this is the cause of many of the problems with planning. Further, we are going to make the assertion that plans are best made by the doers, not by a separate group of planners. There will be more on this subject in the next chapter, "Problems with Planning."

PURPOSES AND TYPES OF PLANNING

Strategic Planning

The purpose of strategic planning is:

> To set the direction of the organization to improve its prospects for long-term survival and prosperity.

Strategic planning focuses on the broadest issues of the business or organization, usually over a relatively long time horizon, typically anywhere from 1 to 10 years. The kinds of issues that strategic planning encompasses are: "What businesses do we want to be in?"; "What are our long-term objectives for growth and profitability, and what must we do to achieve these objectives?"; "What is our long-range product strategy?"; "Should we acquire other companies?"; "Do we have the right set of core competencies?"; "What effect will trends in technology, social structure, politics, regulatory environment, local and global economy, and other areas, have on our future success, or even survival?" And so forth.

Operational Planning

For most organizations, Operational Planning deals with the tactical details of how a business is to be run over a relatively short time frame, typically a year. It is frequently done in the context of having already created a Strategic Plan, and ideally the Operational Plan will reflect important decisions made as part of the Strategic Plan. The elements of an operational plan usually include forecasts of Revenues, Profits, and Cash Flow, as well as detailed plans for employee headcount, operating budgets, project plans, promotional activities, manufacturing capacity, and the like. The focus tends to be financial for most Operational Plans.

Project Planning

Almost all businesses and organizations have projects as part of the system for accomplishing specific objectives, and these can range from the development of a new product, to the construction of a new building, or the installation of a new computer system. Planning and management systems for projects are usually oriented toward the detailed identification and sequencing of all the tasks required to complete the project, and frequently include provisions to predict and track cost and on-time completion of all these tasks. The Implementation Plan phase of Hoshin described in Chapter 11, and the tools and examples of Chapter 13, provide good methods for Project Planning. Excellent software also exists for this purpose, and we recommend its use in conjunction with Hoshin for the planning and implementation of projects.

Financial Plans

Almost all businesses and organizations have financial plans, which are derivatives of the Operational and Strategic Plans. There are various purposes, but the most important are usually that the managers need to make financial projections and commitments to the shareholders or owners of the business or organization, and need to predict cash flow for the purpose of adequately funding the company's activities. Normally, operational and project plans are iterated until satisfactory financial performance is predicted.

The Hoshin system, the subject of this book, applies to all types of planning (strategic, operational, project, financial, and so on), but our emphasis will be on strategic and operational planning.

PLANNING AND THE PDCA CYCLE

The concept of a "closed loop" planning process had its start, for practical purposes, with the teachings of Deming and Juran in Japan in the 1950s. Deming popularized the "Plan Do Check Act" (PDCA) cycle for solving problems and improving processes, and as a result it is widely known as the Deming Cycle. It was originally conceived as the Learning Cycle by John Dewey, the noted early twentieth-century educator, and then adapted by Walter Shewhart of Bell Telephone Laboratories as the Improvement Cycle. We will find that both views, learning and improvement, are important. We will frequently invoke the PDCA cycle, as it is most frequently called, as the logical basis or underpinning of Hoshin Planning.

A simple description of the PDCA cycle is shown in Figure 1.1 (Soin 1992, pp. 96–97). The essential elements are:

1. *Plan*. Determine goals to be achieved and methods to reach them.
2. *Do*. Implement the methods.
3. *Check*. Examine the results: was the goal achieved? Was the improvement hypothesis validated?
4. *Act*. If the goals were achieved, adopt the new methods permanently. If not, determine the cause of failure and return to Plan. Continue this cycle until no more improvement or progress is required.

For some readers, thinking of planning as a means of improvement may be new. But, in fact, a sound plan is the best opportunity the management of an organization has for achieving dramatic improvement in business results.

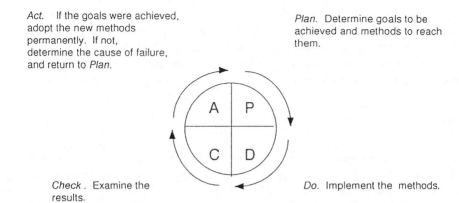

Act. If the goals were achieved, adopt the new methods permanently. If not, determine the cause of failure, and return to *Plan.*

Plan. Determine goals to be achieved and methods to reach them.

Check . Examine the results.

Do. Implement the methods.

Figure 1.1 The PDCA Cycle (Sometimes referred to as the Deming Cycle.) (Soin 1992)

We will see presently that Hoshin is really the application of the PDCA cycle to the regime of planning. Hoshin is a Management System for determining the appropriate course of action for an organization and effectively accomplishing the relevant actions and results.

OBJECTIVES, STRATEGIES, AND HIERARCHY OF PURPOSE

In any planning, especially strategic planning, it is vitally important to select the "right" objectives! In fact, some would insist that this is the primary role of strategic planning.

In addition to setting the "right" objectives, part of the job of planning is to determine the best means of achieving the objectives and, further, to facilitate effective implementation and review of the means as the plan is executed. In order to select the "right" objectives, the planners must, among other things, do their work in the context of the higher-order purposes of the organization. An organization's higher-order purposes will be very specific to its own situation, including the needs and desires of its owners and/or stakeholders (members, in the case of a membership organization; congregation, in the case of churches; and so on).

Examples of higher-order purposes might include "make the owners wealthy," "provide employment for the population of our town," and "provide the best products and services to society." Objectives such as "become profitable in 1997," or "introduce four new products next year," rather than being taken simply as objectives in their own right, need to be viewed as means of achieving the higher-order objectives of the organization in the long-term. Or, in other words, they can be called, quite correctly, strategies for achieving these higher-order objectives. What of the higher-order objectives themselves? Are they strategies for achieving yet higher-order objectives? Yes, probably. And the way to determine what these are is to ask "why?" For example, Why do we want to provide jobs? While this may seem tedious, it is vitally important to develop this context in order to develop the strategic plan effectively. Among other things, the process of asking "why" begins to uncover the true values of the organization.

WHY PLAN?

As we will discuss in more detail in the next chapter, in many organizations planning is everyone's "unfavorite" activity. Can we provide a rationale to support planning that most people can buy into? Perhaps we can; refer to Figure 1.2, which we call the "Highway" or "Road" metaphor for planning.

The metaphor is rich with meaning. First, we need to recognize that, in its most rudimentary form, planning is designed to help us determine how to achieve a desired new state, or objective. For example, you want to learn how to swim. Your present situation, referring to Figure 1.2, is that you lack this skill, and your desired Future State, or Destination, is that you possess it. It is part of your Vision of yourself in the future. Your plan to achieve the

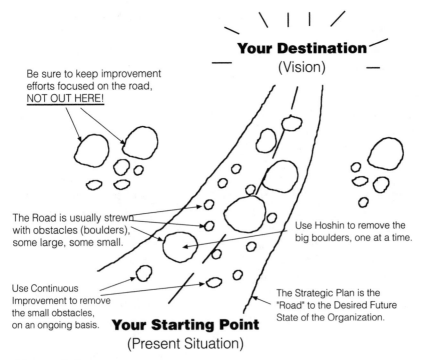

Figure 1.2 The "Road" Metaphor for Planning (Cowley & Associates 1995)

future state is the road leading from your present situation to the desired Future. The boulders are the obstacles or tasks you have to overcome on your journey. The big ones might be "Overcome my fear of the water," or "Take swimming lessons." Some of the small ones might be "Purchase a swim suit"and "Schedule an hour three times a week for this activity."

There are lots of tempting activities off the road, too. For example, "Build a swimming pool" might seem at first like a good idea, but with further thought, it's clear that it is not necessary to achieve the objective of learning to swim. Indeed, it is an expensive and possibly serious distraction from your ultimate purpose. (Although it might be part of a broader vision of how you would like to see yourself in the future.)

No matter how simple or complex an activity might be, the plan is the map of how we expect to get to the desired future state of the activity. It is quite common for important activities, such as businesses, to have neither a concept of the desired future state of the business, nor a plan, beyond the short time frame of an operational plan. Some small businesses may not even have much in the way of a short term operational plan. But if the owners or managers of such businesses were to start off on an automobile trip of several weeks, they wouldn't think of leaving without a map, or without some analysis of how much money they needed, what clothes and recreational equipment to bring, and so forth. Our objective in writing this book is to demonstrate that planning is both valuable enough, and simple enough, that it can be undertaken by any organization that wishes to have the map, and will profoundly enhance its effectiveness in a relatively short time.

STRATEGIC THINKING AND ORGANIZATIONAL LEARNING

Mintzberg has summed up his thinking about Strategic Planning in his article (1994, pp. 107–114) by remarking that it ought to contain two elements:

1. Strategic Thinking, where managers *synthesize* their strategic vision, using intuition and creativity. The outcome is "an integrated perspective of the enterprise, a . . . vision of direction."
2. Conversion of the Vision into actionable steps; "realization" of the vision.

A very important point, also articulated by Mintzberg, in his book, (1994, pp. 209–210) and championed by Senge (1990, pp. 187–188), is that Strategic Planning should contain a component called *Strategic Learning*. That is, recognizing that the future is highly uncertain and usually unpredictable, the sophisticated organization takes the position that as long as it has the broad directions defined in its Vision (Strategic Intent), every unexpected turn of events is an opportunity to learn and adapt. Mintzberg believes that the Japanese, over the last three decades, have tended to be more Strategic Learners rather than Strategic Planners. We agree, and would assert further that this is one of the basic cornerstones of Hoshin.

We worked with a company that operates a group of nursing homes and assisted-living residences. The company leaders said that they did not want strategic planning, because it would prevent them from flexibly responding to targets of opportunity. After considerable discussion, we found out that they feared a strategic plan would require them to take predetermined steps instead of the rapid moves that had been the hallmark of their success.

They found that they already had a strategic plan, to expand through acquisition of targets of opportunity, but that they had never analyzed the competencies needed to execute that strategy well. Improvements in cash-flow management and capital management (so that credit would be available whenever an opportunity arose), and in availability of multi-disciplined technical staff (so that acquisitions that were not providing good care could be turned around quickly), were very quickly identified as the tactics to support the acquisition strategy.

An additional point that perhaps escapes present-day strategic planners is that one of the important purposes of strategic planning, even in an organization that does not face a survival threat, is to find productive and high-leverage directions in which to *stretch* the organization, that is, to force it to renew and reinvent itself in order to preserve its competitive vitality and preempt threatening moves by competitors. As Welch puts it, "A stretch atmosphere . . . asks . . . how good can you be?" (1994; see also Hamel and Prahalad 1993). This view of strategic planning encourages the management team to confront "gaps" in performance and capability that stand in the way of achieving an exciting and valuable Strategic Vision, and to focus the organization on closing these gaps. Hoshin is very much directed at this view of strategic planning, and the most important "gaps" are candidates for "breakthrough" performance improvement.

So, returning to the "Road" metaphor of Figure 1.2, we would assert that the "Why" of planning is simple: Organizations (and individuals, for that matter) need to have a shared definition of *where* they are going (The Vision) and *what they need to do* to get there (The Road and the "rocks"). It is equally important to agree on what will *not* be done to achieve the Vision (The tempting boulders and rocks that lie off the "Road"). The process of planning should provide this complete "map." Furthermore, the process should provide for "rerouting" the road if the chosen path clearly isn't working, and make clear which activities are *strategic* (usually the big "boulders") and which are *tactical* (the small rocks). In Chapter 2 we will discuss some of the reasons that organizations often do not plan effectively, or don't plan at all.

SUMMARY

The management of an organization, whether it be large or small, or a sub-unit of a larger entity, has as one of its principal responsibilities to set the direction of the organization for the future. The "future," for strategic planning purposes, is typically three to five years, but it can be much shorter or much longer, depending on circumstances.

The most effective way to set the future direction is to develop a *shared vision* of what the organization will be in the future, contrast it to the way the organization is *now*, and then create a plan for bridging the gap, or the Strategic Plan. This concept is illustrated in Figure 1.2, the "Road" or "Highway" metaphor for Hoshin. Without a Strategic Plan, the efforts of individuals and departments in the organization are more likely to be "off the highway," and thus have little or no overall impact on achieving the organization's long-range goals. This is one of the reasons "Total Quality Management" and "Business Process Reengineering" efforts have failed in many organizations: they lacked strategic focus.

To carry the "highway" metaphor a step further, the *focus* and *alignment* of the organization is needed to move the large obstacles or opportunities. These large "boulders" are the Hoshin objectives. If the organization tries to move several at the same time, chances are that much energy will be expended, and the boulders will move little, if at all. The focus and alignment of everyone in the organization pushing on one at a time is needed. Further, the smaller obstacles can be moved by local continuous improvement efforts, and do not need the focus of the entire organization; what is important, however, is that these efforts are aligned with the Strategic Plan, that is, they are confined to the "highway."

REFERENCES

Ackoff, R.L. *A Concept of Corporate Planning*. New York: Wiley, 1970.

Hamel, Gary and Prahalad, C.K. "Strategy as Stretch and Leverage." *Harvard Business Review*, March/April 1993, pp. 75–84.

Mintzberg, Henry. "The Fall and Rise of Strategic Planning." *Harvard Business Review*, January/February 1994, pp. 107–114.

———. *The Rise and Fall of Strategic Planning*. New York: Free Press, Macmillan, 1994.

Senge, Peter M. *The Fifth Discipline*. New York: Doubleday, 1990.

Soin, Sarv Singh. *Total Quality Control Essentials*. McGraw-Hill, 1992.

Welch, Jack, CEO. *General Electric 1994 Annual Report*.

Chapter 2

Problems with Planning

Strategic Planning, the original focus of Hoshin, has earned itself a bad reputation among some Western managers, principally because it has become perceived as a rigid, formal, non-value-added activity in many organizations (Mintzberg 1994). These organizations have forgotten that "plans are nothing; planning is everything," a remark attributed to Eisenhower. Eisenhower's remark means that the important product is not the plan itself, but the *ongoing process* of planning.

Mintzberg has written eloquently of the foibles of modern Strategic Planning in his recent book, *The Rise and Fall of Strategic Planning* (1994), but in the end holds out hope that once again it will begin to fill the role for which it was originally intended: to provide a flexible, ongoing, adaptive framework for organizations to realize their Strategic Intent (Vision).

Some of the serious problems we've seen in our own work are as follows:

1. Forecasts or predictions made by managers are frequently unrealistic, but no mechanism exists in the planning process to recognize gaps between reality and prediction, nor are changes made in the plan and targeted outcomes. This tends to lead to disillusionment with the planning process. Even Operational Planning, with its typically short time-frame, is fraught with the risk that *the future really can't be predicted with certainty,* even in the short run. This implies that Operational Planning needs to have a "fall back position" built into it ("What if?"), and that Strategic Planning needs to focus more on competencies and capabilities than on specific outcomes.

2. Goals are set arbitrarily, sometimes without a clear relationship to *need,* or *means* or *feasibility.* This is frequently the result of lack of profound knowledge of the organization's business, or failure to understand the organization as a system, or both. This creates cynicism in managers and employees.

3. A related problem is the *failure to focus* on only a few high-leverage goals; it is a natural tendency to commit the organization to more than it can possibly accomplish. The result is usually that not much progress gets made on any of the goals. This creates stress and discourages managers and employees. It is one of the most common problems we see in organizations.

4. It is common for organizations to *select the wrong goals*. Without a coherent system for relating the higher-order goals of the organization to operational activities, it is easy to do the "wrong" thing and to engage major parts of the organization in low-payback, or even counterproductive, activities. Dr. W. Edwards Deming specified, "Eliminate Management by Objectives. Substitute leadership," as one of his fourteen principles for organizational transformation (1986). The story told about the origin of this principle is that in the late 1970s, Dr. Deming visited a very large company and was told that the reason they needed his help was that the previous year all twenty-two vice presidents had each achieved his objectives, but the company had lost $4 billion! Management by Objectives was not a bad process—using it without a system model of the organization was the problem.

5. There is no "Shared Vision" of the organization's future. The management may know where the organization is going, but no one else does. This tends to lead to people working in an uninspired and uncoordinated manner, or even to working at cross purposes.

6. Planned activities have not been carefully designed to have a strong chance of meeting the goals or targets. The goals then become "wishes." This leads to failure and cynicism.

7. Planned activities are not carefully reviewed on an ongoing basis. This tends to create the impression that the plans are not taken seriously by management. Deviations from the plan and intended results are not systematically identified, and corrective action, if any, is ineffective. Most importantly, systematic weaknesses in the plan and planning process are not recognized and corrected.

8. Plans and/or activities are reviewed, but the process is punitive. This generates an atmosphere of fear, one in which the real facts are not likely to be honestly reported. As a result, the organization fails to "learn." Aggressive planning should lead to occasional, perhaps even frequent, "failure." Innovation, by its very nature, is bound to produce both successes and failures. Sometimes, "failure is the best teacher," and the enlightened management team has the mind-set that good strategic plans should contain a component of experimentation.

9. Many management teams simply have not learned to do effective planning. Planning that is attempted falls far short of their expectations, and there is natural reluctance to repeat the process.

10.   It is frequently not recognized that Strategic Planning is quite different from Operational Planning. The former requires analysis and synthesis, whereas the latter tends to rely mostly on analysis. Many teams embark on Strategic Planning exercises using the methodologies of Operational Planning (analysis) and are disappointed that very little in the way of developing creative new strategies gets accomplished.

11.   Planning is regarded as an event rather than an ongoing process. Remember Eisenhower's remark. The purpose of planning is to create a planning mind-set more than to deliver a plan.

12.   Planning is often done in the absence of adequate factual data about the important factors of planning, especially customer requirements and satisfaction levels. There are frequently no measures of important success factors, such as business processes.

13.   Sometimes the reverse of planning without adequate data occurs, and data about the past is over-analyzed in an effort to predict or influence the future.

14.   Planning is done by a separate planning department; the plans are then implemented by one or more divisions or functional departments. This creates a major motivation problem for most organizations and people, who, for a variety of reasons, prefer to plan their own destiny. "Ownership" for the successful implementation of the plan is not strongly felt by either planners or doers in this case.

Some additional barriers to effective planning that are more related to the thought processes and behaviors of managers are the following:

1. The failure of management teams to admit and confront poor business results. This leads to a never-ending "spiral" of poor results, due to failure to identify and address root-cause issues. Sometimes this is a result of management failing to identify and agree upon the Critical Measures of Success. No planning method can help much until these issues are addressed.
2. Many management teams are reluctant to take inventory of organizational strengths and weaknesses. The reality of business in today's environment is that the typical organization must be able to do many things well in order to survive, and most things well, and some brilliantly, in order to lead.
3. As organizations grow bigger, there is a tendency to continue to use methods that worked well when the enterprise was small, such as informal systems, or "seat of the pants" management. This leads to chaos as the organization grows. As organizations get larger, there is more need to formalize business processes and systems, and to perfect and manage them in order to satisfy customers consistently and meet organization needs.

4. Another frequent mistake as organizations grow is to try to plan and manage financial outcomes without adequate recognition that these outcomes can only be as good as the business processes that deliver them.

DISCUSSION

Both of the authors work as management consultants. The most frequent reason we are retained by our clients is to help them achieve better business results. While we find a myriad of problems preventing good performance, a common denominator in almost all organizations with performance problems is lack of an effective, or for that matter, *any* planning process. While it is sometimes necessary to address serious operational problems immediately, we always try to take the approach of asking why the operational problems occurred in the first place. The reasons are frequently weaknesses in planning, or simply failure to plan. Our argument is that the planning system needs to be addressed or additional serious operational problems are bound to occur, and many of the same problems will occur over and over again.

REFERENCES

Deming, W.E. *Out of the Crisis*. Cambridge, MA: MIT Press, 1986.

Mintzberg, Henry. "The Fall and Rise of Strategic Planning." *Harvard Business Review*. January/February 1994, pp. 107–114.

——. *The Rise and Fall of Strategic Planning*. New York: Free Press, Macmillan, 1994.

Chapter 3

Hoshin Planning Overview

A legitimate question in the face of the issues we discussed in the last chapter, and in view of recent skepticism about the value of strategic planning, is "Is there a Planning Method that solves or avoids these problems?" We believe there is, and the method is Hoshin. Our personal experience with the Hoshin system, and that of our clients, has been that:

- It instills *commitment* to worthy goals in all members of the organization.
- It *focuses* the efforts of the organization on these high-leverage goals, while depriving "the trivial many" of any more effort than they deserve.
- It serves as the best communication vehicle the organization possesses.
- It becomes the focal point for Organization Learning.
- It gets things done faster and better.
- It sets a common direction for the organization.
- It is the path to major improvement in the organization, through the identification of appropriate "stretch" goals.
- It is very flexible, thereby avoiding one of the biggest obstacles to effective planning: the fact that the future environment generally is different from what was imagined when the original plans were created.

HOSHIN AS THE ORGANIZATION'S INTEGRATED PLANNING SYSTEM

We've mentioned that Hoshin can be used for the Organization's Operational as well as Strategic Planning. Let us elaborate on this and put forward the argument that the best planning system is the merging of the two.

Effective Strategic Planning is more about *synthesis* than *analysis*. It is more important to identify creative possibilities for future action than it is to analyze the effects of such actions. This is because when all is said and done, it is difficult to predict the future, let alone analyze it. In many cases, it is as important to develop the basis for sound strategic thinking as it is to develop concrete plans. The development of strategic thinking tends to lead to the development of core competencies and capabilities in the company of the future (such as organizational learning) that allow it to respond quickly and effectively to changes in the business environment. Strategic Planning systems of the future must be flexible and adaptable, allowing continuous improvisation, synthesis, and creativity. While Strategic Planning is the process where intuition and instincts play a major role, we want to stress that it is *not* a substitute for profound knowledge of your business. Rather, it should be viewed as a *framework* for integrating this knowledge, and a way of systematizing your use of the knowledge into truly strategic thinking. Hoshin goes further, in harnessing the abilities of all employees to support the chosen Strategic Direction. The interesting thing is that once the Strategic Intent of the organization is achieved, most organizations find that it is all the more important to improve the systems by which day to day results are achieved—which leads us to operational planning.

Operational Planning generally spans a shorter time-frame, typically one year, and can therefore be more deterministic than Strategic Planning and can benefit from careful analysis of the effects of the proposed actions. Nevertheless, since the outcome of the Operational Plan will still depend greatly on more-or-less accurate predictions of the future, there is still a great need for flexibility and adaptation.

An ideal planning system would provide the flexibility required by both Strategic and Operational Planning, and further, would integrate the two. Integration is important for several reasons: (1) There will be numerous opportunities for leveraging the components of both plans; (2) The components of both plans can be at cross-purposes, unless there is an overt effort to integrate them; (3) The Strategic and Operational Plans usually compete for resources, and intelligent tradeoffs will need to be made.

"Integrated planning" is the common sense "reengineering" of the hodgepodge of planning systems some companies have built up. Thanks to separate systems for research planning, capital equipment planning, human resource planning, and operational budgeting, one team in a large aerospace company had six Ph.D.'s and four technicians wait six months, while $600,000 of new laboratory equipment sat in a warehouse, because there was no budget for $6,000 to install power in the room that was to become the laboratory. This story itself is sad enough, but when we tell it in public seminars, at least one member of the audience can top it with her own story of disintegrated planning.

Hoshin meets the requirements of an "ideal" integrated system. The purpose of this chapter is to describe for the reader what this unique planning system is all about and where it came from. In Chapter 4 we will begin the step by step description of implementing the Hoshin system.

The remainder of the chapter is devoted to:

- A brief history of Hoshin.
- An overview of what Hoshin is and how it works.

THE HISTORY OF HOSHIN AND RELATED DEVELOPMENTS

Hoshin is a planning technique developed in Japan in the 1960s. It is also known as Policy Deployment and Management by Policy. More recently, the phrase "Management by Planning" was coined by Intel (Johnson and Daniel 1993).

Hoshin grew out of the realization on the part of Japanese managers that they needed a more robust and effective form of planning to achieve major improvements and strategic changes of direction in their organizations, and that the quality improvement tools and methods in use at that time were inadequate for this purpose. They used MBO (Management by Objectives) as a point of departure and added their own contributions in the area of participative management practices. To give credit where it is due, many of the basic concepts of Hoshin were published by Juran in his book *Managerial Breakthrough* (1964), but apparently have gone largely unnoticed in the Western business world.

The elements of Total Quality Control (TQC), in particular the Plan-Do-Check-Act (PDCA) cycle (see Chapter 1), were incorporated from the beginning in Hoshin, but an important set of new techniques was added in the 1970s, now known most commonly as the "Seven New Tools." This designation was used to distinguish them from the "Seven Basic Tools" which were by then in widespread use as the "toolset" for problem-solving and process-improvement using the PDCA cycle in Japanese companies. Chapter 13 describes in detail how to use them, in an effort to keep the "how to" aspects of this book as self-contained as possible.

Hoshin was used to focus on areas where major strategic changes, or "breakthroughs," needed to be identified and achieved, and all the discretionary resources of the organization needed to be dedicated to reaching these few, important strategic objectives each year. "Hoshin," literally translated, means "shining metal," or "compass needle," to designate setting the strategic direction of the organization. The methods of Hoshin are used quite widely now in Japan for all levels of planning, but the focus is most commonly on the creation of an Annual Plan (or even a six-month plan) in the context of a long-term, for example three-to-five year, "Strategic Vision." The plan contains both strategic and operational components.

In the United States and Canada, a significant number of organizations have adopted Hoshin. Some of the better-known organizations are Intel,

Hewlett-Packard, Procter & Gamble, Ford, and Xerox. Florida Power and Light (FPL), although not a household name in the U.S., is prominent in the literature as the only American company to win the Japanese Deming Prize—aided in great measure by its effective use of Hoshin.

The "Seven New Tools" were published in 1979, in Japanese, and in 1988 the book was translated into English (Mizuno 1988). A much more readable text was published by Brassard in 1989. Several books now exist on Hoshin and Policy Deployment, and a few of these are listed at the end of the chapter (King 1989; Akao 1991; GOAL/QPC 1990; Collins and Huge 1993; Melum and Collett 1995).

In Japan, the phrase "Total Quality Control" has now largely been replaced by "Total Quality Management" (TQM), reflecting the incorporation of management activities into the Quality improvement programs in Japanese organizations. This phrase is now most widely used in the Western world as well.

OVERVIEW OF HOSHIN

Hoshin was originally developed as a form of strategic planning. It was intended to accomplish the following objectives:

- Identify important areas of necessity or opportunity for the organization to change or improve (Strategic Vision).
- Determine the most effective actions throughout the organization to accomplish these changes.
- Create a detailed plan to implement the actions.
- Provide a mechanism to review and correct the plan, where necessary, and to retain insights and lessons from the planning process.

Hoshin was originally intended to focus only on the very few breakthrough objectives that are regarded by the organization as most important to its future success or survival. However, its methodology can be used to do all of the organization's planning when an organization has become very skilled in its use. This has a distinct value in that it facilitates creating an integrated company-wide plan, as will be discussed later in the book (Chapter 7). Nevertheless, this is a good place to discuss the relationship between Hoshin and Daily Management.

Hoshin and Daily Management

The basic premise of Hoshin is that the organization will identify an area or two each year for special focus and will seek a major improvement in it. The focus and alignment of the organization on this objective will assure that significant progress will get made (that is, a "Breakthrough"). In the meantime, the business of the organization must run on a day-to-day basis, which we refer to as *Daily Management*. Daily Management is the focus of the organization's Operational Plan.

Even though not selected for Hoshin focus, this daily work can be improved in a gradual fashion on a local basis, in other words, not necessarily as part of an organization-wide effort.

The methods used for such improvements are a basic cornerstone of Total Quality Management, and are generally known as *Continuous Improvement*. The methodology of Continuous Improvement differs from the Breakthrough approach of Hoshin, but is a valuable adjunct to it. In fact, these efforts ideally should be closely coordinated with Hoshin. Table 3.1 contrasts the characteristics of Hoshin and Continuous Improvement.

Although the methodology of Hoshin was originally conceived for Breakthrough, many aspects of it can be used to facilitate Continuous Improvement and to manage the organization's efforts to meet its operational goals. The most effective use of both methods is in a coordinated, integrated plan, as we have discussed. We will show how to develop such a plan in Chapter 7.

Table 3.1 Hoshin And Continuous Improvement

Continuous improvement

- Many small ("incremental") improvements.
- Systematic improvement methodology (Mostly Analysis).
- Teams and individuals.
- Should eventually involve all employees.
- Should start with management.
- Tactical.
- Deals with existing systems and methods.
- Part of Daily Management (Process Management).

Breakthrough (Hoshin)

- Major improvement.
- Strategic.
- Focus on one or, at most, a few things: "Strategic Focus."
- Must usually be driven from the top.
- Different methodology from Continuous Improvement (Analysis and Synthesis).
- Will frequently require invention of new systems and methods.
- May only directly involve certain employees, but the entire organization is aligned to the Hoshin objectives.

The Benefits and Advantages of Hoshin

In the last chapter we discussed a number of common problems with planning; the Hoshin process addresses all of these issues. It has the following benefits and advantages:

- It is "Vision-Driven," in that it derives the organization's objectives from its Strategic Intent, or Vision.
- It provides a framework and methodology for the development of "breakthroughs" on a select few of the most important objectives.
- It aligns and focuses the organization on these most important objectives and facilitates development of the most effective means of achieving them. There is a direct link between highest-level objectives and lowest-level activities.
- There is "buy-in" (agreement and commitment) at every level.
- It provides a rigorously structured implementation system that is, at the same time, very flexible. Everyone in the organization has a role.
- It provides a review system that is intimately linked to implementation. Most steps are measured monthly, and all are measured at least four times a year. The review system provides timely corrective actions, an effective assessment of progress, and a method of capturing organizational learning about both the plan content and the planning process itself, so both can be systematically improved. And perhaps most important of all, from a practical standpoint, the review system is the point of departure for the last benefit.
- The process is adaptive and self-healing.

The Hoshin system is based on several important premises:

- The creative talents of the organization can be effectively brought to bear on its problems and opportunities through a structured team process, while at the same time capturing the best ideas and contributions of each individual. Creative methodologies such as those put forward by de Bono (1992) and Nadler and Hibino (1990) are perfectly compatible with Hoshin.
- The creative process needs to be capable of eliciting insights and ideas from all levels in the organization, not just management. The mechanisms for this process are "built-into" the Hoshin approach.
- Planning should be done by those who are expected to implement the plan, not by a special planning group. Mintzberg (1994), however, has made a convincing case that planning organizations can play an extremely vital role in this process, principally in the areas of providing objectivity, pertinent data, and analysis.
- Organizations can only focus strategically on a small number of "breakthrough" goals at one time. All other activity must be relegated to a status of routine ("Daily") management and incremental improvement during this time.

- Planning must be done using verifiable facts and data where possible and appropriate. This leads to the question of what data is needed for the planning process, all of which will be discussed at length in the detailed implementation chapters.
- Implementation and results must be routinely and rigorously measured. "What gets measured gets done."
- Strategic Planning should be treated as a process for facilitating strategic thinking. Strategic Thinking does not happen because we decide to schedule an event called "Strategic Planning"; on the contrary, such an event, if conceived in that fashion, can inhibit strategic thinking (Mintzberg 1994).
- The planning system itself can and must be systematically improved.

The Hoshin process is outlined in Figure 3.1. The elements will be explained in more detail in the next few paragraphs, but notice here the prominent role of the PDCA improvement cycle: improvement takes place in the process and content of the plan, both as the plan is being executed and when next year's plan is being created.

The Planning Team

The usual team for initiating strategic planning, or Hoshin, is the manager of a business or organization entity (corporation, division, section, department, and so on) and his or her staff, with subsequent involvement of all other managers and selected additional personnel in the organization. However, teams comprising much larger parts of the organization, or even the entire organization, can also be appropriate in some cases.

The important point here is that those who will be responsible for implementation must also be responsible for planning. It is appropriate for other individuals and organizations to play a supporting role. For example, in large corporations, it is common for operational entities to attend or charter special briefings by Corporate Research Laboratories staff on the state and trends of emerging technologies that might have an important role or bearing on the entity's future direction. The role of the Financial Community is frequently to keep the entities "honest" regarding their assessment of current performance and the practicality of future plans, at least from a financial point of view. Specific roles might be played by outside experts on important business or technical matters, usually for the purpose of broadening the knowledge and perspective of the management team who will ultimately be responsible for planning.

Regarding roles and responsibilities, it needs to be said that the "right" place for Hoshin to start is at the top of the organization. Hamel and Prahalad (1994) have made an excellent case for recognizing where linkages among the units of a large organization can add enormous value to its overall competitiveness. Hewlett-Packard's "HP = MC^2" concept is a model that recognizes the huge leverage to be realized by linking its core businesses

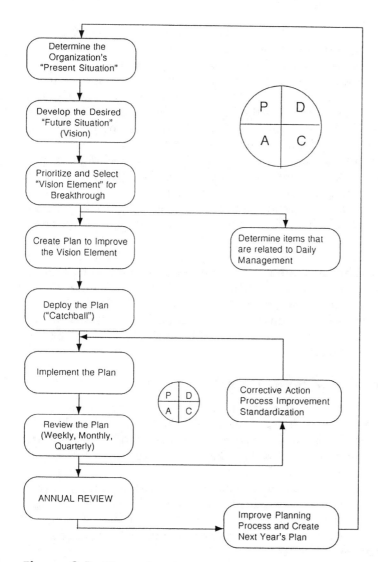

Figure 3.1 The Hoshin Planning Process (Cowley & Associates 1995)

along with Measurement, Computation, and Communication. Using Hoshin, or any other strategic planning system, only at the Business Unit level (or even lower), fails to identify and exploit such leverage, and, indeed, calls into question the added value of Corporate levels of management.

However, it should also be said that even at Hewlett-Packard (HP), Hoshin got its start in the U.S. around 1985 at the division level, three levels down from the CEO, and was effective enough that its value was quickly recognized. By 1988 it became an HP corporate standard, and, as we write this book, Hoshin is being used rigorously and effectively by HP's CEO and all levels of management worldwide.

On the subject of where to start the process, Senge (1990) cautions us that because organizations are really complex, sophisticated, highly interactive systems, it is dangerous to attempt the improvement or change of one of its sub-units without considering the impact on the whole organizational system. This is the downside of Hamel and Prahalad's observation, and again argues for starting Hoshin at the highest level.

If the opportunity exists, however, should you start Hoshin, or any change process, in one department or division of the organization? Tom Peters answers that question frequently in his newsletter (Peters 1994), where the question is raised by department managers who want to change their own departments in companies that are not ready or receptive to change. His reply, which matches the authors' experiences, is that for about eighteen months any one department can improve itself, both by continuous improvement and by breakthrough thinking, before it will find that future improvements require inter-departmental cooperation. By that time, the heroic manager will either be recognized as such, and asked to lead company-wide efforts, or will leave the company in frustration, but will have valuable change management skills for her or his next job. Refer to Ackoff (1981) for further discussion of this issue.

What, How, and "How are we Doing?"

The first three steps outlined in Figure 3.1 may be identified as a synthesis of the organization's Strategic Intent. Collectively, they may be thought of as determining "What the organization needs to do." The fourth, fifth, and sixth steps comprise determining "How should we do it ?" And the last steps may be thought of as determining "How are we doing?" In other words, the process, in its simplest form, may actually be viewed as the three-step process shown in Figure 3.2. By introducing this simple "Three-step" process, we are trying to portray Hoshin as, essentially, a simple process in concept. As we continue this overview, we will give an example of how even a small organization may use the process.

The Present Situation

The planning starts with an examination of the organization's "present situation," as well as that of the environment in which it functions. This includes a careful analysis of the organization's successes and failures (for example its performance against last year's plan), an interpretation of customer surveys or complaints, an analysis of the performance of Critical Processes, and an understanding of competitors' relative strength, as well as important trends in *any* area that might be important to the business in question.

In sophisticated organizations, an examination of the Present Situation is less an event than an ongoing learning process. Throughout the previous

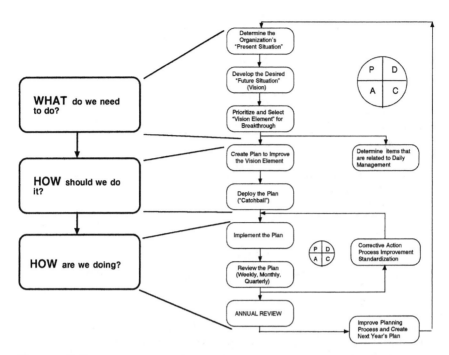

Figure 3.2   A Simplified View of the Hoshin Process shown in Figure 3.1
(Cowley & Associates)

year, the organization has been learning about itself, through tracking its performance against last year's plan, as well as by the identification and analysis of ad hoc events, such as competitor's actions and customer inputs. This analysis is summarized and formalized in the "SWOT" creation process (Strengths, Weaknesses, Opportunities, Threats), which will be described in more detail in the "Step-by-step Procedure" in Chapter 4. A checklist of items that should be considered in Present Situation analysis is shown in Table 3.2.

For some organizations, assessment of the "Present Situation" may simply take the form of an informal discussion session about the above issues, using Table 3.2 as a checklist. This will be especially true of very small organizations, where more formal approaches are not feasible. An important aid to such discussions is the development and documentation of the team's ideas using simple tools, like the Management and Planning Tools described in Chapter 13. A case study will illustrate this process.

A Small Business Example: The Silhouette Shops

THE "SILHOUETTE" SHOPS is a specialty lingerie business consisting of two stores, located in Downingtown, Pennsylvania, and Wilmington, Delaware, cities

Table 3.2 Elements that Go Into the "Present Situation" Analysis

Elements that Go Into the "Present Situation" Analysis

- Mission.
- Employee Feedback.
- Performance vs. last plan.
- Higher Level Objectives.
- Organization Values.
- Critical Process Performance.
- Competitor Performance.
- Customer's Needs & Satisfaction.
- Current and required Products and Services.
- Markets (Applications).
- Distribution Channels.
- Geographic Areas served.
- Critical Success Metric performance.
- "STEEP" Factors: Social, Technological, Economic, Environmental, Political.

which are about 40 miles apart. They are owned by a single proprieter, Claire. Claire and her husband, Bruce, are not happy with the performance of the business, which has been barely breaking even since the acquisition of the Wilmington store three years ago. For the preceding seven years, since the inception of the business, the single Downingtown store had been modestly profitable, with an improving profitability trend year by year.

Claire and Bruce decided one day to take advantage of the offer of one of the authors to discuss possible ideas for improvement of the business. In about two hours, we completed the discussion of all the elements of the "Present Situation," and wrote down the following:

Present Situation

- On its own, the Downingtown store is profitable, with an improving trend.
- The rent on the Wilmington store is quite a bit higher than the rent in Downingtown.
- The Wilmington store, while not profitable, is on a trend which will get it to profitability in about four to five years.
- Claire, who is 60 years old, intends to run this business for the foreseeable future.
- Claire is stretched in trying to manage both stores, although each store has a manager running the day to day business.
- Bruce, while supportive, is concerned about the overall negative cash flow of the business.
- Bruce is the original investor in the business and provides additional cash when needed.
- Bruce runs a successful, one-man Manufacturer's Representative business, and intends to retire in a few years. He is 62.

- All customers for both stores are captured and profiled in a mailing list.
- The mailing list allows sorting by product purchased, store location, special preferences, and so on.
- Advertising is done almost entirely by periodic mailings.
- Claire does all the buying for the stores, takes care of accounting and the mailing list database, as well as other miscellaneous overhead tasks.
- The economies of both locations are healthy and growing.
- In some cases, clientele travel considerable distances (30–40 miles) to shop at the stores.

The SWOT analysis was done by brainstorming the Strengths, Weaknesses, Opportunities, and Threats on Post-its™, and simply grouping them:

Strengths

- Strong position in specialty (prosthetic) lingerie market
- Excellent store locations
- Loyal clientele
- Lots of repeat business
- Business is growing five percent a year
- Downingtown store is generating cash
- Inventory is interchangeable between stores
- Highly personalized service is provided to all customers

Weaknesses

- Claire is the only one who knows the accounting system
- Business currently has a negative cash flow
- Claire is very stretched
- Wilmington store is a cash drain
- Inventory obsolescence is high

Opportunities

- Improve profitability of Wilmington store
- Improve inventory management
- Broaden the product line
- Advertise more widely

Threats

- Rents could go up
- Alternatives to radical breast surgery could decrease prosthetics business
- Claire could get sick
- Local economies could weaken

The Strategic Vision

Later, after reflecting on the SWOTs, Claire and Bruce "brainstormed" answers to the following question: "What is our ideal vision of what this business, and our situation, will look like in the future?" The answers were directly recorded on Post-its™, and these were grouped and titled, according to the Affinity Diagram process described in Chapter 13. The results were as follows:

- Claire and Bruce are happy with the business
  Claire has plenty of free time to travel with Bruce
  The business is providing Claire with a real purpose in life
- The business is profitable
  The business has positive cash flow
  The business is self-sustaining
- The business is more independent of Claire
  Claire is working about 2 days per week
  Claire can turn the business over to her managers for a few weeks at a time
- The business is growing
- Claire can devote significant time to creative strategic thinking about the business
- The staff are well-trained
- Customers are very loyal
- Service is excellent
- Merchandise is attractive and current

Each of the bulleted items is a Vision Element. These are potential areas for strategic focus. Through a process we will discuss more fully later in the book, Claire and Bruce decided to focus on "The business is more independent of Claire" and "The business is profitable."

They considered a number of possible "Breakthrough" actions to help realize these Vision Elements, and settled on trying to sell the Wilmington store as the single most effective action. This became their "Hoshin" Objective. They worked on it diligently for a year, with disappointing results.

After reviewing the first year's progress, the Hoshin objective was changed to "Close the Wilmington store." The target date was set for the following year, when the lease ran out, and the strategies to accomplish an effective closing were developed as follows:

- Consolidate useable inventory in the Downingtown store.
- Move obsolete inventory to the Wilmington store.
- Have a series of aggressive sales to get rid of obsolete inventory.
- Retain Wilmington customers by offering an incentive discount, via special mailings, to attract them to the Downingtown store.
- Have a special sale of store furnishings.
- Remove useable fixtures and furnishings to the Downingtown store.

These six strategies were carried out, and the store closing was a great success. About twenty percent of the Wilmington customers were retained, and the resulting revenue increase in the Downingtown store dramatically improved profitability. Cash flow received a big, one-time positive improvement as a result of the special sales, and a number of new customers were gained. Obsolete inventory was eliminated. The burden on Claire was reduced, as hoped for, and this set the stage for realization of the other Vision Elements in a relatively short time.

Development of the Strategic Vision

Development of the Present Situation through SWOTs sets the stage for the creation of the organization's "Vision." The Vision is a comprehensive portrayal of the organization as its members would like it to be in the future. The process of "Visioning" is fundamentally different from the analytic techniques we use to make sense out of the past or present. Visioning is a *synthesis* process and is the first chance the planning team will have to identify opportunities for true organizational breakthrough. Other opportunities will occur later in the process. The Vision is comprised of "Vision Elements," each of which is a brief statement of an aspect of the organization in the future. It is developed through the use of the Affinity Diagram, one of the Seven New Tools, described fully in Chapter 13. Suffice it to say here that the Affinity Diagram is an advanced form of "Brainstorming" in which, in the case of "Visioning," the features of the "Ideal Future State of the Organization" are brainstormed by the management team. See the example in the lingerie shop case study.

Setting the Breakthrough Objectives

The practice we recommend for beginning users of Hoshin is to select one of the Vision elements in a given year for "Breakthrough" focus, although more than one element might be chosen by an organization very skilled in the use of the process. If the Vision has already been developed in a previous year, it might only be necessary to "revisit" it, and perhaps select a new Element for Hoshin focus. It is also common to select the same Vision Element several years in a row, working on different aspects of the Element each year.

In a large organization it is usually appropriate for Visions to be created at several levels. The Visions, of course, need to be consistent, and generally they will become more detailed and explicit at lower (for example, Business Unit) levels in the organization.

When a Vision Element has been selected, the team will then determine the aspects of the Element that they wish to improve ("Breakthroughs"). The Breakthroughs will be stated in the form of actions or objectives, for example, "Improve Service to Customers." Having done this, they will use prioritization techniques to select the breakthrough with the biggest strategic impact. Metrics (quantitative measures of progress or completion), and goals (numeric targets for the metrics), should be selected for the Breakthroughs.

After selection of a Breakthrough area and appropriate metrics and goals for it, we show the process branching to the step "Determine items related to Daily Management." This simply means determining whether or not the routine management systems in place for the organization ("Daily Management") have any connection with the Vision Elements. They usually do, and some of the relevant business processes might be special candidates for continuous improvement.

Developing the First Level Strategies

The team will now begin the process of developing Strategies to reach the selected Hoshin goals. A typical goal might have three to five strategies, sometimes more or less.

The strategies at the first level are arrived at by the team in a variety of ways, depending on the circumstances. A common way is brainstorming and prioritization, supported by facts and data obtained from careful research and study of the relevant technical and/or managerial disciplines. The creative techniques of de Bono (1992), and Nadler and Hibino (1990), can frequently be appropriate for this purpose.

Tentative strategy sets are assigned metrics and goals, just as for the objective, and the team carefully examines and analyzes the strategies to verify that they have a good chance of meeting the objective. If they do not, new strategies may need to be developed, or the goals of the existing strategies may have to be set more aggressively.

The process of selecting strategies to meet an objective at any level is sometimes known as "catchball," which is a method of dialog between managers and their teams to reach agreement on the strategies and their goals. Perhaps a better name for it is "Collaborative Goal-Setting." Whatever the term used, we stress that agreement is important at this point, because at least some of the team manager's subordinates must take full responsibility, or "ownership," for one or more strategies. At the same time, the manager has the responsibility for "integration" of the plan at his level. All this means is that the Objective and the Strategies are self-consistent, and that the strategies will in fact, with high probability, deliver the objective. Reaching agreement will frequently call into question the assessment of organizational capability in one or more areas; this can be one of the most valuable aspects of Hoshin. It is even more valuable if the organization is taking a system view of itself, which we will discuss further in Chapter 5.

Deliberate and Emergent Strategies

If the capability required to meet an important objective does not exist, then a creative way to develop or acquire it may be needed. In fact, a breakthrough may be needed at the strategic level.

Realistically, however, many capability shortfalls may not be recognized until implementation is underway. In that case, the plan may have to be amended. Mintzberg (1994) discusses "deliberate" and "emergent" strategies: deliberate strategies are conceived in the process just described, whereas emergent strategies may be determined only after some effort to reach the objective has been exerted, and the team has learned a great deal more about what works and what doesn't (as in the case of the lingerie shop). In addition, some assumptions made by the team about the environment may have changed, or may be found to have been wrong from the start.

Deployment of the Plan

When the management team has selected a Breakthrough (Hoshin) objective and a set of appropriate first-level strategies, the strategies themselves now become objectives, and second-level strategies must be developed to achieve the first-level strategies. In the lingerie shop case study, for example, only one level of strategies was developed.

The people who report to the team manager's direct reports now play "catchball" and take ownership for the ensuing strategies. This process will repeat itself until strategies become clearly definable tasks which can be assigned to individuals. At that point, they are called tactics and become part of the Implementation Plan for the Hoshin objective.

Frequently, management teams will recognize that an objective or strategy warrants a cross-functional, or cross-organizational approach, to achieving it, for one or more of the following reasons:

1. The selected issue involves a Business Process that is cross-functional or cross-organizational.
2. The expertise needed spans more than one function or business unit.
3. It is pretty clear that successful implementation of the objective or strategy will directly affect people in more than one function or business unit.

Ideally, the Objective and strategies in this chain of events have metrics, goals, and a definite completion time. Tactics do not have metrics per se, but they have definite completion times.

The overall process of developing the "cascade" of strategies and tactics to achieve the objective is called Deployment of the Objective. The term "catchball" signifies the give-and-take that must occur between and among levels of management to develop strategies (means) at each level, which are capable of implementation and will achieve the objectives.

This system makes it absolutely clear how every individual involved in the plan has agreed to contribute, and it assures focus and convergence of all of these individuals' efforts on the objective. This is one of the most powerful features of Hoshin.

Documentation

The plan, up to this point, must be carefully documented, by preserving and distributing the notes of all meetings, and by use of a concise set of forms to record the key decisions and plan elements—mainly the record of what all the objectives, strategies, goals, tactics, and completion times are, and who is responsible for each. We will introduce examples of appropriate forms; most organizations customize forms for their own use.

Depending on the resources available to the organization, documentation can be done on spreadsheets, Lotus Notes, or similar groupware, or simply by photocopying and reducing the flipcharts from meetings and distributing them, along with copies of filled-out forms.

The plan is now ready for implementation.

Implementation and Review

As implementation takes place, the plan is formally and rigorously reviewed. At the tactical level, the plan will be reviewed at least once a month,
and possibly as often as once a week. At the strategic level, plans should be
reviewed monthly and/or quarterly. After the end of the third quarter of the
year, an "Annual Review" is conducted to serve as the starting point for the
next year's plan.

In all reviews a concise format is used, and the "learnings," both in
terms of content and process, are documented and preserved. Special forms
are provided for this purpose, and an example is shown in Figure 3.3.

Note that in the simple case of the lingerie shop, the Hoshin objective
itself was changed after progress was reviewed. A new Hoshin was adopted,
and was successfully implemented.

The "learnings" are used to improve the next planning cycle, and,
where possible, to improve the existing plan. The review process, as we will
describe later, is very efficient; reviews at any level can be accomplished in
several hours.

This completes the overview of the Hoshin process. We need to discuss
some other important issues now, namely, Timing, Roles and Responsibilities, and the Calendar that should drive the process.

HOSHIN TIMING ISSUES

Hoshin is commonly used to develop Breakthrough plans for implementation over a one-year period, but since it is part of a long-term process, it is

REVIEW   TABLE

Review Date_____ By_____ Plan Date_____ Year_____					
Strategy or Objective	Goal	Actual Performance	O = Made ● = Missed	Reasons for Deviation (Root Cause)	Corrective Measures and Implications for Next Year

Figure 3.3   Review Table (Cowley & Associates 1993)

quite common to have objectives, strategies, and tactics which span multiple years. In such cases, it is mandatory to have interim goals, at least at yearly intervals. In fact, it is desirable in general to have measurable goals at even more frequent intervals, such as every quarter. We should also point out that in some Japanese companies, the Hoshin plan is renewed every six months, reflecting a response to the increased speed of change in today's world.

ROLES AND RESPONSIBILITIES

It is probably pretty obvious that in the use of Hoshin, managers and their teams play important roles. They are the key participants in the content of the planning. The *process* of planning, however, is of equal importance in Hoshin, and there are several additional roles that emerge as a result:

Process Owner   One person, usually a member of the manager's staff, needs to take overall responsibility for the implementation of the process. This includes scheduling of meetings, creation and maintenance of the Planning Calendar, delegation of the other important roles, and taking the lead in improving the process itself.

Scribe   Every aspect of the planning process should be documented and distributed to all those involved in the plan. In most cases , the documentation can be done on "flipcharts," which can later be photocopied and reduced to $8\frac{1}{2} \times 11$-inch format. This is the responsibility of the Scribe. For long planning meetings, this responsibility can be shared among several people.

Facilitator   For some management teams, it may be prudent to have a facilitator for at least some of the meetings. The responsibility of the facilitator is to help keep the meeting process on track, without getting involved in the content.

Leader   Usually the team manager, but at his or her discretion, some of the leadership tasks may be delegated to other team members.

Some of these roles (for example, Scribe, Leader, Facilitator) will need to be replicated for lower-level management teams in the organization. It is the responsibility of the managers to help the Process Owner keep the whole activity coordinated.

PLANNING CALENDAR

Hoshin is a time-driven process. It works, in part, because the people involved commit to a predetermined schedule of events. The generic events are usually driven by a Planning Calendar. A typical planning calendar is shown in Figure 3.4.

The "Process Owner" is responsible for creation and refinement of the planning calendar, and for seeing that the events on it are entered into the calendars of all participants on the appropriate dates. As part of the Annual

Implementation Calendar-Hoshin Planning

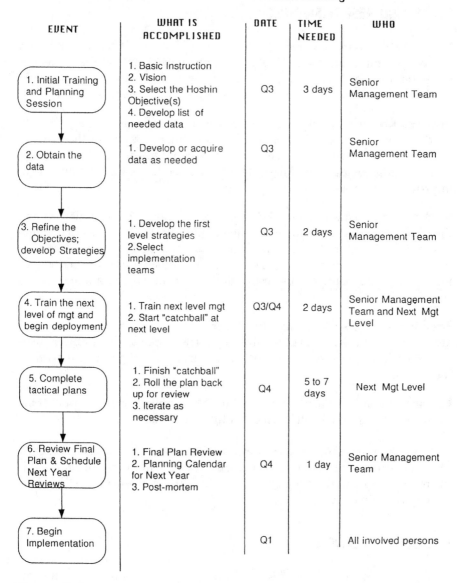

EVENT	WHAT IS ACCOMPLISHED	DATE	TIME NEEDED	WHO
1. Initial Training and Planning Session	1. Basic Instruction 2. Vision 3. Select the Hoshin Objective(s) 4. Develop list of needed data	Q3	3 days	Senior Management Team
2. Obtain the data	1. Develop or acquire data as needed	Q3		Senior Management Team
3. Refine the Objectives; develop Strategies	1. Develop the first level strategies 2. Select implementation teams	Q3	2 days	Senior Management Team
4. Train the next level of mgt and begin deployment	1. Train next level mgt 2. Start "catchball" at next level	Q3/Q4	2 days	Senior Management Team and Next Mgt Level
5. Complete tactical plans	1. Finish "catchball" 2. Roll the plan back up for review 3. Iterate as necessary	Q4	5 to 7 days	Next Mgt Level
6. Review Final Plan & Schedule Next Year Reviews	1. Final Plan Review 2. Planning Calendar for Next Year 3. Post-mortem	Q4	1 day	Senior Management Team
7. Begin Implementation		Q1		All involved persons

Figure 3.4 Typical Implementation Calendar (Cowley & Associates 1995)

Review, the Planning Calendar should be revisited for any problems that arose due to scheduling, and appropriate changes in the calendar should be made for the next planning year.

SUMMARY

The intent of this chapter is to give the reader a "holistic" idea of the Hoshin process, without going deeply into the details. The "Silhouette" lingerie shop example has two purposes:

1. To illustrate with a simple example how the basic process works.
2. To demonstrate that the process can work very well for small organizations, and even for individuals. In later chapters, we will show examples of its use in medium and large organizations. The principles remain precisely the same.

Of course, the details *are* important ("The devil is in the details"). But we want to emphasize that the reader must understand the *purpose* of each of the detailed steps, rather than the exact way we describe its implementation. Most organizations develop their own highly individualized approaches to the detailed steps, using what works best for them, without compromising the basic intent of the process.

Now, on to the details. Chapters 4 through 11 describe the process in enough detail that many organizations will be able to implement it using their own internal resources. To be realistic, however, many organizations will find that the services of an experienced consultant to facilitate and monitor progress will repay the cost many times over.

REFERENCES

Ackoff, Russell L. *Creating the Corporate Future*. New York: Wiley, 1981.

Akao, Yoji, ed. *Hoshin Kanri: Policy Deployment for Successful TQM*. Cambridge, MA: Productivity Press, 1991.

Brassard, Michael. *The Memory Jogger Plus +*. Methuen, MA: GOAL/QPC, 1989.

Collins, Brendan and Huge, Ernest. *Management by Policy*. Milwaukee, WI: ASQC Quality Press, 1993.

de Bono, Edward. *Serious Creativity*. New York: HarperBusiness, 1992.

GOAL/QPC Research Committee. *Hoshin Planning: A Planning System for Implementing Total Quality Management*. Methuen, MA: GOAL/QPC, 1990.

Hamel, Gary and Prahalad, C.K. *Competing for the Future*. Boston: Harvard Business School Press, 1994.

Johnston, Catherine G. and Daniel, Mark J. *Setting the Direction: Management by Planning*. Ottawa: Conference Board of Canada, 1993.

Juran, J.M. *Managerial Breakthrough*. New York: McGraw-Hill, 1964.

King, Bob. *Hoshin Planning: The Developmental Approach*. Methuen, MA: GOAL/QPC, 1989.

Melum, Mara Minerva and Collett, Casey. *Breakthrough Leadership*. Methuen, MA: American Hospital Publishing and GOAL/QPC, 1995.

Mizuno, Shigero, ed. *Management for Quality Improvement: The Seven New QC Tools*. Cambridge, MA: Productivity Press, 1988.

Nadler, Gerald and Hibino, Shozo. *Breakthrough Thinking*. Rocklin, CA: Prima Publishing, 1990.

Mintzberg, Henry. "The Fall and Rise of Strategic Planning." *Harvard Business Review*, January/February 1994, pp. 107–114.

——. *The Rise and Fall of Strategic Planning*. New York: Free Press, Macmillan, 1994.

Peters, Tom. *The Tom Peters Newsletter*. San Jose, CA: Tom Peters Group, 1994.

Senge, Peter M. *The Fifth Discipline*. New York: Doubleday, 1990.

Chapter 4

Preparation

Converting the organization into one that effectively uses Hoshin Planning as an ongoing process requires careful thought and preparation—and planning in its own right. This chapter will help get the process started, while Chapter 12 will elaborate on the deeper cultural issues involved in converting an organization's planning system to Hoshin.

THE PLANNING TEAM

We mentioned in Chapter 3 that the usual team for initiating strategic planning, or Hoshin, is the manager of a business or organization entity (corporation, division, section, department) and his or her staff, with the subsequent involvement of all the other managers, as well as select additional personnel in the organization.

The executive or manager who decides to embark on the use of Hoshin would do well to read this book in its entirety before proceeding, and to make the book available to the planning team as well. An informal meeting should then be held for the purpose of determining:

1. The level of team commitment to making the effort to implement the Hoshin system. Figure 3.4 gives a rough idea of the required time commitment.
2. A rough schedule of events for the team's planning efforts. Use the Planning Calendar (Figure 3.4) as a guide.
3. Decide who should play the roles of Process Owner, Scribe, Facilitator (if any), and Leader.
4. The time and place for the first meeting (usually three days).

SCHEDULING

As a starting point, we would recommend scheduling five days, as follows: an initial three-day session, as described above, and a two-day session about four to six weeks later. This is detailed in Figure 3.4. If work still remains, additional one-day sessions may be scheduled as needed. When the management team feels comfortable with the results at this point, they can schedule the additional time necessary to deploy the plan.

The rationale is to spend the first session developing the basic mind-set of thinking strategically. Only enough data to support this effort should be reviewed. The emphasis should be on trying to integrate the information available into a coherent picture of the present and, later, an exciting, compelling Vision for the future. Major "gaps" in the available information should be identified and, where feasible, filled before the second session. It is important not to get bogged down in too much detail during these meetings. Table 4.1 lists some questions that many organizations will find useful to reflect upon before starting the planning process.

The outcome of the second session should be a preliminary set of objectives and strategies. Some useful reading in preparation for this session is *Six Thinking Hats* (de Bono 1985). It is important to remember Mintzberg's remark that "strategic thinking can't necessarily happen 'on schedule'." The management team may need more time for this part of the process, and it might be better for some teams to do the initial session in three or more

Table 4.1   Important Strategic Questions

- Are you working to achieve an understanding of the future as a time when many of the competencies and capabilities that are now serving us very well might not work?
- What new core competencies and strong capabilities will be needed?
- Are you working diligently to understand who your customers will be 5 years from now? 10? 20? Their needs?
- What new products and services need to be brought to market to satisfy current customers and attract new ones?
- Will channels of distribution need to be expanded and/or changed?
- Who will our competitors be?
- What will the "crisis" issues of the future be?
- Are new Business Processes needed?
- We will review Social, Technological, Economic, Environmental, Political trends that are important to the organization's future. ("STEEP" factors). It would be helpful to give some thought to these prior to the meeting.
- Will employee feedback or other knowledge of their needs dictate any radical departures from current employee development practices in the future?
- We will list organization Strengths, Weaknesses, Opportunities, and Threats (SWOT's). What will you be putting on each list 5 years from now? 10?

separate days, spaced a few days apart. The first three steps in the process are intended to "catalyze" strategic thinking. We should also point out that focusing too much on an analysis of data can impede the synthesis processes of strategic thinking. More on this later when we begin to develop the Vision in Chapter 6.

Between the first and second sessions, try to acquire the missing information and data as best as can be done. It may be prudent to impose a time limit on this effort. If the outcome is that the data or information requires a major effort, the responsible parties should come to the second meeting with that assessment, rather than the data itself. This is an area where strategic planning professionals, if they exist in the organization, should assist, especially if the plan being developed is the corporate one.

In the second meeting, the data (or lack thereof) is discussed, and its impact on the Vision is assessed. Amendments are made accordingly. In some cases, it may be decided that the organization is so "data poor" that the ensuing year should be spent gathering the data necessary for a good strategic plan (this is the "zero'th year" discussed in Chapter 12).

All of the forgoing is well and good, but, in the true spirit of this process, it ought to be recognized that for many organizations this schedule may not work. Our advice is this: use it as a starting point, and as it becomes clear that something isn't working, make a conscious decision to make a change. To this end, do an evaluation of the process at the end of each day, and capture your "learnings" (that is, write them down!). Thus, you will have all valuable insights relating to how the process worked, and even if it is not done until next year, you will be able to avoid this year's mistakes and improve the process next year.

CROSS-ORGANIZATIONAL ISSUES

Sometimes it becomes obvious, either before planning starts, or even after it has begun, that there are issues critical to the organization's success that are the purview of another unit in the larger organization, or even an entirely different organization. This may be a sign that the process should start at a higher level in the organization, but if that is not possible, then the planning team needs to agree on an effective way to link the other organization to its planning process. Occasionally the best way to start is by inviting the responsible executive to the second planning session, after a briefing on the outcome of the first. But there are many effective variations on facilitating cross-organizational communication. The important point is to make the interaction with your team a time-efficient one for the visiting executive, but at the same time to have the highest-level decision-maker from the other organization present so that an appropriate level of cooperation is obtained from the other organization. This is likely to be a very fluid arrangement until more is learned by both parties from the initial sessions.

FACILITIES AND LOGISTICS

We can save many planning teams a lot of "cut-and-try" headaches regarding facilities and logistics with a few guidelines in the area of meeting setup and required materials. While almost any well-equipped meeting room will do, we highly recommend the following:

Meeting Room　It should be large enough to accommodate the participants, seated in groups of four to six at separate tables, and should have plenty of wallspace to hang flipcharts. Typically, about fifteen flipcharts will be generated each day. For ten participants, for example, about 500 square feet is required.

Flipcharts　Three or four will be needed for a typical planning team. We have found that full-size, 27 × 34-inch, 1-inch quadrille ruled flipcharts, with perforations for easy tear-off, work best (for example, TOPS Business Forms #7900).

Overhead Projector　Have one handy for presentations.

Meeting Materials
- Masking tape to hang flipcharts (one roll).
- Post-it pads, 3 × 3-inch or 3 × 5-inch, one per participant.
- Flipchart pens, one or two new four-color sets (red, green, blue, black).
- Bold, felt-tip pens for Post-its™ (0.8mm), one per participant (for example, SANFORD "Sharpie" Fine Point, black).
- Calculators, two or three, simple four-function.
- Adhesive Labels, 3/4-inch round (such as AVERY T-5467 Red Glow), one pack of 1,000.

Facility Location　Our feeling about facility location is that best results are obtained if an offsite facility free from distractions is used. The team should discuss this in its initial informal meeting. It is obviously a tradeoff, both economically and in terms of preferred style of running meetings.

REFERENCE

de Bono, Edward. *Six Thinking Hats*. Boston: Little, Brown, 1985.

Chapter 5

Analyzing the Present Situation

For many organizations, doing a thorough job of assessing the Present Situation can be a valuable exercise in its own right. Frequently, it will reveal obvious problems that can be addressed without a great deal of formal planning. Its primary purpose, however, is to establish the "starting point" of the journey described in the "road" metaphor described in Chapter 1. We will later suggest that this assessment should be "refreshed" frequently as part of the Review process, because two things will happen:

1. Things will change.
2. Even if they don't change, your perception of them will change as you grow more sophisticated in thinking strategically.

For most organizations, the checklist shown in Table 5.1 contains the vital components of the Present Situation for Strategic or Operational Planning. We describe in detail how to accomplish these steps in this chapter.

Before we get into the details, however, we encourage the reader to review Figures 3.1 and 3.2. We are at the first step, "Determine the Organization's 'Present Situation'." Figure 5.1 puts this step in a better perspective with respect to the rest of the process; assessment of the Present Situation may be viewed as a "Wide Scan" appraisal of both internal and external information. The objective is to get a broad rather than a highly detailed view of the world in which the organization functions, as well as a broad appraisal of the organization itself. The information so gathered will be filtered and focused somewhat by the "SWOT" generation process, and then again by the Visioning and Objective-setting processes.

DEVELOPING THE MISSION

The first task of the initial planning meeting should be to develop, or revisit, the organization's Mission.

Table 5.1   Reviewing the Present Situation

- Develop the organization's Mission, or revisit it, if one already exists. The Mission is a simple statement of what the organization does to add value for its customers. Or in other words, it describes the organization's purpose.
- Revisit or develop the organization's values.
- Review existing data and trends on performance against Critical Measures of the organization's success. Are there any "crisis" issues?
- Review performance versus last year's Strategic Plan.
- Review Customers needs and satisfaction levels.
- Review performance of Products and Services.
- Assess performance of the organization's Distribution Channels, if any, and examine performance in the geographic areas served by the organization.
- Review alignment of the organization's Products and Services with the needs of the markets served.
- Review performance of Critical Processes.
- Review Competitor performance compared to the organization's.
- Review Social, Technological, Economic, Environmental, Political trends that are important to the organization's future. ("STEEP" factors). This can take a variety of forms, including briefings or educational sessions by in-house or outside experts.
- Review employee feedback.
- Make a list of areas where data or information is needed, but isn't readily available. Update this list as the initial planning proceeds. Assign individuals to make an effort to acquire this data, as appropriate.
- Determine Strengths, Weaknesses, Opportunities and Threats. (SWOT's). This should include a review of the organization's Core Competencies (Hamel and Prahalad 1990) and Capabilities (Stalk, Evans, Shulman 1992).

The definition of Mission is very simple: it is the purpose of the organization, the reason the organization exists. It is common, but not mandatory, for mission statements to define the scope of the company's activities (geographical or customer-market, for example), the reason that the purpose is important to the customer, and even *how* the mission is to be accomplished. Some examples follow (Abrahams 1995):

> To meet our customers' ongoing needs for economical and reliable electric service in ways that merit the trust and confidence of our publics.
>
> Pennsylvania Power & Light

> The mission of Mid-America Dairymen is to provide each member market security, by providing a market for all the milk he or she desires to produce and marketing that milk in the form and market channels providing maximum returns consistent with long-term stability.
>
> Mid-America Dairymen, Inc.

Here are some other mission statements:

Plan, design, build, and operate space needed by our customers.
The internal building services department of a large telephone company

We are a company whose primary business is the design, construction, and maintenance of the lighting, electric power, data, communication, and control systems in industrial plants, commercial buildings,

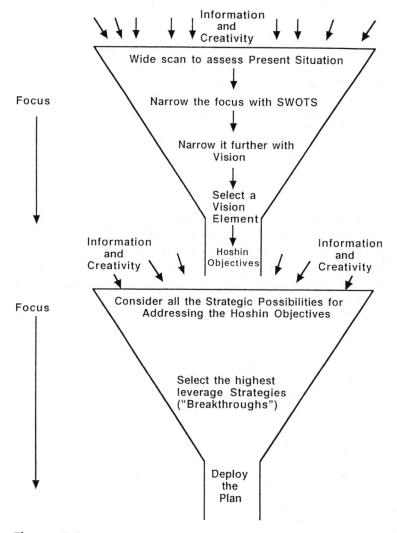

Figure 5.1 Gathering Information for the Present Situation (Cowley & Associates 1993)

hospitals, substations, and power distribution systems. We will do work wherever a customer asks us, provided we feel we can do a good job for them while minimizing our risk and making a good profit.

Power City Electric, Spokane, WA

The point here is to be specific about what the organization does to bring value to its customers. Simple language is best. The target audience for the mission statement is management, employees, customers, and shareholders. The purpose of the mission statement is to have a common view of what the organization does and, perhaps even more important, what it does not do.

Mission statements are generally stable, but they should be changed when the management and ownership of the organization agree that the mission has changed. Here is an example from the 1995 Annual Report of Cadence Design Systems; the current Mission Statement is:

> We provide services and software that help our customers meet their product development goals.

Five years ago the Mission Statement was:

> We make tools for people who design integrated circuits.

The mission was changed to reflect a change in the scope of the company's business, the addition of outsourcing of design services and design consulting, to complement their continuing business in design tools.

A surprising number of organizations do not have mission statements, or, if they do, they are obscure and have little impact on organizational behavior. Creating one, or modifying one that has somehow become relegated to the shelf where strategic plans used to be kept, is a simple process. We recommend that it be done by the top management team by having each team member print what he or she thinks the mission statement ought to be on a Post-it™ and posting it on a flipchart easel. Use Abrahams' book (1995) for ideas on wording, length, and format. Agreeing on the final wording can be an iterative process, which may be facilitated by having the team vote for the one or several versions they like.

The "Hundred-Dollar Test"

The voting can take the form of giving each team member "one hundred dollars" in the form of "ten-dollar bills" (actually, round colored labels) that may be "spent" in any way the team member wishes (for example, all on one mission statement, or distributed over the best three, and so on). The top-scoring several candidates can then be "synthesized" into the final statement.

Before adoption of the final statement, it is desirable to "try out" the mission statement on a sample of employees, stockholders, customers, and lower-level mangers.

It has been our experience that development of the Mission Statement, for an organization that has not had or used one, is far from a "no-brainer." Frequently, interesting disagreements arise about the major parameters of the organization's business, such as what products will be offered, or what markets and customers will be served by the organization, appropriate geographical limits, and so forth. Obviously, these issues have to be resolved before an organization can proceed with effective planning. One of the authors spent almost a day with the counseling department of a major University before agreement could be reached on its mission. For further arguments in support of the vital importance of having a mission, see Ackoff (1981). Robert (1993, Chapter 6) presents a useful process for deriving the organization's Mission from the basic parameters describing the organization's business.

VALUES

Values are defined here as the fundamental beliefs that influence individual and organizational decision-making and behavior. Bean (1993) observes that "values drive actions." Therefore, it is important in the planning process to acknowledge these values, to agree on what they are, and, more importantly, how they will guide policies and actions.

For example, an important value for the Hewlett-Packard organization has been the recognition that talented people are the company's most valuable asset. This has led to a collection of principles, polices, and other values called the "HP way," which govern how the company treats its employees and expects managers and employees to behave.

Another important basic value at HP is Integrity in dealing with every person and entity outside the company, which has led to a documented set of policies for dealing ethically with suppliers. Abrahams (1995) give numerous examples of such values.

In many respects, the Values of an organization are the most powerful and enduring determinant of its performance over the long run, so we do not mean to give them short shrift here. We mentioned earlier, in the section on "Objectives, Strategies, and Hierarchy of Purpose" in Chapter 1, that asking "why" the organization has specific objectives frequently leads to the organization's values. The important issue is that the organization *articulates* and *lives* its values, and explicitly uses them to evaluate the appropriateness of policies and strategies. If the values have not been articulated, then time needs to be set aside to do so.

CRITICAL SUCCESS MEASURES

At this point, one of the most important steps must be completed: the management team must agree on the metrics (measures) that describe how well the organization is meeting its business objectives, and then assess the organization's performance against them. Or to put it another way, How does the management team know that it is achieving its Mission, day-in and day-out? Are there any "crises," existing or imminent?

For a profit-making business, it is certainly clear that some financial measures are appropriate. In fact we would argue that all organizations must have appropriate financial measures. But there is more to it than that. Hronec (1993) has written that the organization's performance metrics are the "Vital Signs" by which the ongoing health of the organization may be measured. Most businesses have in place financial measures, like profitability and cash flow, but it is the non-financial measures that are frequently missing or inadequate.

Some examples at the organization level:

- Operating profit margin = profit before taxes/sales
- Orders booked per month = $
- Shipment volume per month = $
- On-time delivery = percent of product delivered on time
- Customer satisfaction = aggregate score of a customer satisfaction survey
- Innovation = percent of this year's sales contributed by products introduced in the last three years
- Customer loyalty = (# of customers − lost customers) / # of customers
- Employee Satisfaction = Score on Attitude Survey
- Employee Turnover = percent of employees leaving in a year

Note that financial measures tend to be lagging indicators, that is, they really measure the result of actions taken by the company in the past, perhaps decades in the past, including such things as winning a proprietary position in a technology or product, developing the products in the first place, and manufacturing them at a competitive cost, as well as other investments. The financial indicators are necessary for any business, but are not very good indicators of things to come, which will be the result of how good a job is being done *now* on developing competitive products, attracting and retaining customers, entering new markets, and so on.

Some of the other examples, like Innovation, Customer Satisfaction, and Customer Loyalty, are better predictors of the future, and hence might be called leading indicators. They are indicators of the organization's ability to remain competitive and, hence, to succeed in the future.

The subject of appropriate measures of success for organizations is treated elegantly by Kaplan and Norton in their *Harvard Business Review* articles (1992, 1993, 1996). The point we want to make here is that these measures need to exist, and be agreed upon, before meaningful planning can take place. The reason for this is that one of the first elements of determining the "Present Situation" is to baseline performance against these measures, so that we can subsequently set goals for future performance. We will later argue that not only must performance at the organization level be measured, but also strategies and business processes lower in the organization, for these measures must be linked to the overall organization measures.

The job that must be done at this point is to review the organization's performance against these measures, look at trends, and analyze any short-falls or future risks. The "Review Table," shown in Figure 5.2 and described in the next section, is an effective format to use for this purpose.

Thought also ought to be given at this point to adopting additional measures, especially "leading indicators." In Chapter 7, on Analysis of the Vision, we will discuss ways of identifying where such leading indicators would be helpful, and how to identify them.

PERFORMANCE AGAINST LAST YEAR'S PLAN

Even if a different planning method was used for the previous year, it is very useful and constructive to review that plan using the Hoshin review format and methodology. The methodology is simple: refer back to Chapter 3, and use Figure 3.3 to examine performance against the plan. The concept is simple and is embodied in the form. The first column is used to record the description of what was to be done or accomplished. The second column is used to record the numeric goal, if there was one. The third column is used to record the actual performance or accomplishment—in numeric terms, if available, in words if not. The fourth column is a simple "flag" to indicate whether or not the objective was met. The fifth column is intended to be a brief summary of any analysis that was done to determine why the goal was or was not met. Finally, the intent of the last column is to provide space to indicate what will be done in the future, whether it be corrective measures if the goal wasn't met, or adoption of the results if the objective was success-fully met, or follow on actions in either case, and so on.

An example of an actual filled-out form is shown in Figure 5.2. The team was the building services management team whose mission was used as an example earlier. What we see is pretty typical of the result for a team that did make an effort to plan, but with a planning process that was not very rigorous. Their own appraisal of these results is shown verbatim in Table 5.2.

All in all, this is a pretty profound set of observations by this team, triggered entirely by the simple process of reviewing their previous plan. The review took about an hour to prepare and discuss. Many of the observa-tions support the need for a more rigorous planning process, and it will be instructive to comment on each of them.

REVIEW   TABLE

| Review Date April 5, 1993 | | By Planning Team | | | |
| Plan Date Late 1991 | | Year 1992 | | | |
Strategy or Objective	Goal	Actual Performance	O = Made ● = Missed	Reasons for Deviation (Root Cause)	Corrective Measures and Implications for Next Year
1. Increase internal Share of Market	"Increase"	?	●	No numerical goal was set	Set numerical goals next time
2. Increase client satisfaction	"Increase"	?	●	Our customers' perception is that we did improve, but no hard data	Do a baseline and end-of-year survey next year
3. Establish global benchmarks	Complete the project	Partially complete	●	Higher priorities intervened	Do a formal resource allocation next year
4. Get an award outside America		Got a local award	O	Plan changed mid-year	
5. Reduce waste	144k savings	100k	●	Goal too ambitious. No analysis.	Analyze what is possible or feasible next year before setting goal
6.Optimize assets		?	●	Intent not clear. No metric or goal.	Define intent. Establish metric. Set numeric goal.

Figure 5.2   An Actual Review Table (Cowley & Associates 1993)

Table 5.2   What Did We Learn From the Review Process That Will Help Us Improve Next Year's Planning?

1. We must set specific numerical goals, which means we must have metrics for each objective and strategy.
2. Set a few, important objectives.
3. Substantiate the objectives with profound knowledge.
4. Objectives have to be realistic and attainable.
5. Those who will have to help achieve the objectives must buy in and participate (in the planning as well as implementation).
6. Objectives must be more focused and precise.
7. Objectives must reflect need rather than present capability.
8. Objectives should be customer driven.
9. There must be a process to measure actual performance versus the objectives. Critical metrics (for example, Key Processes) should be measured on a routine basis.
10. The objectives at one level must support higher-level objectives.
11. Further, our objectives ought to improve our business.
12. Objectives should be team-developed, not developed by a single individual, because no individual can know enough by himself to have the "right" answer, and the team has to share a vision in order to feel "ownership" for the objective.
13. The team had no ownership of the planning process.

Observations #1 & 6 It was difficult for the team to do this review, because, save for one objective, there were no measures and, therefore, no quantitative indicator of success. There were also no completion times specified for objectives. Lastly, because of not having metrics, the last two objectives lacked precision as to exactly what was intended.

Observations #2, 10, & 11 The plan reviewed was a hodgepodge of objectives, some of which, in retrospect, didn't seem too important, or were somewhat disconnected from each other. Moreover, their business purpose didn't seem clear. These points highlight two important issues. First, there should be a clear hierarchy of purpose in any plan, as we described earlier. In other words, any objective ought to be traceable upwards in the scheme of things to a clear business purpose, like improvement of performance in the future against one or more Critical Success Metrics (CSMs) for the business. (Keep asking, "Why are we doing this ?" to get to the higher-level purpose.) The CSMs hadn't been explicitly identified in the previous planning exercise (although Objective #3 implicitly addressed one of them), and no effort was made to relate the objectives to a higher business purpose; the objectives just seemed like good things to do in their own right.

The second important issue is that of focus. Generally, organizations cannot make significant progress on more than a few major objectives outside of the scope of day-to-day business in any given time period. This suggests that the few objectives chosen should be very important to the organization, which further implies that some tough prioritization choices must be made.

Observation #3 argues for setting objectives and numerical goals based on facts and data, that is, profound knowledge of the specific issue and its relationship to business performance.

Observations #4 & 7 are related, and conflicting. #7 should take precedence, while #4 is a prescription for going out of business. The purpose of planning is to determine what must change in order to be able to meet needs not provided by current organization capability.

Observations #5, 12, & 13 support the premise that the people who are expected to implement a plan must be involved in the planning in some way. They also speak to the value of the team developing a shared vision of what needs to be achieved.

Observation #8 makes the argument that plans should be customer-driven and, indeed, we would agree. But we would also add that most organizations, businesses in particular, must satisfy a number of important groups—in addition to customers—simultaneously, notably owners or shareholders, regulators, governments, and employees, in order to achieve business success. In the long run the CSMs of the organization must reflect this reality.

Observation #9   argues for an effective Review Process. Again, we would have to say "right on!" and remark that surprisingly few organizations have such a process.

We have, perhaps, digressed here, but with a purpose. The purpose is to show how effective it is to use the Review Process, not only to reveal operational problems and challenges, but, as was the case here, to reveal shortcomings in the planning process itself.

CUSTOMER NEEDS AND SATISFACTION LEVELS

In our discussion of elements that ought to be addressed in any Strategic Planning process worthy of the name, we are beginning to touch on things for which there is an enormous pool of published information about what to do, how to do it, and who should do it to whom. We will need to describe enough about the subject to show clearly how customer-related issues must be dealt with in the planning process. Some of these points are detailed further in Chapter 14.

First of all, lets define our terms. We will be talking about two broad classes of customers: external, or those people or entities who purchase the goods and services of the organization, and internal, or those people, functions, and departments, to whom each person, function or department provides information, materials, service, and partially completed product in the normal course of conducting business.

A useful concept for identifying and communicating with customers (Rummler and Brache 1990), is to describe the organization as a set of business processes, each intended to provide products or services—some to internal customers, some to external, some to both. All are supposed to add value for the customer.

It is going to be important to be able to view the organization in this way when we discuss Critical Processes, and the best view for the purposes of Planning at the highest level in the organization will be the organization's Process Map. An example is shown in Figure 5.3. It is in such a construct that we can begin to see who the customers are, and how they are supplied with goods and services.

At any level in the organization, it is important that the needs and satisfaction levels of external customers be dealt with first. Generally, they "pay the bills," and problems and opportunities there need to have top priority. At very high levels in the organization, a fundamental issue should be, "Do we have effective systems for capturing the voice of the customer, and how do we know they are effective?" In fact, we will argue that a system for capturing, integrating, and transforming customer "voices" into action-

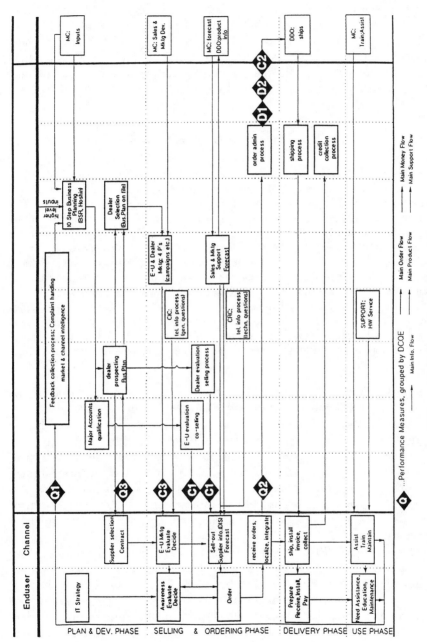

Figure 5.3 Process Overview Map

49

able plans is, or should be, one of the Critical Processes of all organizations. At the highest levels in the organization, a key responsibility is to assure that this process is working properly and is being used effectively. As we move closer to operational processes that "touch" the external customers, the focus should be more on what the operational implications of customer inputs are; for example, where do we need to improve, and by how much? Chapter 14 expands on this theme, and the following example illustrates how a customer dissatisfaction issue led to the complete overhaul of a critical Business Process for one company.

"On-time Delivery"

A major semiconductor company, "ABC Semiconductor," on the basis of its routine Customer Satisfaction Survey and supported by frequent complaints by its salespersons, concluded that it needed a major improvement in its delivery performance. An important customer segment expected the company to commit to delivery within a fairly narrow "window" in time, typically a three-day period. The expectation was that the company would meet this commitment "most" of the time, which was translated to a goal of "more than ninety-five percent of the time." We will describe later in the book the details of the company's analysis of this situation, but the point we wish to make here is that the company's performance fell far short of customer expectations, and an analysis of the existing systems of acknowledging orders and scheduling the flow of newly manufactured parts disclosed that these systems were not sophisticated enough to deliver the desired performance. Achieving the required performance eventually became the company's Hoshin objective.

From a much more strategic point of view, the question of who the organization's customers are expected to be in the future needs to addressed. Or, more importantly, who does the organization *want* to serve in the future, and why? And what will motivate these customers to buy from us? Unfortunately, as Hamel and Prahalad (1994) have pointed out, it isn't sufficient to be "customer-driven"; even if you know who your future customers are, it isn't enough to respond to their expressed needs. The company who hopes to be growing and competitive must cater to a broad spectrum of customer benefits, many of which cannot be, or are not, articulated by customers.

But so what? What are the planning implications? At the outset it may be sufficient to recognize which of these issues isn't even currently on the organization's radar screen, and to put plans in place to address them. If there isn't evidence that customer voice plays a strong role in the organization's operational and strategic decisions, a resolution to change drastically should be drafted. At a more tactical level, the information that is available from customers should be used to formulate actionable objectives. This might take the form of first using management instinct to formulate tentative plans, but then gathering real data quickly on an *ad hoc* basis to support or challenge the decisions.

Products and Services

The organization's Mission, and its customers' expressed and deduced needs, should influence the design and delivery of its Products and Services. Sometimes, however, the connection is weak, especially in the area of using customers' needs and satisfaction levels to improve existing products and design new ones. If competitors are doing it better, then the organization faces some serious problems.

Many organizations are product-driven, in that they depend on a steady stream of competitive new products and services to generate growth and maintain profitability. This means that the New Product Development process is one of the most important Critical Processes, and it behooves such companies to continually monitor and improve this process, including benchmarking competitors' processes.

An important issue that needs to be addressed in the planning process is whether or not the products and services that the organization plans to offer will be able to produce the revenue and profit required by the organization to meet its growth objectives. An ongoing appraisal of the financial performance of each product and service provided is a standard part of the reporting procedure for many companies; this is usually done on a quarterly basis. Performance of products is an important retrospective measure of the New Product Development process. This concern will also lead many companies to examine its distribution channels, and the geographic areas they serve.

Distribution Channels and Geographic Area Served

For many organizations, the channels of distribution need to be treated as another customer, with needs and satisfaction levels. The question of whether these channels reach the target-end customers, and whether the cost structure of the company's products can provide adequate profits for both company and channel, are also key.

Marketing a company's products in a new geographic area is an important strategic decision, and in many cases might require a period of major investment before returns are realized. Careful planning, and analysis of risks and rewards is needed.

When a company markets its products in multiple geographic areas, and through more than one channel, the financial performance of the products should be monitored by channel and geographic area, taking into account the real costs associated with the different channels and areas. This analysis frequently leads to the realization that ongoing management of the products needs to be different for the different channels and areas, especially in the area of pricing. This can have important strategic as well as operational implications.

Markets

In addition to having customers, products, and services, the organization must understand the application of their products, and how and why customers use them. There must be a clear and unambiguous understanding of the segmentation of the markets served and the positioning of the organization's products or services within those segments. The decisions regarding markets and segments to be served should be reflected in the Mission, and naturally will have a profound effect on Product and Service offerings. For example, in many high-technology products, such as printers, the manufacturer must decide whether to be the high-volume low-cost producer (like Hewlett-Packard), or a high-performance, high-price producer (like Tektronix). These are two different market segments with vastly different requirements for technology competencies, manufacturing expertise, and distribution strategy.

PERFORMANCE OF CRITICAL PROCESSES

As we saw in the preceding section, it is helpful to view the organization as a set of interactive Business Processes. The view we see in Figure 5.4 is a variant of the Rummler and Brache Relationship Map (1990). It shows Business Processes and their interdependencies at a macroscopic level; all of the processes, as shown here, contain sub-processes, and even lower levels of processes beyond. Being able to express how the organization "works" at this level is very helpful in identifying customer-supplier relationships, flow of information and material, and potential "disconnects," that is, flows that should exist, but don't. It also sets the stage for identifying high-level measures for the processes themselves. For very small organizations, the Process Map is optional, but we feel it is an essential tool once the organization reaches 100 employees or more.

In the ideal case, with no disconnects, the task of managing all of the routine affairs of the organization comes down to managing these processes and their interactions effectively, to achieve the mission of the organization day-in, day-out. Even high-level strategic activities can be managed effectively by, among other things, the Planning Process. Many of the eagerly sought-for improvements in Business Performance can be accomplished by understanding the Business Processes that have the highest leverage on the Critical Success Metric needing improvement, and improving those processes. This can be done both on the basis of gradual, incremental improvement, or by Breakthrough improvement (the big boulders and smaller rocks in Figure 1.2). From a strategic point of view, management will also routinely

LEVEL 4 TELEPHONE ORDERING PROCESS - TELESALES MANAGER

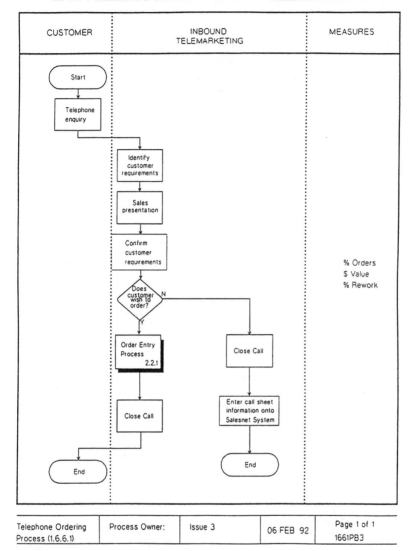

Telephone Ordering Process (1.6.6.1)	Process Owner:	Issue 3	06 FEB 92	Page 1 of 1
				1661PB3

Figure 5.4 Process Flowchart Example

consider whether there are processes that need to be added to the organization's repertoire, or whether some processes might be, or become obsolete, and whether in fact the requirements of the future will dictate a different "wiring diagram."

If the observation at the highest levels in the organization is that this view doesn't exist, then a clear strategic question arises for the next planning period: whether or not to put forth the effort to adopt it, along with its important ramifications. Some of the considerations that might come to bear include the following:

1. In order to consider any sort of "reengineering" of important organization business processes, this view is essential.
2. Even if reengineering doesn't turn out to be a priority, the process view of things makes it much easier to run most organizations with higher quality and lower cost.
3. A process view greatly facilitates diagnostic efforts if something goes wrong, or if something needs improving.
4. Performance measurement of all activities in the organization is greatly facilitated.
5. Relative priorities for improvement can be more easily ascertained.

For the organization that has taken the Process view, this part of the planning process should be devoted to highlighting the need or opportunity for process improvement. This could be driven by a clear need to improve an organization CSM, or by the perception that improvement could yield a significant competitive advantage. It might also be driven by the observation that current performance can't adequately support a desired new organization direction for the future, such as expansion into a new market. And, of course, many improvements may be driven by customer dissatisfaction issues (such as the "On-time Delivery" example), or by the perception that the competition is doing it better. At any rate, without the Process and system view, it is much more difficult to focus improvement efforts.

Furthermore, since organization processes tend to be so highly interactive, it is very likely that the desire to improve a given process or performance area will cause major perturbations in other processes linked to it. These can't be seen easily without the "map." Refer back to our discussion in Chapter 3 on "The Planning Team" for additional discussion of this point. We will develop some of the other concepts important to the process view in the following sections.

Operational Definitions

We need to define our terms so that we can intelligently discuss the concept of Process review. A process will be defined here as "a series of steps designed to produce a product or service" (Rummler and Brache 1990). Processes have defined inputs and desired outputs, as well as defined steps and procedures describing how the inputs get transformed into the outputs. Most processes have equipment, supplies, people, training, and documentation associated with them. Figure 5.4 shows a common way of depicting and documenting a process: the Process Flow Chart. Each box represents a process step, and the flow of material, information or events is from left to right.

Metrics

Metrics for processes serve the same function as for the organization; they indicate whether or not the process is functioning properly. A very simple example of a process might be the recipe for baking a cake. Some of the data that will be of importance within this process will be oven temperature, time of baking, and perhaps temperature of the ingredients during mixing. These are called process metrics, whereas measurements of the end result, such as height of the cake, moistness, and taste, are called results, or output metrics. This is illustrated in Figure 5.5. The results metric for the "On-time delivery" example is "Percent of shipments that are on-time"; the goal for the metric was ninety-five percent.

Its probably obvious that both results and process metrics are important, and that they are analogous to the leading and lagging CSMs we talked about earlier. When we get to the section on creation of strategies, we will enlarge on the subject of metrics, and we will find that they need to be used for measuring the effectiveness of strategies, just as they are used for measuring the effectiveness of the organization and its Business Processes. We should point out that customers of the process should play a major role in defining output metrics and setting performance levels. The employees using the process should play the major role in defining process metrics and performance levels.

Process Management and Improvement—the Connection between Hoshin and Daily Management

There is an entire science devoted to the management and improvement of processes, called Statistical Process Control (Grant and Leavenworth 1980). It will suffice for our purposes to note that the measurements of a metric of a process "under control" will almost always lie within prescribed boundaries, called control limits. An "out of control" process will show excursions from time to time outside these limits. The implications of this can be very important: an "in control" process has outputs that are predictably within the

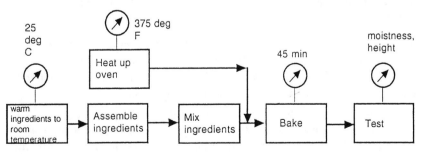

Figure 5.5 Process Example: Baking a Cake

control limits, and conversely, the outputs of the "out of control" process might be anywhere.

Although in many cases it might not be necessary to invoke strict statistical measurement of Business Processes, the concept of predictability is usually very important. For example, in the case of the semiconductor company just described, the customers were expecting what they defined as "on-time delivery" more than ninety-five percent of the time, with continuously improving performance. Quite a bit of statistical data was needed to monitor and control this process, and, as was mentioned, performance was not adequate.

It is important to recognize that some businesses processes may be much more important to certain organizations than others, and that this may depend on the size of the organization. For example, in a "high-technology" startup company, the New Product Development process will probably be by far the most important, and the Core Competencies relating to the company's technical discipline will be critical. As the company matures and grows, it will need more balance in its repertoire of business processes. For one of our clients, a mortgage banking company, the most important processes were the loan initiation and loan servicing processes, and the critical core competency was the Data Processing (Information Technology) skills that the company possessed.

Planning Implications

With these few concepts in mind, the issues that need to be considered by the management team are: "Is this organization managing itself largely through the management of its Critical Business Processes? If not, do we need to lead it in this direction? If so, are we doing our part to understand and improve our results through the intelligent use of Process and Relationship maps and related tools?"

A further and fundamental argument for using Process Management to continuously improve Business Processes, is illustrated in Figure 5.6. It depicts the activities of various levels of employees and managers in the organization, and the relative time spent on each. The basic ideas embodied are several:

1. Responsibility for Business Processes should be that of the employees using the processes. All employees, even executives, use processes; therefore, even executives have this responsibility. This includes regular performance monitoring, as well as continuous improvement.

2. Managers have an additional responsibility, namely looking to the future. This we can describe as strategic thinking. This is where strategic planning should be focused, and the higher the level in the organization, the more time ought to be spent on this activity. If business processes are not working well, then managers will be continually distracted by "firefight-

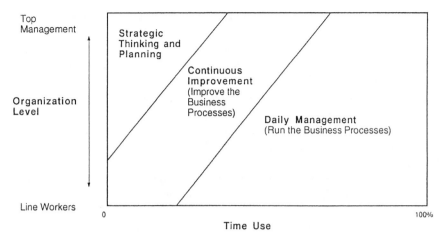

Figure 5.6   Time Use in the Ideal Organization, also known as the "Itoh" model for time management (Soin 1992)

ing," and won't have time to be strategic thinkers. This can be fatal in the long run.

3.   If a company has a robust Process Management and improvement program, and most Business Processes are performing at or near optimum levels, then managers will understand very well what their process capability is and will, therefore, understand that further major improvements might require breakthroughs. As we have pointed out, a common term for the use of Process Management, and continuous improvement in the routine management of an organization, is Daily Management.

4.   If an organization does a good job in defining, managing, and improving its Business Processes, and they are managed at the appropriate level in the organization (the point of use), then the management as a whole will have more time to manage the future, which is the activity shown in the upper left-hand area of Figure 5.6.

ANALYSIS OF COMPETITORS

As in the case of customer information, there is a rather large pool of knowledge and services centered around "Knowing your competitor." The planning team has to make some careful choices about what information is needed, and how much time, effort, and expense is justified in getting it.

The section on Benchmarking in Chapter 14 describes the process and value of this activity. Suffice it to say here that any planning, at any level, potentially needs to use "competitor intelligence" as an important planning factor. We say potentially because there are different points of view on this subject, ranging from, "If we are far enough ahead of our competitors, we don't have to worry too much" (which begs the question of how you know), to "We need to be able to convince ourselves that our core processes and products are best in their class." How important or valid either approach is depends on the organization. Maintaining current "competitor intelligence" is not without cost, so that cost-effectiveness is an issue.

In the Hewlett-Packard Components business, we generally conducted detailed competitive product analysis when we either perceived a threat from a competitor's product, or when we intended to develop a competitive product. On an ad hoc basis, we occasionally benchmarked the cost and profitability structure of competitors, or worthy companies in similar, but not directly competitive, businesses. On a routine basis, as part of the Product Management process in the Marketing function, we would track competitor pricing, which would serve as part of the data used to adjust our own pricing.

At a higher level in HP, we benchmarked important processes (like Human Resources Management and General Accounting) to uncover opportunities for improvement, in other industries as well as competitive companies. Some of this work can be done with the help of consultants specializing in either the discipline of interest, or in benchmarking, or both.

In certain industries, like consumer products, it usually makes sense to have in place more formal systems to monitor competitor behavior on an ongoing basis. For guidance in these matters, we recommend Fuld (1995), a valuable overall resource dealing with the basic concepts of Competitor Intelligence, all the way to the "how to" of obtaining and analyzing competitor data in a systematic fashion. Rausch also lists the common elements of an analysis of Competitive Factors (1982).

While not purely a competitor issue, the organization needs to be sensitive to trends in society or markets that might lead to a decline in need for their products or services, or to an increase.

Planning Implications

Running a business is a series of decisions. Planning has to do with decisions you will make in the future, and how you will make them. For most organizations, there are competitors, and their mission is to be successful at your expense. Knowing something about them can, therefore, be of the utmost importance. The question of what needs to be known depends on what kinds of decisions need to be made.

For new products that are contemplated, for example, knowledge of your competitor's current offerings, and more important, any likely next offerings, will be useful. Predicting next moves might be educated "guesswork," but frequently this is better than proceeding in a complete vacuum. Sometimes it may suffice to know something about your competitor's core competencies to predict any next moves. For example, if a competitor is known to be good in the area of low-cost manufacturing, then the chances are good that this weapon will be used against you. Your next product offerings should reflect countermeasures, if possible.

Competitive analysis should be broad and deep, near term and far term. Two examples from relatively low-technology areas can illustrate the need to take account of competition in the broad sense.

A paper-coating company sold its product for many years to a manufacturer of vinyl flooring. The paper was used in one step of the flooring production, then discarded. The flooring manufacturer developed a technology that did not need the coated paper as an intermediate agent during production. The "competition" was not another paper company; it was the new technology developed by its customer.

Does the customer want a quieter lawnmower? A safer lawnmower? One that uses less (or no) gasoline? Short term, lawnmower developers compete on these issues. But the customer really wants nice grass. Farsighted lawnmower companies have recently acquired seed companies that are developing tailored-DNA grasses, that stop growing at a pre-determined height, and are sponsoring University research on plant hormones that stop growth at a specific height.

STEEP FACTORS

STEEP stands for Social, Technological, Economic, Environmental, and Political elements of the environment in which the organization functions (Rausch 1982, p. 46). It is also symbolic of any other factors that may need to be understood well, because of their potential impact on the organization's success or competitiveness. For many organizations, for example, regulatory issues are very important.

As is true for customers and competition, evaluation of STEEP factors should be an ongoing process, rather than an event. The basic motive in this evaluation is to try to predict possible future trends and events so as not to be "blindsided" by them, and to have the capability for quick response if any such events occurs. A simple example might be to have a contingency plan in place in case of severe economic downturn. Another might be to have a plan in place to take advantage of an expected technology advance when it happens, even though the exact timing may be unknown.

As in the customer and competitor realm, evaluation of STEEP factors requires some level of prediction. Mintzberg, in his book (1994), cites predictability as one of the great fallacies of planning; many, if not most, of the great changes in the world as we have known it in our lifetimes were not predicted even a few years before their occurence. Hence, the prediction of important STEEP factors is perhaps more art than science. Nevertheless, the concept still has value, if only to create the mindset that these factors can make or break a business, and, albeit difficult, it is imperative to be watching for the signs of impending change in those factors with a large impact.

Many organizations take a multi-faceted approach to keeping their managers and executives current on the important STEEP factors. For areas that are judged to be high-risk or opportunity, a special effort to "get up to speed" and then to stay current may dictate educational seminars and self-study, perhaps organized and led by internal experts, outside consultants, or a combination of the two. In the late 1970s, in the Components Group of Hewlett-Packard, we perceived ourselves as not very conversant in the technology of Microprocessors, at least at the higher management levels. We believed there were both risks and opportunities for us in this new technology. Consequently, we chartered a series of seminars and workshops, both to educate us in the theory, and to give us some "hands-on" experience. Even executives learned to program in Assembler language! It was time well spent, because we later introduced a number of products incorporating microprocessor technology, and, as it turned out, sold most of our product into applications that required them to interface with microprocessors. Finally, we made a decision *not* to try to directly compete in this market. A simple anecdote, but we hope it illustrates that some creativity, planning, and extra executive effort may be required to deal with the important STEEP factors of Strategic Planning.

As another approach to STEEP factors, it sometimes makes sense to charter a special study or research project, possibly in collaboration with consultants or universities, or just with the use of internal resources, if they can be spared and possess the needed expertise.

To get a "feel" for the operating environment, many executives accompany sales personnel on customer visits, to get the customer's point of view on possible future developments and trends.

The above approaches are intended not so much to lead to predictions of the future as to prepare managers, with education and information, to imagine for themselves what *might* happen in the future.

EMPLOYEE FEEDBACK AND DEVELOPMENT

The management of any organization should have a good sense of the attitudes, morale, needs, and wants of the organization's employees. Some companies use numerous mechanisms for this purpose, such as employee surveys, lunch meetings with top management, formal development evaluations, and so on. Since employees should be thought of as one of the most important assets of an organization, it follows that their professional and personal development ought to be an integral part of the Vision and the Strategic Plan.

Further, when we speak of Organizational Learning, we should be quick to point out that organizations really don't learn, it's the people in the organization who learn. There are many who say that the only competitive edge left in the future will be the ability of the organization to learn, that is, the ability of its people to learn faster than its competitors' people. Senge (1990) asserts that this capability is a strong function of enlightened leadership. We would take this thought a step further by saying that Organization Learning is a Core Competency and a process that must be continually improved and developed as part of an organization's ongoing operations and strategy.

As we will see, a good first step in creating the "Learning Organization" is a robust planning process. The diligent creation, execution, and review of a good strategic plan can be a profound and valuable learning experience.

For the purposes of reviewing Employee Development and Feedback, some questions that can be addressed are the following:

- Does the organization survey employee opinion in a systematic way?
- Does a formal employee development program exist?
- Is employee training regularly conducted, and is it closely coupled to the organization's strategic needs?
- Are there any quantitative measures of employee attitude, learning, and morale?
- Are employees intimately familiar with the Vision, Mission, and performance of the organization, and do they clearly know their roles in achieving them?
- Does two-way communication between employees and management occur on a regular basis? Is it having the desired effect?
- Do most employees participate in continuous improvement efforts?
- Is the degree of participation measured?
- Are the effects measured?

The creative management team can doubtless think of many additional questions, but this list can get the dialog started.

SWOT ANALYSIS

Using the information gathered in the efforts to assess the Present Situation, the Planning team needs to digest it and to extract elements of special importance to the organization. This process is called SWOT analysis (Strengths, Weaknesses, Opportunities, Threats). The idea is to take some time to reflect on and to discuss the information and its implications, and then to brainstorm specific observations on Post-its™. The Strengths and Weaknesses comprise what may be called an internal scan of the organization, while the Opportunities and Threats are an external scan of the organization's operating environment. To make the SWOTs more useful, an

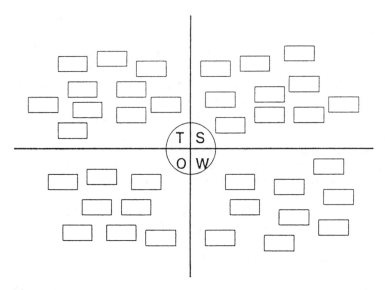

Figure 5.7 Typical SWOT Diagram: Strengths, Weaknesses, Opportunities, Threats (Cowley and Associates 1993)

Affinity Diagram (Chapter 13) of the information can be done. Figure 5.7 shows the SWOT diagram for a typical planning session.

Small Organizations

We mentioned earlier that for smaller organizations, the development of the Present Situation might simply be a conversation among the management, or even all employees, with someone recording important observations on flipcharts or Post-its™, and later duplicating them. Table 5.1 can be used as a checklist. The conversation can culminate in the SWOT exercise, just as for a more formal Present Situation analysis. This approach is illustrated in the lingerie shop example in Chapter 3.

ASSESSMENT TOOLS

Many organizations use either internal or external assessment methods (for example the Malcom Baldrige National Quality Award Application) for supporting the Present Situation analysis. We certainly endorse that practice as long as the management team is careful to see that all the important "bases" are covered in the assessment. Our experience is that such assessment tools sometimes lack sufficient emphasis on business results, such as profit performance. But, in general, we find them very valuable and, with the forgoing caveat, endorse their use as a collateral method to the approach we've described in this chapter.

MISSING INFORMATION

Usually it will be clear to the Planning team that there are significant pieces of data or information missing, after they have begun to try to assemble what they know and have available into a coherent picture of the Present Situation. In fact, this is an almost inevitable occurrence in any planning effort. The solution is to record these discoveries of inadequate or missing information as they happen, and then to reserve time at the end of the meeting to decide which items are essential. Assignments are then made to planning team members to acquire this data for the next meeting.

SUMMARY

A thoughtful assessment of the organization's Present Situation is an important first step in any planning endeavor. We hope the reader will appreciate the spirit of this chapter as describing a process of inquiry, whose primary function is to get at the truth of the organization's current state of competitiveness. The objective is to form a reasonably accurate and, more importantly, *shared* view that can be the basis for future operational and strategic efforts to improve and advance. The methodology can range from structured and formal, to a simple several hour conversation.

Further, it is hoped that the reader and practitioner will recognize that the best of all worlds is that this assessment becomes an *ongoing* rather than static (such as once per year) effort. Use of the Review Process described in Chapter 11 provides a way to accomplish this state of continual renewal of important information. In the next chapter, we will move on to the Vision development for the organization.

REFERENCES

Abrahams, Jeffrey. *The Mission Statement Book.* Berkeley, CA: Ten Speed Press, 1995.

Ackoff, Russell L. *Creating the Corporate Future.* New York: Wiley, 1981.

Bean, William C. *Strategic Planning That Makes Things Happen.* Amherst, MA: Human Resource Development Press, 1993.

Fuld, Leonard R. *The New Competitor Intelligence.* New York: John Wiley, 1995.

Grant, Eugene L. and Leavenworth, Richard S. *Statistical Quality Control.* New York: McGraw-Hill, 1980.

Hamel, Gary and Prahalad, C.K. *Competing for the Future.* Boston: Harvard Business School Press, 1994.

———. "The Core Competence of the Corporation." *Harvard Business Review,* May/June 1990, pp. 79–92.

Hronec, Steven M. *Vital Signs.* New York: AMACOM, American Management Association, 1993.

Kaplan, Robert S. and Norton, David P. "The Balanced Scorecard—Measures that Drive Performance." *Harvard Business Review*, January/February 1992, pp. 71–79.

——. "Putting the Balanced Scorecard to Work." *Harvard Business Review*, September/October 1993, pp. 134–147.

——. "Using the Balanced Scorecard as a Strategic Management System." *Harvard Business Review*, January/February 1996, pp. 75–85.

Mintzberg, Henry. *The Rise and Fall of Strategic Planning.* New York: Free Press, Macmillan, 1994.

Rausch, Bernard A. *Strategic Marketing Planning.* New York: AMACOM, American Management Association, 1982.

Robert, Michel. *Strategy Pure & Simple.* New York: McGraw-Hill, 1993.

Rummler, Geary A. and Brache, Alan P. *Improving Performance: How to Manage the White Space on the Organization Chart.* San Francisco: Jossey-Bass, 1990.

Senge, Peter M. *The Fifth Discipline.* New York: Doubleday, 1990.

Soin, Sarv Singh. *Total Quality Control Essentials.* New York: McGraw-Hill, 1992.

Stalk, George, Philip Evans, and Lawrence E. Shulman. "Competing on Capabilities: The New Rules of Corporate Strategy." *Harvard Business Review*, March/April 1992, pp. 57–69.

Chapter 6

The Strategic Vision

When we were young, most of us were told at one time or another to "set goals." Better advice would have been to "Create a Vision," to form the context for goal-setting. The Vision is the *reason* for the goals, as we will see.

The management of an organization, whether it be large or small, or a sub-unit of a larger entity, has as one of its principal responsibilities to set the direction of the organization for the future. The "future" for strategic planning purposes is typically three to five years, but it can be much shorter or much longer, depending on circumstances. A typical time frame for Operational Planning is one year.

The most effective way to set the future direction is to develop a shared vision of what the organization will be in the future, contrast it to the way the organization is now, and then to create a plan for bridging the gap—the Strategic Plan. This concept was introduced in Figure 1.2 as the "Road" metaphor. In that metaphor, the Vision is the organization's destination, the "Present Situation" is the starting point, and the "highway" represents the plan for getting to the destination or Vision.

In Chapter 5, we described the first important step in the process, the assessment of the organization's Present Situation, culminating in a summary of the organization's most important Strengths, Weaknesses, Opportunities, and Threats, or "SWOTs." This is the point of departure for the creation of the Strategic Vision.

WHAT IS A VISION AND WHY DO WE NEED ONE?

A vision is a statement (or a picture) of an ideal state of being or existence in the future that is inspiring and empowering for the stakeholders of the

65

organization. It creates the context for the process of planning the future for the organization. In a real sense, it *is* the future of the organization, and from it can be derived the "goals," the important strategic objectives of the organization (sometimes referred to as the strategic direction or strategic intent). We saw an example of a Vision in the lingerie shop example of Chapter 3. It is reproduced in Figure 6.1.

Notice that the vision, even though it describes the future, is expressed in the present tense. The idea is to imagine you are in the future, and to visualize what that ideal future is like.

We will see another example later in the chapter, but we ought to touch on why it is desirable to have a vision. There are several reasons:

- The process of developing a vision is in itself a team-spirit enhancing activity. (We should point out here that a Vision can also be created by

---

- *Claire and Bruce are happy with the business*
  Claire has plenty of free time to travel with Bruce
  The business is providing Claire with a real purpose in life

- *The business is profitable*
  The business has positive cash flow
  The business is self-sustaining

- *The business is more independent of Claire*
  Claire is working about 2 days per week
  Claire can turn the business over to her managers for a few weeks at a time

- *The business is growing*

- *Claire can devote significant time to creative strategic thinking about the business*

- *The staff are well-trained*

- *Customers are very loyal*

- *Service is excellent*

- *Merchandise is attractive and current*

Figure 6.1 Simple Example of a Strategic Vision

an individual, for his or her own future.) The Vision inspires: "A task without a vision is drudgery."

- The Vision represents a shared expression of the future desired by the members of the organization. It is an essential step toward the creation of unity of purpose in all their endeavors.
- The Vision makes it relatively easy to determine the strategic priorities for the organization, and to develop specific plans for its eventual realization: "A vision without a plan is a dream."
- The Vision creates a context for objectives, so that their relationship to the entire organization is clear. It is frequently the starting point for developing the "systemic" view of the organization, that is, a view of the organization as a unified whole, rather than the sum of parts "flying in formation."

CHARACTERISTICS OF A GOOD VISION

The Vision should meet several tests:

- It should be grounded in the reality of the organization's Present Situation; that is, it should recognize challenges that the organization now faces as having somehow been addressed in the ideal future.
- As a result of the previous point, the Vision ought to create some problems for the organization.
- The stakeholders (Employees, Customers, Owners, Suppliers) of the organization must be able to see themselves or their interests represented in the Vision.
- The Vision should be the result of the integrated thinking of the management team, rather than a collection of individual visions. We call this a shared vision.
- The Vision should invite and inspire people to want to bring it to fruition.

TIME HORIZON

Regarding the time-frame of the Vision, we take the position that it depends on the issue at hand. For strategic planning, some would argue that the Vision should be timeless; we have found that most executives prefer a finite time-frame, usually in the three to five year range. For some businesses or organizations, there may be good arguments for a much longer time-frame (utilities or public transportation agencies, for example) or for a much shorter one (a small startup venture with a first product yet to be introduced). The "Visioning" process can also be used for numerous other planning endeavors, such as new product planning. Clearly, in this case, the time-frame will be dictated by the desired product release date.

OTHER KINDS OF VISIONS

Besides the strategic Vision, there can be a great variety of applications of the visioning process incorporated into planning. Examples are the vision of an ideal process, the vision of an ideal product strategy, the ideal product for a specific purpose, indeed, any business issue can be approached using the visioning process.

On a personal level, one might envision the perfect career, the perfect education, the perfect vacation. When we were young, parents, teachers, and perhaps clergymen told us we needed to have goals in life; what we really needed was a vision. On a political or philosophical level, perhaps we can envision the perfect world, the perfect healthcare system, the perfect educational system, and so on.

While, of course, the process doesn't guarantee success, it is the first step in constructing a systemic framework for meaningful objectives, around which teams, families, political parties, and others can rally.

THE VISIONING PROCESS

The process of "visioning" is fundamentally different from the analytic techniques we use to make sense out of the past or present. "Visioning" is a synthesis process. Synthesis is generally more difficult than analysis; however, we will describe a process that can be readily learned by anyone, using the Affinity Diagram tool described in Chapter 13.

Our process for Visioning is quite easy—and fast. For most organizations it can be accomplished in an afternoon. However, we wish to caution the reader that creating the Vision without taking the time to assess the organization's Present Situation is a bad idea. It will result in a Vision that is shallow and superficial, and is likely not to meet the tests outlined above. For a small organization or an individual, the assessment of the Present Situation can be done in a few hours. For a large organization, it might take several days or even weeks.

So How Do We Do It?

The first step in the process is to develop a "Vision Question." This should be a question that invites the participants to contribute any thoughts they have about the nature of their "ideal future." For example, the "Vision Question" for a medium-range strategic planning session might be:

> It is 1999 and we are very pleased with our strategic success; what do
> we look like and how did we get here?

For a more tactical issue, like a project to design an employee survey, the
question might be:

> We have designed the ideal Employee Survey Process; what does it
> look like and what effect is it having on the organization?

The team then brainstorms answers to the Vision Question and records them
on Post-its™ with a bold pen, preferably in block-letter printing. The usual
rules of brainstorming apply (no comments or criticism of anyone's ideas, no
discussion). In addition, the participants are asked to express their ideas
concisely but completely, using phrases of typically five to seven words,
with a noun and verb, expressed in the present tense.

For the case where a considerable body of information has been
developed in preparation for the Visioning process (such as the Present
Situation in Strategic or Operational planning), the participants are asked to
carefully review and reflect on that information as they develop their
responses.

The Post-its™ are placed on a flipchart easel as they are developed.
This serves as the "group memory" for the brainstorming process, and
allows people to build upon others' ideas (one of the principal purposes of
brainstorming).

The team then proceeds with the Affinity Diagram process, as described in Chapter 13, culminating in the Vision. The inset shows an actual
example of this process.

Visioning Process Example

The example we'll use to illustrate the Visioning process is one that was done at
the strategic level for an actual organization, but we would like to emphasize
again that the method can be used at any level of planning with excellent results.
This example is an excerpt (with permission) from the Strategic Planning done by
Power City Electric. The Vision was created in July 1993.

After a thorough discussion and analysis of the "Present Situation," and
development of the company's SWOTs, the executives started the "Visioning"
process by brainstorming answers to the following question:

> It is 1997 and we feel we are very successful; what do we look like,
> and how did we get here?

In the brainstorming of answers to this question, the executives were asked to
project themselves into the future and imagine how the company would look,
ideally, in the future. For example, what would have been accomplished
(weaknesses overcome, opportunities taken advantage of, and so forth), how

customers and employees would perceive the company, how the company would be performing, and any other characteristics that would be part of an ideal, attractive future for the company. Their thoughts were printed on Post-its™ and placed at random on a flipchart. The five executives generated 109 responses in about half an hour.

After the brainstorming was completed, the executives put all the Post-its™ on a wall and arranged them in groups expressing the same theme or idea. Then titles for each group were developed and placed at the top of the groups, outlined in bold pen. The result is shown in Figure 6.2.

The titles in Figure 6.2 represent the company's Vision. They are called Vision Elements. Together they represent the executives' view of an exciting, desirable "state of being" to aspire to in the future. The managers noted at this point that the vision element reflecting their greatest desire for maintaining and improving business performance was Element #9, "We have safe and strong financial growth."

Comparing the Visions depicted in Figures 6.1 and 6.2, note the difference in format. This reflects the transcription of the original Post-it™ version of Figure 6.1 to a typed, outline format. The process used for both Visions was identical, and in each case was felt by the creators to represent a compelling, exciting mental picture of an ideal future for the organizations.

As can be seen from the examples shown here, Visions are a complex mosaic of desired or desirable outcomes. Referring back to our discussion of hierarchy of purpose in Chapter 1, it is important for teams to reflect on the Vision they have created and to question why certain elements are there, and, in particular, to challenge whether or not the Vision, and all its elements, are consistent with the values of the team and organization.

It is also advisable to test the Vision using the criteria mentioned earlier in this chapter, and further, to ask, "Is this the Vision we really want for our organization?" Some "fine-tuning" may be in order, and, occasionally, a team will notice an omission or a major inconsistency that will require changing, adding, or deleting a title Post-it™ (Vision Element). All of this is permissible. The ultimate test is that the Vision truly reflect the team's desired future for the organization.

"It's not what the Vision is, it's what the Vision does."

This observation was made by Senge (1990) in his discussion of Vision and the fact that visions cause creative tension in the individual or organization when the envisioned state is compared to the Present Situation. This is why we observed earlier that visions should cause some "problems" for the organization. Perhaps "challenges" is a better word. In the next chapter we will introduce methods for prioritizing the "problems" or "challenges," so that the team is not faced with the prospect of working on all of the Vision Elements at once.

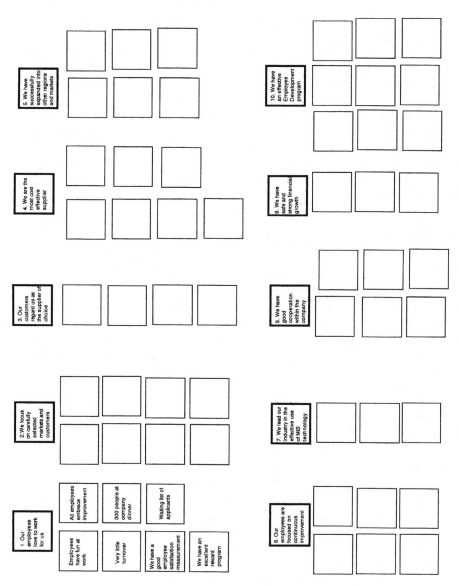

Figure 6.2 Vision Example (Cowley & Associates 1995)

COMMUNICATING THE VISION

The initial work on the Vision is generally done by an executive or manage-rial team, and this is appropriate. However, to be fully effective, the Vision must be "bought into" by all members of the organization. An effective way to do this is to share the Vision in its "Post-it™" version, or any other convenient form, with all other members of the organization, and to encour-age additions to the preliminary version (for example, by using different colored Post-its™). Our experience has been that this is always a positive experience and frequently results in valuable contributions to the Vision. It is always greatly appreciated by the other organization members and gives them a genuine sense of "up-front" participation in designing the organization's future. Many executive groups take this opportunity to ex-plain the planning process to the other organization members and preview their role in it.

CREATING A VISION STATEMENT

The Vision in the form shown in Figures 6.1 and 6.2 can be converted into a Vision Statement by simply incorporating the information in the Title Post-its™ into a narrative or outline form ("bullets"). This creates a form more suitable for brochures, Annual Reports, banners, posters, and so on. Generally, we suggest that a member of the team who is good at "wordsmithing" takes a first cut at this, with the team taking the role of critics. Usually, a good Vision Statement emerges after two or three rounds of this process.

DISCUSSION

Referring to Figure 1.2, the Vision is the organization's destination in the future. We encourage teams who develop Visions to be pretty daring—and perhaps even a little unrealistic. The Vision should be driven more by what's *desirable* than by what *seems possible*, because time and again, creative teams and individuals will figure out how to do the seemingly impossible if they see in the Vision what the benefits can be.

The Visioning process is one of the steps in Hoshin Planning that calls on the "right brain," the creative side, to help synthesize ideas for the future. This is one of the areas in planning where intuition and instinct play impor-tant roles. Profound knowledge of the matter at hand is also vital; therefore, it is important that the composition of the team reflect the knowledge re-quired. On the other hand, since we are seeking emergent thinking, that is, ideas and concepts that have perhaps never been thought of by this organi-zation before, there is a role for creative individuals who are unconstrained

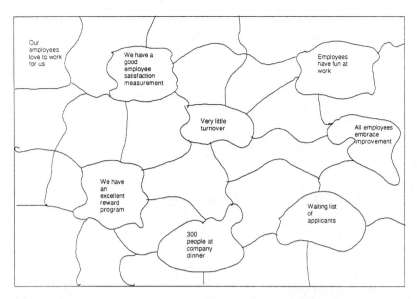

Figure 6.3 Synthesis of High Level Ideas or Concepts from Fragments Using the Affinity Diagram. Possible overall theme: "We have a happy and productive workforce." (Cowley & Associates 1995)

by "what worked in the past" in their thinking. This will become even more important as we develop strategies to achieve the Vision.

The Affinity Diagram method seeks ideas "trying to be born," helping the team to synthesize them from the fragments assembled in the grouping process. Referring to Figure 6.3, the process is something like partially assembling a puzzle and then trying to identify what's in the picture. So the whole (the title) is greater than the sum of the parts, and frequently represents an idea that is at a higher level of abstraction than any of the fragments.

Is it necessary to have a Vision in order to set good objectives? We would have to be honest and say "no." Occasionally, an individual or management team might have enough deep knowledge of an issue that it is obvious that it needs to be addressed; if that is truly the case, then we say "get on with it." However, we would make the observation that the visioning process is so straightforward, that if any risk exists of failing to take a "systemic" view, then a vision will pay back the effort to develop it many times over.

REFERENCE

Senge, Peter M. *The Fifth Discipline*. New York: Doubleday, 1990.

Chapter 7

Setting the Breakthrough Objectives

ANALYSIS OF THE VISION

In Chapter 6 we described how to develop a Vision for the organization. Many organizations have created Visions for the future, but do it in isolation from a planning process, or lack the understanding of what to do next, or have deployed weak and ineffective plans to realize the Vision. In this chapter we will begin describing how to set focused, high-leverage objectives to work on the Vision, starting with the highest-leverage elements. These objectives are called Breakthrough, or Hoshin, objectives. There can be more than one in a given year, but we generally recommend starting with one per year for organizations using Hoshin for the first time. We also recommend setting Hoshin objectives that can be completed in a year or less. If this is not possible, then the project should be divided into sub-projects that can be completed in a year.

A major theme we'll be emphasizing from this point on is that organizations need to focus. The biggest mistake organizations make is failing to focus on the high-leverage actions that really make a difference in the organization's long-term competitiveness.

To identify where the highest leverage is, we need to analyze the Vision in several ways. A useful first step is to correlate the Vision with the way the organization is currently being managed. We will call this the Correlation to Daily Management. A second step is to get some idea of how far the Present Situation is from the envisioned state; in other words, how big is the "gap" separating the desired future state from current reality. To do this we will use a tool called the Radar Chart. Finally, we will find in almost all cases that there are strong cause and effect relationships among the Vision Elements. We will identify these using a tool called the Interrelationship Digraph, or "ID" for short. The methods we will use, the Matrix Diagram, Radar Chart, and the ID, are all described in Chapter 13, and are part of the Management and Planning Toolset.

CORRELATION WITH DAILY MANAGEMENT

In Chapter 5 we discussed Critical Success Metrics and the concept of Business Processes. These are the tools that the organization uses every day to manage and measure its ongoing business, and it behooves the team to know how these relate to the Vision just developed. In particular, we will want to know if the metrics being used to judge performance of the organization are, or could be, measures of how well the Vision is being realized. We also wish to know which Business Processes have an impact on the Vision, in order to align improvement efforts.

To put what has just been said on a practical footing, we have created the matrix shown in Figure 7.1. It is simply a graphic way of showing the answers to two questions: "To what extent do the organization's Business Processes support the Vision Elements?" and, "How well do the Critical Success Metrics of the organization measure the Vision Elements?" We are using the example of the Electrical Contractor, Power City Electric, whose Vision we described in Chapter 6. Two conclusions are apparent upon a quick inspection of the matrix: (1) The CSMs don't measure the Vision very well, and (2) The Vision is potentially well supported by the Business Processes. The implications are that in order to measure progress toward real-

Critical Processes: To what extent do the CP's support the Vision Elements?											Vision Elements	Critical Success Metrics: How well do they measure the Vision Elements?				
Sales/Marketing	Project Management	Estimating	Purchasing	Quality Management	Planning	Accounting	Employee Development	Communications	Safety	Equipment Management		Revenue	Backlog	Profitability	Project OPM	Sales
				O	O		◉	◉	◉		1. Our employees love to work for us					
◉					◉		Δ	◉			2. We focus on carefully selected markets and customers			◉	◉	
O	◉			◉	O		O	◉			3. Our customers regard us as the supplier of choice					O
	◉	◉	◉		◉	◉	◉	O	Δ	O	4. We are the most cost effective supplier			◉		
◉					◉			◉			5. We have successfully expanded into other regions and markets	O				O
				◉	◉	O	◉	O			6. Our employees are focused on continuous improvement			Δ	Δ	
					◉		◉				7. We lead our industry in the effective use of MIS technology					
				◉	◉		◉	◉			8. We have good cooperation within the company					
O	◉	◉	◉	O	◉	◉	O	O		Δ	9. We have safe and strong financial growth	O		◉	◉	O
					O	◉		◉	O		10. We have an effective Employee Development program					

◉ Strong
O Medium
Δ Weak

Figure 7.1 Correlation of the Vision with Daily Management (Cowley & Associates 1995)

ization of the Vision, additional measures will be needed, and some well-directed work on the Business Processes can contribute to moving the organization toward realization of the Vision.

USING THE RADAR CHART TO PERFORM "GAP ANALYSIS"

We will return to the Power City Electric example to illustrate how "gap analysis" is accomplished with the Radar Chart. The completed Radar Chart is shown in Figure 7.2. It was constructed by placing the Vision Elements around the rim of a circle (the "Radar Screen"), and representing the present state of the organization on a scale of 0–10. Here, 10 is at the rim of the screen and represents "perfect" current performance, that is, equal to the ideal performance envisioned in that Vision Element. It is common practice to

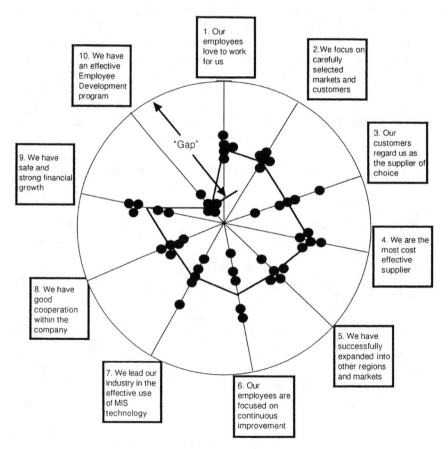

Figure 7.2   Using the Radar Chart to Perform "Gap Analysis" (Cowley & Associates 1995)

draw the Radar Chart on a flip chart, then to use colored labels (dots) to allow each team member to "vote" by placing a dot on each "spoke" of the chart. The team then discusses each item and agrees on a single value for each Element. This tool is frequently called the "gap analysis" tool, because the most useful interpretation of it is that the largest "gaps" between current and desired future performance (for example Element 10) are possibly the greatest opportunities for improvement.

Another benefit of the Radar Chart is that it reveals significant differences of opinion among team members as to the current state of the company, while providing an opportunity to discuss different points of view. Good examples in this chart are elements 3, 6, and 7.

ANALYZING CAUSE-EFFECT RELATIONSHIPS USING THE INTERRELATIONSHIP DIGRAPH

Additional insight can be obtained from the Interrelationship Digraph (ID). It is frequently called the "Root Cause tool," because it helps identify the deep, causal issues that are frequently not apparent in the Vision. The ID for Power City Electric is shown in Figure 7.3. It was constructed by comparing each Vision Element with every other Element and asking the question, "Does Element A cause or enable Element B, or vice-versa ?" If element A is believed to be a cause or enabler of Element B, then an arrow is drawn from it to Element B. Only relatively strong relationships are considered. In addition, arrows are allowed in only one direction between two elements, so that in the case of causal or enabling relationships in both directions, the team is asked to determine the stronger or more fundamental relationship.

Interpretation of the ID is straightforward. Elements with a large preponderance of outgoing arrows are called primary causes or drivers. *They are the most influential elements in the overall success of the Vision.* Those Elements with a preponderance of incoming arrows are usually the desired outcomes in the Vision. Elements with both incoming and outgoing arrows will usually be important means of achieving the Vision.

The outcome Elements in the ID almost always relate to some or all of the organization's Critical Success Measures, like profitability (#9), growth (#9), cost (#4). Its interesting to note that outcomes are usually measured routinely by organizations, but drivers and intermediate steps frequently are not. Referring back to the discussion of leading and lagging performance indicators in Chapter 5, this observation may represent an opportunity for the organization to improve its business reporting and control systems.

SELECTION OF A VISION ELEMENT FOR STRATEGIC FOCUS

Selection of the most appropriate Vision Element to focus upon requires careful judgment of the team, supported by the information provided by the

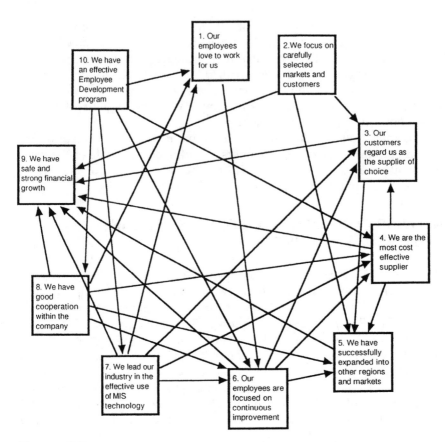

Figure 7.3 Using the Interrelationship Digraph to Reveal Cause-Effect Relationships Within the Vision (Cowley & Associates 1995)

Vision itself, the Radar Chart and ID analyses, and the Correlation Matrix, Figure 7.1. In the case of Power City Electric, the decision wasn't too difficult: the team observed that Element 10, "We have an Effective Employee Development Program" was a strong "Driver" (lots of outgoing arrows), and was also relatively weak on the Radar Chart (large "gap"). They also felt that it was the right thing to work on to improve their financial performance in the long run. So, without too much debate, they agreed that they should focus for at least the next six months or so on Employee Development issues, and the objective was stated as "Improve our Employee Development Program."

Determining the Most Effective Breakthrough for the Vision Element

Our example company has learned a great deal about itself in a short time (approximately three total days invested to this point), has set its direction through the creation of its future Vision, and even knows where work should start to clear the road to success. However, the chosen area of focus is still quite broad ("Improve the Employee Development Program"). Before a specific plan is developed, the team needs to narrow the focus to a more specific shorter-term goal.

An effective way to do this is to have the team revisit the Present Situation information used to develop the Vision, and, in particular, look at the relationship of the chosen Vision Element to the desired improvement in performance (financial performance, ultimately). This was done (in about an hour) by the electrical contractor team. The managers then brainstormed a large number of possible breakthrough actions that would address Employee Development. These were organized into Affinity groupings, just as was done in the Vision development, and the results are shown in Figure 7.4.

The team used the "$100 Test" to express their opinions about the relative value of these potential "Breakthroughs." The method is simply to give each team member ten adhesive labels ("$10 bills") to distribute any way desired among the options, reflecting their relative value. The results are shown at the top of Figure 7.5. "Project Manager Development" received the most votes in the $100 Test. After reflecting on this result, the team agreed unanimously to focus on this as the Hoshin objective. The observation had been made earlier that a particular area of weakness in the company was Project Manager performance and availability of potential new project managers from the employee pool; this had a detrimental effect on cost effectiveness (Vision Element #4), which in turn affected profitability (#9).

The Hoshin objective was restated as "Improve Project Manager Performance." In effect, the team decided that this was the first big "boulder" to be attacked on the road to their Vision (Figure 7.5).

Other Ways to Set the Breakthrough Objective

We mentioned in the last chapter that the management team, in the assessment of the Present Situation, may see something so obvious and so serious, that it needs immediate, focused attention. This could range from a serious financial loss situation, to a serious product failure. In any case, it may be obvious without going through the Visioning Process; if so, the management team might elect to identify it right away as the Hoshin objective. An example of such a case was the "On-time Delivery" problem described in Chapter 5.

METRICS

The next important step is to establish Metrics for the selected objective to facilitate determining progress on and completion of the objective in the planned time-frame. A metric is something tangible about the Breakthrough

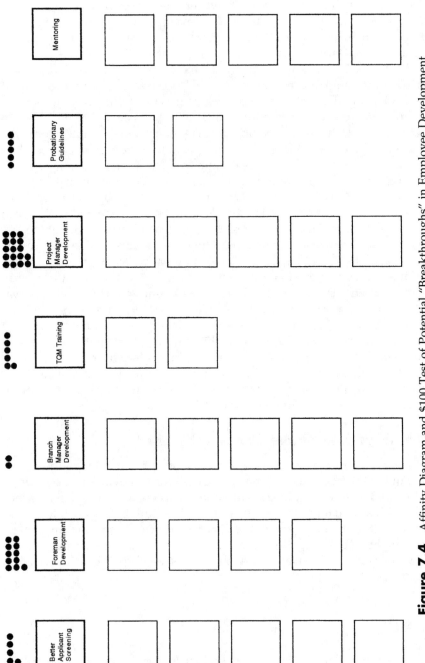

Figure 7.4 Affinity Diagram and $100 Test of Potential "Breakthroughs" in Employee Development (Cowley & Associates 1995)

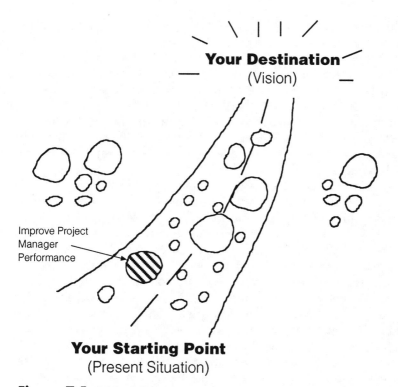

Figure 7.5 Identifying the First "Boulder" in the "Road" (Cowley & Associates 1995)

(or any other objective) that can be measured in a unambiguous way, and that can serve as a numeric indicator of the degree to which the breakthrough objective has been achieved. For example, if the Breakthrough selected was "Improve Employee Morale," then the metric could be the score on a simple Employee Survey designed to measure Employee Morale. In this case, an existing survey might be used by selecting an appropriate subset of questions from it.

In general, metrics fall into four classes:

- *Quality metrics,* which are measures of how well a task or strategy was done.
- *Delivery metrics,* which are measures of on-time or timely performance, and/or capacity.
- *Cost metrics,* which can include cost of plan implementation and ongoing cost of an improved operation.
- *Employee metrics,* including training, safety, and morale.

The team should select from this list the types of metrics they believe are most important to the success of the Objective. More than one metric may be used, and the above list ("QDCE") should always be used as a "checklist" when choosing metrics.

In the example of the electrical contractor, the metrics chosen for "Improve Project Manager Performance" were "Gross Profit Margin per Project Management Hour," and "Estimate Accuracy." Both of these metrics were easily obtained derivatives of the company's standard financial data, and, more important, were deemed to be critical measures of success for the Project Management process. It was unanimously felt that Breakthrough improvement in these measures would have a profound effect on the future success of the company.

Having selected a suitable metric, a numeric goal for the metric must be developed. Usually it is necessary to do some level of analysis (for example, trends of previous years' performance, if they exist) in order to set appropriate objectives, especially if the intent is to achieve true breakthrough. The analysis would, in this case, be directed at forecasting what GPM per project manager hour and Estimate accuracy would be in the absence of a Breakthrough improvement effort, so that the "breakthrough increment" could be added to form the goal. This process is depicted in Figure 7.6, and is an example of the principle of using "facts and data" to understand the present situation and to set goals. In setting "breakthrough" objectives, the idea is to set goals which are out of reach of the current set of management practices, so that the organization will be forced to consider innovative new approaches to the issue at hand. The goals must also be aggressive enough to meet the desired overall performance level embodied in the Vision.

WHERE DO BREAKTHROUGHS COME FROM?

As we stated in the last section, the process of obtaining breakthrough performance starts with setting an aggressive goal that forces the organization to consider new approaches to doing the task in question, in this case Project Management. The goal has to be seen by managers and employees alike as a worthy and necessary or highly desirable one, or commitment to it will be inadequate and of short duration. The managers setting the goal must be able to demonstrate a clear need or desire to meet the goal, and this is part of the role of the Vision.

But beyond setting a challenging goal, the issue of meeting it will normally require something different in the approach to doing the task. Our experience is that sometimes surprisingly basic, focused changes in the way of performing a task or basic business process can achieve the required improvement in performance, but sometimes a dramatic new invention or approach is required. In the case illustrated in Figure 7.6, the team determined from data and past experience that ten percent improvement was feasible with modest continuous improvement efforts, but the remainder of

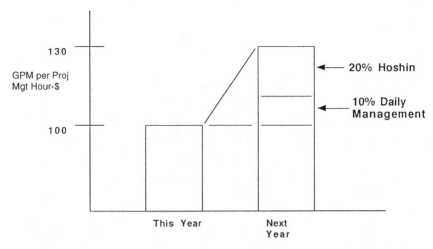

Figure 7.6 Setting the Breakthrough Objective for "Improve Project Management." Ten percent improvement can be achieved with the existing system, but a Breakthrough is needed to achieve the full thirty percent, based on the organization's understanding of their facts and data on the Project Management Process.

the desired thirty percent improvement would have to be contributed by a major change in method. We will pursue this further in the next chapter when we discuss strategies. In the "On-time Delivery" example of Chapter 5, the goal of ninety-five percent was needed to satisfy the company's customers. It was also challenging, and, when it was first set, was not clear how to achieve it, or that it could be achieved at all. This is characteristic of breakthrough objectives.

WHAT HAPPENS TO THE REMAINING VISION ELEMENTS AND OPERATIONAL OBJECTIVES?

An important feature of the Hoshin approach is to identify high-leverage areas for special, breakthrough focus. But in any organization, the day-to-day running of the business will usually occupy most of the time of most employees.

An additional element is introduced by the Vision; we've now opened "Pandora's box" and the management team is aware of many attractive opportunities for attention and effort. There needs to be an effective way to maintain an appropriate balance of time, effort, and attention among all of these components of managing the organization's activities.

A first step is to recognize that the day-to-day running of the business ("Daily Management") is usually based on established methods, the organization's Business Processes. We discussed this concept in Chapter 5.

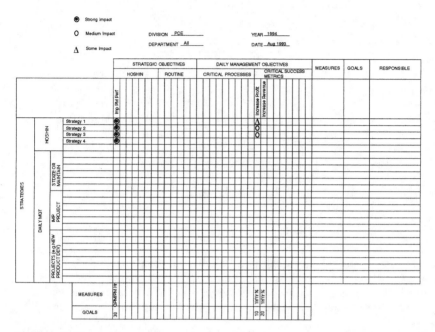

Figure 7.7   Operational and Strategic Goals on the same form, The Annual Business Plan (Cowley & Associates 1993)

Even for organizations which haven't consciously recognized Business Processes as such, the methods do exist, and the assumption can normally be made that these processes will either continue to run "as is," or will be subjected to incremental, continuous improvement efforts. So, the planning of the day-to-day activities of the business usually can be reduced to a simple statement of new goals for the organization's Critical Success Measures. The option also exists to include continuous improvement of Business Processes. The important thing to recognize is that *no new methods or processes have to be invented*; the methods already exist, and planning, for the most part, consists of agreeing on the performance goals for the business and their important resource implications. Figure 7.7 shows a method of displaying the Operational Planning goals of the organization, along with the Strategic goals, on one sheet of paper.

In contrast to Daily Management objectives, Hoshin objectives do require the creation of new approaches and methods. The organization must align itself to these objectives and create special strategies and tactics to achieve them. This is the purpose of the structure that Hoshin brings to bear on such objectives, and is the reason we usually recommend that only one Hoshin objective be undertaken in each planning period. Most organizations simply cannot successfully cope with more than one such objective, in addition to the demands of Daily Management. Figure 7.7 provides a special place to record Hoshin objectives, and other strategic objectives.

We will have more to say about Figure 7.7 in the next Chapter, but at this point, note that the columns are used to record objectives and the rows are used to record the strategies for meeting the objectives. The symbols in the cells defined by the rows and columns describe the impact each strategy has on each objective. Note that the special rows designated for Hoshin strategies contain 4 strategies (we'll show how these strategies are developed in the next chapter) that each have a strong impact on the Hoshin objective. This is expected, because they were designed to achieve the objective. What is interesting is that these strategies also have measurable impact on one of the operational objectives, "Increase Profit." This kind of leverage is common, and is especially visible in the matrix format of Figure 7.7.

Another reason we strongly recommend the use of a document like Figure 7.7 is that management teams almost always have difficulty "juggling" their strategic goals with their operational goals. We have found that a vital first step in resolving this difficulty is getting clear visibility of the total plan in a simple format. If the entire plan is visible, it is usually much easier for the management team to get a sense of how their time needs to be allocated, and whether the potential exists for overcommitment of the organization. We'll show in the next chapter how to extend this concept further to the strategy level, and in Chapter 11, to the Review Process.

In the meantime, what of the other Vision Elements? The team has made the decision to focus on only one of them, as we discussed earlier in this chapter, but the option exists to begin tracking some of the others through the organization's Critical Success Measures or Process Measures, using the information in Figure 7.1. We would caution the reader not to allow this activity to distract the team from the Hoshin objective, however.

DISCUSSION

In this chapter we have taken the first important step in developing the organization's Hoshin Plan, development of the Hoshin Objective, and also have shown how to integrate it with the Operational Objectives. We should stress again the importance of using the tools we have introduced to focus the organization on a very limited number of Hoshin objectives, preferably one for organizations using Hoshin for the first time. In the next two chapters, we will work on deployment of the plan into the organization, using the concept of "catchball." We will also show some simple, basic methods of dealing with the issue of resource allocation and organizational capacity.

Chapter 8

Developing the High-Level Strategies

In Chapter 7 we discussed how to select the objective for Breakthrough focus. In this chapter we will describe methods for achieving the objective. The methods will be applicable to *any* objectives the organization wishes to achieve, not just Hoshin objectives, but since there is quite a bit of rigor involved, our recommendation is to confine their use initially to the Hoshin objective. When the organization has achieved skill and confidence in their use (usually after a year or so), the methods can be applied more widely.

The actions required to achieve an objective are generally called strategies. However, we should also keep in mind that the achievement of objectives in the realm of day-to-day business (Daily Management) may not require special strategies; the existing business processes may do nicely. Generally, a combination of existing processes (which can be thought of as repetitive strategies) and special strategies is required to meet Hoshin objectives.

FIRST-LEVEL STRATEGY DEVELOPMENT

The Planning Team needs to identify first the high-level strategies for meeting the Hoshin objective. These are the major thrusts, or broad directions, the organization must take to achieve the objective. As such, they can be very difficult to develop. We have had success with an approach that is quite simple; it is identical in concept to the method used to develop the Vision, using the Affinity Diagram.

To illustrate the approach, we will use again the example of the Electrical Contractor, Power City Electric. The Hoshin objective was "Improve Project Management." The first step in developing strategies is to formulate an appropriate question to drive brainstorming, in this case, "What are all the things we can do to improve Project Management?"

The next step is to brainstorm answers to the question. These answers, recorded on Post-its™, are then grouped and titled, as described in Chapter 13, the Affinity Diagram process, and the titles are candidates for the first-level strategies we seek. The actual results are shown in Figure 8.1.

The team is then asked to examine the strategy candidates, and to arrange them as shown in Figure 8.2. This arrangement is called a Tree Diagram and is another one of the Management and Planning Tools described in Chapter 13. Specifically, the team is asked to form a judgment, using data if possible, on whether each of the candidates is necessary to meet the objective. After discussion, they are asked to remove any strategies that are not believed to have a strong impact on the objective. Some teams prefer to use the "$100 Test" to make this decision, and this approach is shown in Figure 8.3.

What are all the things we need to do to Improve Project Manager Performance?

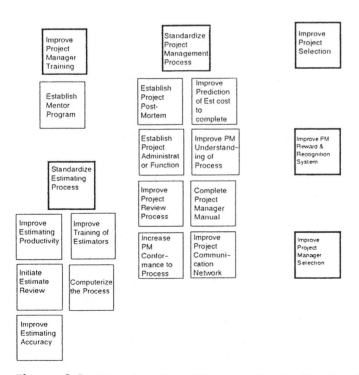

Figure 8.1 Using the Affinity Diagram to Develop First-Level Strategy Candidates (Cowley & Associates 1995)

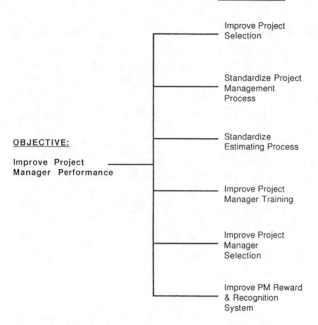

Figure 8.2 First-Level Strategy Candidates Arranged on a Tree Diagram (Cowley & Associates 1995)

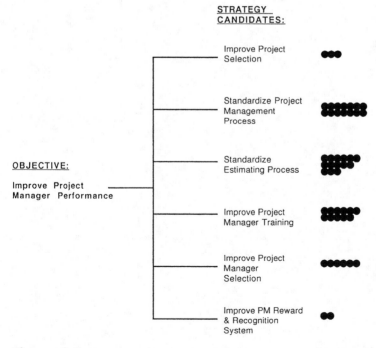

Figure 8.3 Using the $100 Test to Select the First-Level Strategies (Cowley & Associates 1995)

For the surviving strategies, the team is now asked to examine if these strategies together are sufficient to meet the objective, based on common sense and their specific business and technical knowledge of the situation. In some cases, more in-depth analysis may need to be done, and experts outside the planning team may have to be consulted. Sometimes, teams will recognize at this point that something important is missing and will add it to the Tree Diagram; teams may need additional time to reflect on the strategy set before committing to it. Figure 8.4 illustrates the completed Tree Diagram.

METRICS AND GOALS

Just as for the Hoshin Objective, the Strategies need to have numerical measures to allow judgment of how well they need to be done, at what cost, and by what completion date. The goals for these metrics, especially completion dates, might be tentative, pending development of the lower-level details.

TIME SEQUENCE OF STRATEGIES

Generally there will be some dependency among the Strategies, that is, some might need to be completed before others can start. It is useful to lay them

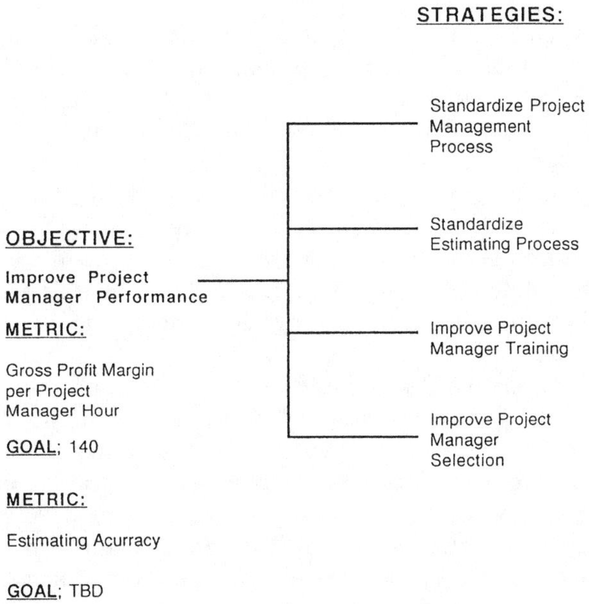

STRATEGIES:

OBJECTIVE:

Improve Project Manager Performance

METRIC:

Gross Profit Margin per Project Manager Hour

GOAL; 140

METRIC:

Estimating Acurracy

GOAL; TBD

- Standardize Project Management Process
- Standardize Estimating Process
- Improve Project Manager Training
- Improve Project Manager Selection

Figure 8.4 Final First-Level Strategies (Cowley & Associates 1995)

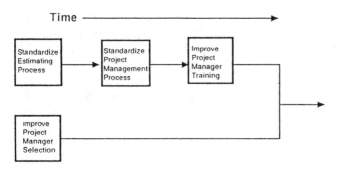

Figure 8.5   Sequencing the First-Level Strategies (Cowley & Associates 1995)

out on a timeline, on Post-its™ as shown in Figure 8.5, to see these dependencies and to arrive at logical sequencing. The method we have used is another of the Management and Planning Tools, called an Activity Network Diagram. It is a version of the Critical Path Method (CPM), probably familiar to many as a project management tool, and available in many off-the-shelf software packages.

BREAKTHROUGH AT THE STRATEGY LEVEL: CREATIVE THINKING

We mentioned in the last chapter that setting an aggressive goal for the Hoshin Objective was only the first step in the process, and that it would force the organization out of its current mind-set. Part of the process for doing this can be addressed by having the Planning team address some basic questions.

If what we are trying to achieve is a major improvement in something we are currently doing, do we understand fully why our current approach or process can't deliver the desired performance? For example, in the case of the Project Management objective, the team examined this question by doing a post-mortem on a number of poorly-performing projects, and a number of relatively successful projects, to get ideas for improvement.

If what we are trying to achieve is something we've never done before, has anyone else done something similar that might apply to our situation? For example, in the case of the "ABC Semiconductor Company" trying to achieve breakthrough improvement in on-time-delivery, one of the team members noticed that what they were trying to do resembled very closely the concept of an airline's seat reservation system. They were able to apply this model to a redesign of their order acknowledgment and production scheduling systems, thereby making the systems interactive and obtaining an elegant and effective solution.

Is what we are trying to do different from anything that has ever been done, to our knowledge? In this case, techniques have been developed (de Bono 1992; Nadler and Hibino 1990) to assist in the process of inventing new approaches and methods. The work of de Bono is especially interesting in that he examines the processes our brains use to solve problems and asserts that, unfortunately, our brains are inherently "programmed " to avoid going down unfamiliar, untried paths in search of innovative solutions. He discusses ways of overcoming this tendency.

Realistically, though, we have to take to heart the observation that many of the most profound inventions and discoveries down through the ages have been accidents or chance occurrences. It would seem that this implies that an approach to creativity could be to provide a mechanism for sorting quickly through many events and experimental results that could have applicability to the Hoshin Objective, by consulting experts, on-line searches, focused brainstorming sessions with any and all in the organization, and so forth, to come up with ideas. Many Japanese companies use sophisticated Employee Suggestion Systems to enhance the brainstorming approach. Concepts and applications from other disciplines sometimes help to break "paradigms" in the organization's primary discipline.

Another reality in seeking "breakthroughs" is that the organization will have to go "beyond brainstorming." Research and profound knowledge in the subject disciplines is necessary, although perhaps not sufficient, to produce breakthroughs. One type of research is benchmarking, described in Chapter 14.

HOW TO RECOGNIZE AND ADDRESS CROSS-ORGANIZATIONAL ISSUES

One of the most powerful features of Hoshin is its ability to address cross-organization or cross-functional issues. The existence of such issues can frequently be recognized at lower-levels of the organization as "lack of cooperation," or inability of the organization to solve basic problems for lack of coordination between departments, divisions, or functions. What is usually not apparent, however, is the opportunities that can exist to make "the whole greater than the sum of the parts" through creative combination of the capabilitites and competencies in the organization. These can frequently only be seen when the organization is viewed as a system, as we discussed in Chapter 5.

Using the high-level Process Map we introduced in Chapter 5 is one of the best ways to identify these issues and to determine who must be involved to address them. A classic example is New Product Development. This process is frequently viewed as the province of the "R & D" Department, but is really a cross-functional process involving heavy contributions from Research & Development, Marketing, and Manufacturing functions, with participation from the Finance and Quality Assurance functions, as well as from the Sales and Distribution functions. In the normal course of running this activity, or in any effort to improve it, the leadership of all these functions should be deeply involved.

Another example of a cross-functional issue is the "On-time Delivery" case we discussed. In this case, the Manufacturing (scheduling), Sales (order acknowledgment), and IT (computer system development) functions were involved, and a cross-functional leadership team consisting of managers from each of these departments was given joint ownership of the project.

The spirit that such teams need to generate is one where the successful creation of the ideal solution becomes the team's focus and transcends any local or departmental priorities. Involvement of the Functional Managers in a Steering mode is often helpful, to overcome any barriers that might arise because of functional priorities.

Figure 8.6 shows how the management of the "On-time Delivery" project was handled in the semiconductor company. Note that the General Manager's direct functional reports play the "Steering" role, while selected next-level managers have day-to-day responsibility for leadership of the project.

Existing Processes and Systems May Be Part of the Problem

In the preceding discussion, it should be recognized that the High-Level Process Map represents the existing organization and how it works. The planning team should be open to the possibility that this current system

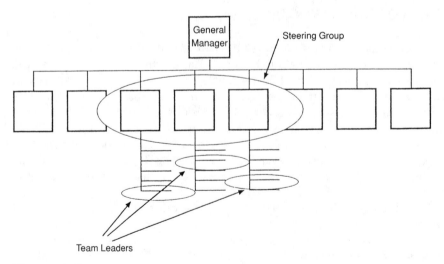

Figure 8.6 Organization of the Effort to Address a Cross-Functional Issue
(Cowley & Associates 1995)

could be "part of the problem," that is, a barrier to a creative solution, and hence should be open to creative ways of eliminating this obstacle by organization and/or business process changes or additions, replacements, or deletions.

DELIBERATE AND EMERGENT STRATEGIES

The intent in planning is to identify at the outset the objectives and the means (strategies) for achieving the objectives. This is frequently very difficult, because in the planning phase the problem or challenge of the objective is not nearly as well understood as it will be after some, possibly considerable, effort has been invested. In the example of the small lingerie shop (Chapter 3), the team struggled for a year before concluding that the current plan wasn't going to work, and the plan was changed to one that did work. In that case, it was the objective itself that was not feasible.

An important feature of Hoshin is that the process requires frequent in-depth reviews to check progress and to continually evaluate the feasibility of the strategies and objectives. The review process will be described in detail in Chapter 11, but the point we wish to make here is that the planning team must continuously be prepared to abandon strategies and objectives that, in the light of new knowledge and insight, are seen to be unworkable. New objectives and strategies must then be sought. These are called emergent strategies.

OWNERSHIP OF STRATEGIES AND OBJECTIVES

The responsibility and accountability for every element of the organization's plan must be clearly assigned to an individual, or, occasionally, a small team of people. This includes objectives, strategies, and tactics. The form of Figure 8.7 is designed with spaces for filling in the names of the owners. Usually ownership is hierarchical, that is, the CEO will own the objectives and his/her direct reports will own strategies as individuals, or as teams, but other arrangements are also possible.

In the next chapter we will introduce some alternative forms for documenting objectives, strategies, metrics, owners, and goals, and we will elaborate on the responsibilities of owners in the Hoshin system of planning.

ALIGNMENT

It is normal for organizations to have projects going on at the time of planning, for a variety of reasons: new products, improved processes, new capa-

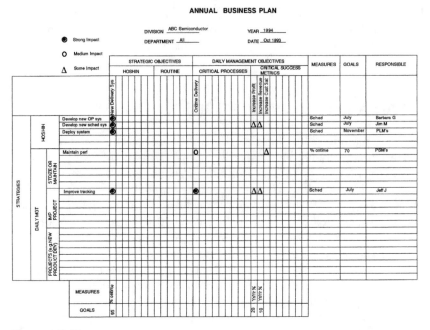

Figure 8.7   High-Level Plan on the Annual Business Plan Matrix (Cowley & Associates 1993)

bilities, expansion of existing capacity, and so on. When the Hoshin Objective is developed, the leaders of these efforts should look carefully for opportunities to align these activities to the Hoshin Objective.

For example, in the "On-time Delivery" example, an improvement team was working on the existing process and were able to make a major contribution to the Hoshin effort by contributing the ongoing Delivery Performance tracking system that they had developed. Some members of that team transferred to the Hoshin team, while others remained and continued to hold the existing process to its best possible performance while the new process was being developed, a two-year period. They became part of the transition team when the new process was introduced.

This situation is depicted on the form introduced in Chapter 7 (Figure 7.7) and used here as Figure 8.7. Here we see the key Hoshin strategies, concerned mostly with creation of the new scheduling and order-acknowledgment systems, as well as the On-time Delivery Improvement Project, which had been ongoing, both supporting the Hoshin objective.

Again, the utility of this format is that it is easy to list all of the organization's objectives across the top of the form, and all of its ongoing projects and activities down the left side, and then to see the extent to which the activities support the objectives. This can serve as a crude indicator of any activities that might be considered for termination, on the grounds that they compete for resources with activities that strongly support the organizations Strategic and Operational Objectives.

THE "THREE DS": DELETE, DEFER, DELEGATE

As we mentioned earlier, the biggest temptation executives will have in this process is biting off more than the organization can chew. A simple discipline to help avoid this is to use the "Three Ds": Delete, Defer, Delegate. All existing and proposed projects and activities should be examined for alignment with either the Hoshin or essential Operational objectives, then three questions should be asked:

- Can we delete it?
- Can we defer it?
- Should we delegate it?

Figure 8.7 can be helpful for this purpose. If an existing or proposed activity can't be shown to have strong impact on the high-level objectives, then the questions need to be asked. Some organizations like to add a fourth "D": Do. If it is obvious that something needs to be done, simply do it.

DISCUSSION

In this chapter we have shown how the Hoshin process can be used to develop the organization's High-Level Plan. This plan now needs to be further deployed into the organization, to the managers and individuals who will perform most of the work.

REFERENCES

de Bono, Edward. *Serious Creativity*. New York: HarperBusiness, 1992.
Nadler, Gerald and Hibino, Shozo. *Breakthrough Thinking*. Rocklin, CA: Prima, 1990.

Chapter 9

Deployment of the First-Level Strategies (Catchball)

The Hoshin Objectives and first-level strategies developed in Chapter 8 are called the High-Level Plan. In many organizations the executive team would "hand-off" the high-level plan at this point and expect the organization to somehow execute the strategic intent of the planning team. In the Hoshin process, this step is a formal part of the process, and until concrete strategies and tactics are developed to support the high-level plan, the executive team is not finished. This process is called deployment of the plan.

In Figure 9.1 we have shown a Tree Diagram of the type developed in the last chapter, with the addition of the supporting strategies and tactics (tactics left blank for now). As each strategy level is developed, there is a need for a convenient way to record all the important information, beyond what can be conveniently placed on a Tree Diagram. A form for doing this is shown in Figure 9.2 and is called the Annual Plan Table. Each objective and strategy has its own Annual Plan Table. The concept is that the objective or strategy being documented is recorded in the "Objective" box in the upper left hand corner of the form, with its metrics and goals in the boxes below it, and the strategies that support it are listed on the right side of the form, together with their owners, metrics, and goals. The Hoshin Objective and the first-level strategies (the high-level plan) for the example of Figure 9.1 are shown in Figure 9.2.

We will describe the process of developing the supporting strategies and tactics later in the chapter, but it is useful to develop the overview of the process at this point. The first important point in the overview is that the scheme that we developed in the last chapter to develop the first-level strategies is simply replicated at lower levels in the organization. The first-level strategies become the objectives for the next level of strategies, meaning

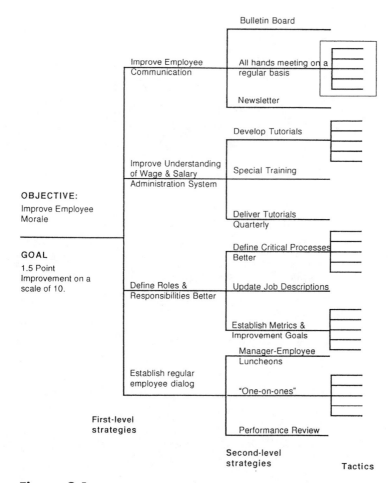

Figure 9.1   Supporting Strategies and Tactics shown in "Tree" Format (Cowley & Associates 1993)

that the second-level strategies are what must be done to achieve the first-level strategies. Similarly, the third-level of strategies are what must be done to achieve the second-level strategies, and so on. When strategies become detailed, well-defined tasks, they are called tactics. The tactics are the last items in the Tree Diagram, on the right hand side. *All plans must be developed to the point of having the tactical details.* Figure 9.1 depicts the existence of a second-level strategy set, which are directly deployed to Tactics.

The second point in the overview is that the entire plan will need to be developed by a series of meetings at successively lower levels in the organization until the tactical details are developed. Then, the plans must be reviewed starting at the bottom of the organization, working up until the entire plan has been reviewed and is judged to be self-consistent. The de-

Date October 15, 1991	By Joe Smith	Year 1992	Theme: Our employees are committed and satisfied	
Objective	Strategies	Owners	Measures	Goals
Improve Employee Morale	Improve Employee Communication	Mary I.	Relevant Survey Question Score Improvement	4.0
Measure	Improve Understanding of Wage & Salary Administration System	Jim S.	Relevant Survey Question Score Improvement	4.0
Employee Survey Score (10 question survey)	Define Roles & Responsibilities Better	Jerry K., Stan G., Jim L.	Relevant Survey Question Score Improvement	4.0
Goal				
1.5 Point Improvement on a scale of 10.	Establish regular employee dialog	George C.	Improvement in Score for remaining survey questions	1.0

Figure 9.2   First-Level Strategies Recorded on an Annual Plan Table (Cowley & Associates 1993)

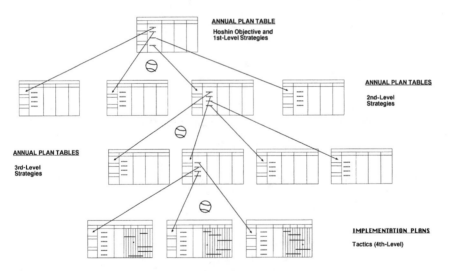

Figure 9.3   Hoshin Deployment Using Annual Plan Tables (Cowley & Associates 1995)

ployment process is depicted in Figure 9.3. Here the reader should note the following: (1) In the interests of saving space, the entire plan is not shown; for example, only one set of second-level strategies is shown being deployed to the third-level, and only one set of third-level strategies is shown deployed to the Implementation Plan (Tactical) level. (2) We have shown three strategy levels, with all strategies being deployed to Tactics at the fourth-level. In other situations, there may be more or fewer strategy levels, and the tactical level may be different for different strategies.

The process described in Figure 9.3 is called "catchball" by the Japanese. This term emphasizes the fact that its purpose is to give all the participants in the process the opportunity to throw ideas back and forth, at each level, about what can be done to achieve each strategy, where there might be problems in capability or capacity, and what commitments need to be made to address these problems. The intent is to get a true picture of organizational capability, and to get the focus of the organization on those areas where the biggest obstacles or opportunities lie, relative to the achievement of the Hoshin. This requires, at all levels, an attitude of honesty on the part of employees, and a willingness to listen and believe on the part of supervisors and managers.

Figure 9.4 shows the process of "rolling up" the first version of the plan, which is a review of the plan at each level until it reaches the top of the organization. At this point it is theoretically possible that the entire plan will need to be "rolled down" and back up again, but typically a few adjustments of the plan suffice to make it final.

"Catchball" is the biggest difference between Hoshin and Management By Objectives (MBO). In Hoshin the planning process isn't complete until the Objectives *and* all strategies and tactics are agreed to and thought to be self-consistent by the entire organization. Effective use of this concept requires both clarity of organizational capability, and recognition of where the current capability isn't sufficient and improvements are needed. Managers and employees must feel challenged and inspired by the prospect of being able to achieve things that are out of the ordinary, not fearful of failure if they don't. For many organizations, instilling these attitudes requires a major culture change. We'll discuss this at greater length in Chapter 12. Meanwhile, we will proceed to the details of deploying the first-level plan, starting with communication to the remainder of the organization of the intent and results to date of the planning effort.

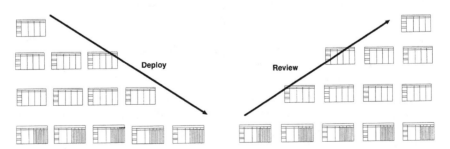

Figure 9.4   Hoshin Deployment and Plan Review (Cowley & Associates 1995)

COMMUNICATION OF THE HOSHIN PLAN

The Hoshin system is different enough from past practice for most organizations that some preparation is required before deployment is started. Managers and employees who are expected to participate in Hoshin planning need to understand the intent and basic philosophy of the process, and also need to be aware of the results that were achieved at the initial planning meetings. We will leave the details of doing this to the reader, but a successful general approach is to let it be known at the outset that the senior team is working on the high-level plan, and that there is an expectation of participation by the other organization members, followed by forwarding the notes of the initial planning meetings to all participants. Training on the Hoshin concepts can be provided by the senior managers as they conduct their deployment meetings, as we will describe below.

DEVELOPMENT OF THE SECOND-LEVEL STRATEGIES

The process of developing the second-level strategies is conducted by each of the first-level strategy owners with their direct reports, and/or cross-functional teams, using a process identical to that used to develop the first-level strategies. Each strategy owner holds an initial meeting (one or two days) for this purpose. Part of the meeting will be devoted to a review of what has been done to date. This review will be facilitated by the fact that all the attendees will have received notes of the high-level management meetings. Training on Hoshin principles can be combined with this review. Our experience is that, while all the details may not be clear at this point, the meeting attendees will quickly grasp the concepts as they develop their plan.

The first-level strategy owners will have thought of some of the second-level strategies that are required. But in light of the new insights brought to the process by their teams, it is better to start the strategy formation process from scratch, with the brainstorming and Affinity Diagram process we described in Chapter 8, so fresh new ideas can be contributed. Owners for the second-level strategies should be sought and decided upon, and the owners tasked with committing to metrics and goals that collectively assure achievement of the first-level strategies, as before. This process is called "catchball," since it involves "tossing" ideas back and forth to finally arrive at those which are mutually agreeable as strategies, metrics, and goals. The managers will need to challenge their teams with difficult goal proposals to assure breakthrough thinking. It is the first-level strategy owner's responsibility to lead his/her team in the examination of the second-level strategies, to assure that they are both necessary and sufficient to meet their objectives, the first-level strategies.

Frequent outcomes of these meetings, and of "catchball" meetings in general, are:

- The team will discover a major capability shortfall in their ability to meet their objective (the first-level strategy). They may have to make an agreement to accept the challenge, while making it clear that they can't see an obvious path to success, and hope that a creative solution will be found somewhere in the next levels of "catchball," or during implementation.
- It may become obvious that some cross-organizational cooperation is needed to address the main strategy, or one of the sub-strategies. The strategy owner might take the responsibility to acquire the necessary cooperation.
- A variant of the last point is that the team may decide that a key participant is missing (for example from another department) and invite that participant to join the team.
- The team might feel confident that it can meet the objective, and might even suggest raising the goal.

The team may need subsequent meetings to finalize its thinking, but, ultimately, they will emerge with the second-level of strategies, with metrics, goals, and owners. Their counterparts for the other first-level strategies will be doing the same thing concurrently, and, where necessary, will have been working collaboratively on cross-organization issues as they are identified.

The next step will be for the second-level strategy owners to assemble their own teams and begin the process of developing third-level strategies, using the identical set of procedures. And so forth.

TACTICS

When the deployment process has come down to a level where strategies are becoming clearly defined projects, or where the actions to achieve them are clearly defined tasks that can be accomplished without further definition, or a combination of the two, we call these projects, or tasks, tactics. There is no further need for deployment using the Hoshin formal process, but these tasks and projects can be planned using conventional project planning methods (CPM, Microsoft® Project, etc.). We will show in the next chapter how these items are deployed in an Implementation Plan. The Implementation Plan level may be different for different branches of the planning "tree."

TIMING OF THE DEPLOYMENT (CATCHBALL) PROCESS

The first time Hoshin is used, it might take two weeks or more to perform each level of the catchball process. With practice, and excellent planning and coordination, most organizations can manage about a week per level. Thus, the entire deployment process for a plan with three strategy levels should take about two months, including development and review of the final tactical level (the fourth-level in this case).

DOCUMENTATION

The Tree Diagram (Figure 9.1) is a useful tool for summarizing the entire plan. It shows clearly the linkage of each strategy, project, and task to the final objective. It should be used as a unifying document to explain and discuss the plan. The format of Figure 9.2, The Annual Plan Table, has the virtue that it is easily understood. The same form can be used to document the plan down to the Implementation Level, which we will describe in the next chapter.

At the next level (Figure 9.5), the Strategies from Figure 9.2 become the Objectives on the Annual Plan Tables and the strategies are the second-level strategies, and so on, to the lowest-level strategies. The last strategies are deployed to an Implementation Plan, which contains the tactics required to achieve each strategy. The inset shows the continuation of the two-strategy-level plan described in Figures 9.1 and 9.2. This is an actual example, used with the kind permission of one of our clients.

Improving Employee Morale

This example is an actual case, in which the management team decided to work on a Vision Element entitled "Our employees are committed and satisfied." Observation and data (an employee survey) showed that the actual situation was far from that described in the Vision, and this element turned out to be a strong driver for the Vision. The objective agreed upon was "Improve Employee Morale," and the metric was the score on the Employee Survey. The goal was a 1.5 point improvement on a scale of 10, in one year (from 6.5 to 8.0). Figure 9.5 shows the Tree Diagram with the first- and second-level strategies. The second-level strategies, enclosed in the box in Figure 9.5, are shown in the Annual Plan Table in Figure 9.6. We will show one of these second-level strategies ("Establish 'all hands' meeting") deployed to an Implementation Plan in the next chapter.

Matrices

The matrix format of Figure 7.7 is also useful for summarizing the entire high-level plan, and for showing the relationships among the Operational and Strategic elements of the plan.

This matrix leads to an alternative, or additional, method of documenting strategies. The matrix equivalents of Figures 9.2 and 9.6 are shown in Figures 9.7 and 9.8, respectively. Note that symbols are now used to denote the connections between objectives and strategies, and strategies and owners. Similar symbols, with a different meaning, are used to denote responsibility for each strategy.

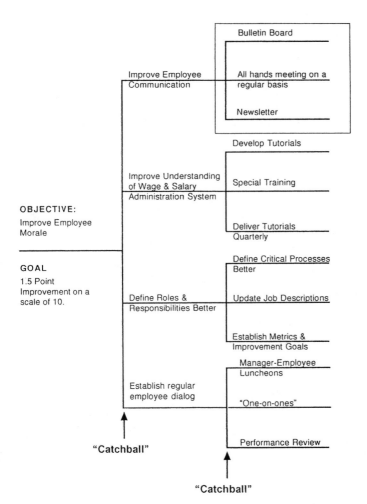

Figure 9.5   Second-Level Strategies (Cowley & Associates 1993)

The matrix method may be a little confusing at first, but it allows the strategies at any level to be recorded on one form, albeit large, and it adds a powerful new capability, which can be seen in Figure 9.9. In Figure 9.8, the first three strategies were originally developed for the first objective, "Improve Employee Communication." The fourth through sixth strategies were developed for the second objective, "Improve Understanding of the Wage and Salary System," and so forth. But in Figure 9.9, we notice that some strategies have impact on objectives other than the ones for which they were originally developed. For example, the first strategy, "Develop a Bulletin Board," was originally conceived to support "Improve Employee Communication," but is also judged by the team to have substantial potential impact on "Establish Regular Employee Dialog." With some minor "tuning" of Bulletin Board content, this potential was realized and enhanced the "Establish Regular Employee Dialog" objective, as well as supported "Improve

Date ___October 22, 1991___ By ___Mary I.___ Year ___1992___   Theme: Our employees are committed and satisfied

Objective	Strategies	Owners	Measures	Goals
Improve Employee Communication	Develop Bulletin Board	Freda	Coverage of Work Areas	90%
Measure	Establish "All Hands" Meeting	Edith	Frequency	1/month
Relevant Survey Question Score Improvement	Publish Newsletter	Theresa	Frequency #Pages	1/Quarter >6
Goal				
4.0				

Figure 9.6 Second-Level Strategies Recorded on an Annual Plan Table (Cowley & Associates 1993)

ANNUAL PLAN MATRIX

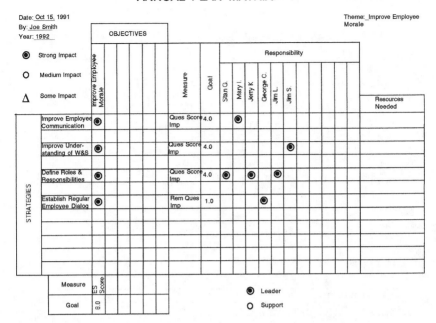

Date: Oct 15, 1991
By: Joe Smith
Year: 1992

Theme: Improve Employee Morale

◉ Strong Impact
○ Medium Impact
△ Some Impact

OBJECTIVES

Responsibility: Stan G., Mary I., Jerry K, George C., Jim L., Jim S.

Resources Needed

STRATEGIES	Improve Employee Morale	Measure	Goal	Stan G.	Mary I.	Jerry K	George C.	Jim L.	Jim S.
Improve Employee Communication	◉	Ques Score Imp	4.0		◉				
Improve Understanding of W&S	◉	Ques Score Imp	4.0					◉	
Define Roles & Responsibilities	◉	Ques Score Imp	4.0	◉		◉		◉	
Establish Regular Employee Dialog	◉	Rem Ques Imp	1.0				◉		

Measure: ES Score
Goal: 8.0

◉ Leader
○ Support

Figure 9.7 The Matrix Equivalent of Figure 9.2 (Cowley & Associates 1993)

ANNUAL PLAN MATRIX

Date: Oct 15, 1991
By: Joe Smith staff
Year: 1992

Theme: Improve Employee Morale

◉ Strong Impact
○ Medium Impact
△ Some Impact

OBJECTIVES

Responsibility: Freda, Edith, Theresa, All FM's, All mgrs/sups, Joe

Resources Needed

STRATEGIES	Improve Employee Communication	Improve Understanding of W&S	Define Roles & Responsibilities	Establish Regular Employee Dialog	Measure	Goal	Freda	Edith	Theresa	All FM's	All mgrs/sups	Joe
Bulletin Board	◉				Coverage	90%	◉				○	
All hands meeting on a regular basis	◉				Frequency	1/mo		◉		○		○
Newsletter	◉				Frequency / # pages	1/Q >6			◉		○	
Develop Tutorials		◉			Eval score	>8		◉				
Special Training		◉			Eval score	>8	◉					
Deliver Tutorials Quarterly		◉			Frequency	1/Q				◉		
Define CP's better			◉		% CP's Documented	90					◉	
Update Job Descriptions			◉		% Documented	90			○		◉	
Establish Metrics & Imp Goals			◉		% Established	30					◉	
Manager-Emp Luncheons				◉	Frequency	1/mo		○			◉	
"One-on-ones"				◉	Frequency	1/mo					◉	
Perf Review				◉	Frequency	1/yr	○				◉	

Measure: Ques Imp, Ques Imp, Ques Imp, Rem Q Imp
Goal: 4.0, 4.0, 4.0, 1.0

◉ Leader
○ Support

Figure 9.8 The Matix Equivalent of Figure 9.6 and Counterparts (Cowley & Associates 1993)

ANNUAL PLAN MATRIX

Date: Oct 15, 1991
By: Joe Smith staff
Year: 1992

Theme: Improve Employee Morale

◉ Strong Impact
O Medium Impact
Δ Some Impact

STRATEGIES	Improve Employee Communication	Improve Understanding of W&S	Define Roles & Responsibilities	Establish Regular Employee Dialog	Measure	Goal	Freda	Edith	Theresa	All FM's	All mgrs/sups	Joe	Resources Needed
Bulletin Board	◉			O	Coverage	90%	◉				O		
All hands meeting on a regular basis	◉			Δ	Frequency	1/mo	◉		O		O		
Newsletter	◉			O	Frequency # pages	1/Q >6		◉		O			
Develop Tutorials		◉			Eval score	>8		◉					
Special Training	O	◉		Δ	Eval score	>8	◉						
Deliver Tutorials Quarterly		◉		Δ	Frequency	1/Q				◉			
Define CP's better	O		◉	O	% CP's Documented	90					◉		
Update Job Descriptions		◉			% Documented	90			O		◉		
Establish Metrics & Imp Goals	O	◉			% Established	30					◉		
Manager-Emp Luncheons	O			◉	Frequency	1/mo	O				◉		
"One-on-ones"	O	O	O	◉	Frequency	1/mo					◉		
Perf Review	O	O	O	◉	Frequency	1/yr	O				◉		
Measure	Ques Imp	Ques Imp	Ques Imp	Item Q Imp									
Goal	4.0	4.0	4.0	1.0									

◉ Leader
O Support

Figure 9.9 Annual Plan Matrix of Figure 9.8 Showing Cross-linking of Second-Level Strategies (Cowley & Associates 1993)

Employee Communication." There is synergy among strategies, which can be recorded on the matrix form, but which is harder to discern in the Annual Plan Table. Such synergies can be significant, and can substantially increase the overall impact of the plan. In addition, this format makes it easier to spot redundancies at any strategy level.

The Tree Diagram, Annual Plan Tables, and Annual Plan Matrices are all somewhat redundant, but each contributes a unique view of the plan. Our advice is to use, as a minimum, the Tree Diagram, for a broad overview of the plan, and either the Annual Plan Tables or the Annual Plan Matrices for the detailed view. As we will see in the next chapter, the Implementation Plan is also mandatory. The Performance Measures Table is optional, for clarification if needed.

For a fast but effective method of documenting plans, try using the Outline capability that exists in most word processing packages. An example is shown in Figure 9.11 for the "Employee Morale" example. Finally, most spreadsheet programs lend themselves pretty readily to creation of either the Annual Plan Table or the Annual Plan Matrix. Examples are shown in Figures 9.12 and 9.13.

For a very small company on one site, the bulletin board might be the most effective way to communicate the plan. For larger organizations, e-mail, groupware, or "Intranet" approaches are appropriate, if they exist, or the old-fashioned paper hardcopy works fine, if they don't.

Date Oct 15, 1991 By Joe Smith Year 1992

Strategy or Objective	Performance Measure	Goal	Action Limits	Review Period	Control Documents	Formulas, Remarks, etc
Improve Employee Morale	Employee Survey Score	8.0	+0.5 / -0.2	1/Year	Employee Survey July 1990 Version	Score=Average of the responses to Questions 41-50 inclusive
Improve Employee Communication	Survey Question Score	9.0	+/- 0.5	1/Q	Employee Survey July 1990 Version	Ques # 42 score
Improve Understanding of W&S	Survey Question Score	8.0	+/- 0.5	1/Q	Employee Survey July 1990 Version	Ques # 44 score
Define Roles & Responsibilities	Survey Question Score	9.0	+/- 0.5	1/Q	Employee Survey July 1990 Version	Ques # 47 score
Establish Regular Employee Dialog	Survey Question Score	8.0	+0.5 / -0.0	1/Q	Employee Survey July 1990 Version	Average score of remaining questions

Figure 9.10 Performance Measures Table. This table provides a place to define or clarify Performance Measures.
(Cowley & Associates 1993)

Improve Employee Morale

1. Improve Employee Communication
   1.1. Bulletin Board
   1.2. All hands meeting on a regular basis
   1.3. Newsletter
2. Improve Understanding of Wage & Salary Administration System
   2.1. Develop Tutorials
   2.2. Special Training
   2.3. Deliver Tutorials
3. Define Roles and Responsibilities Better
   3.1. Define Critical Processes Better
   3.2. Update Job Descriptions
   3.3. Establish Metrics & Improvement Goals
4. Establish Regular Employee Dialog
   4.1. Manager-Employee Luncheons
   4.2. "One-on-ones"
   4.3. Performance Review

Figure 9.11   Outline Method of Documenting Hoshin Plan (Cowley & Associates 1996)

ANNUAL PLAN TABLE				
Date: October 15, 1991	By: Joe Smith	Theme: Our employees are committed and satisfied		
Objective:	STRATEGIES	OWNERS	MEASURES	GOALS
Improve Employee Morale	1.Improve Employee Communication	Mary I.	Score Improvement	4
Measure:	2.Improve Understanding of Wage & Salary Administration System	Jim S.	Score Improvement	4
Employee Survey Score	3.Define Roles and Responsibilities Better	Jerry K./StanG./Jim L.	Score Improvement	4
Goal:	4.Establish Regular Employee Dialog	George C.	Score Improvement	1
1.5 point improvement				

Figure 9.12   Spreadsheet version of an Annual Plan Table (Cowley & Associates 1996)

RESPONSIBILITIES OF STRATEGY OWNERS

Strategy owners in the Hoshin methodology have responsibilities that are probably quite different from planning processes they've been involved in before, so it seems appropriate to summarize them:

- To organize the appropriate team to develop the strategies or tactics to achieve the strategies they own (which are their objectives!).
- To lead the team effectively in the formation of the strategies, including fostering an atmosphere of trust, honesty, creativity, and risk-taking in the team meetings.

Theme: Our employees are committed and satisfied.

Date: October 15, 1991 By: Joe Smith	Objectives	Measures	Goals	Owners: Mary I	Jim S	Jerry et al	George
	Improve Employee Morale						
1. Improve Employee Communication	###	Score Improvement	4	#			
2. Improve Understanding of Wage & Salary Administration System	###	Score Improvement	4		#		
Strategies:							
3. Define Roles and Responsibilities Better	###	Score Improvement	4			#	
4. Establish Regular Employee Dialogue	###	Score Improvement	1				#
Measure:	Employee Survey Score						
Goal:	1.5 point improvement						

Figure 9.13 Spreadsheet Version of an Annual Plan Matrix

- To ensure that these strategies are necessary and sufficient to meet the objective.
- To ensure that each strategy has an owner, metrics, and goals.

Later, during implementation:

- To prepare for and conduct the review meetings on progress of the strategies and the objective. This will be discussed in detail in Chapter 11.

DISCUSSION

This chapter contains the essence of how Hoshin differs from other planning methods, such as MBO. The biggest difference is the concept of "catchball." In "catchball," the managers at each level have to play the role of effective team leader in helping to understand the capabilities of his or her organization, leading to a two-way commitment to overcome shortfalls and synthesize capabilities that didn't exist before. The manager of each team must have a good idea of what it takes, in aggregate, to meet the objective, so that preliminary integration of the strategies can be performed, that is, confirmation that the strategies, with their goals, will meet the objective and its goal. This will generally take some analysis, or, in some cases, mathematical or logical modeling, using data from past experience and from others in the organization as a guide. The use of data, the responsibility to be accountable for the integrity of the plan, balanced with trust and assignment of similar ownership to subordinates, are all major changes in style for many managers, and constitute a challenge that might not be overcome in a single year. The required skills will be acquired gradually, as the process is replicated year after year.

Chapter 10

Implementation Plans and Final Plan Review

T he last step in the Deployment or "Catchball" process is development of Implementation Plans. It is tempting for executive teams to imagine that they don't need to be involved in the "details" of developing tactical plans, and in a very mature organization with an excellent, proven planning system, maybe they don't. However, for every organization we have encountered, without some executive involvement and formalization of the details, the tactics of their plans don't get developed with much rigor. The reasons are simple: in many organizations, tactical detail has never been required for their plans, and most people tend to be preoccupied with the Operational "doing" of the organization. There is nothing wrong with being focused on the "here and now," except that usually the strategic plans get short shrift. Many organizations are not even very rigorous about operational plans, and the methods we'll describe here can apply to operational plans as well. We would further make the observation that plans without the tactical detail don't usually get implemented very well, sometimes not at all.

A key step in the Hoshin process is the solution to this dilemma: the creation of Implementation Plans. A typical format is shown in Figure 10.1, and shows the tactical details ("Implementation Items") of one of the strategies for our Electrical Contractor example (Figure 8.4). In this particular example, the first-level strategies are directly deployed to Implementation Plans, with no intervening strategy levels. The strategies from Figure 8.4 are shown in Annual Plan Table format in Figure 10.2.

The Implementation Plan (IP, as it is called) is the plan from the point of view of those actually executing it, the owners of the Implementation Items. All of the important details are there, including completion dates. A very effective way to create the tactical detail is to use the brainstorming method with Post-its™ that we used for strategy formation, recognizing that

Plan Date Sept 16, 1993	By Ray	Year 1994				
Strategy	**Implementation Item**	**Owner**	**Q1**	**Q2**	**Q3**	**Q4**
Standardize the Estimating Process	1. Assemble team	Ray				
	2. Assign system administrator (SA)	Ray				
	3. Develop list of key assumptions	Ray				
	4. Create structures notes	Buzz				
Measure	5. Ray get familiar with system	Ray				
1. Completion Date	Progress Reviews	Ray				
2. Accuracy	6.Implement Estimate "Post-Mortem" process	Buzz				
Goal	7. Review & revise Data Base Labor Units	Buzz				
1. June 1994	8. Establish 3 "Gold" Estimates	Buzz				
2. +/- 2%	9. Create pre-bid checklist	Buzz				
	10. Data base development	SA				

Figure 10.1 Implementation Plan for "Standardize the Estimating Process" (Cowley & Associates 1993)

Date August 31, 1993	By Dave	Year 1994	Vision Element:	We have an effective Employee Development program	
Objective	**Strategies**	**Owners**	**Measures**		**Goals**
1.0 IMPROVE PROJECT MANAGEMENT PERFORMANCE	1.1 STANDARDIZE PROJECT MANAGEMENT PROCESS	Dave	Publication Date of PM Manual		12-31-93
	1.2 STANDARDIZE ESTIMATING PROCESS	Ray	Completion Date		June 94
Measure			Estimating Accuracy		+/- 2%
1. GROSS PROFIT MARGIN PER PROJECT MANAGER HOUR	1.3 IMPROVE PROJECT MANAGER TRAINING	Mark	Pilot training package available		2-15-94
2. ESTIMATING ACCURACY	1.4 IMPROVE PROJECT MANAGER SELECTION	Dave	PM Selection process draft complete		10-31-93
Goal					
1. $140					
2. TBD					

Figure 10.2 First-Level Strategies of Figure 8.4 on an Annual Plan Table (Cowley & Associates 1993)

what we are brainstorming now is the individual tasks required to implement the strategy. The implementation team and the strategy owner should do the brainstorming together. After brainstorming, the team arranges the Post-its™ on a timeline corresponding to the expected or hoped for completion time-frame, in their logical order of completion. Figure 10.3 shows this process.

Figure 10.3 is basically the Activity Network Diagram described in Chapter 13. It is important to assign owners to each task early in the process, so that the owners can have the job of estimating the duration of each task, as well as identifying necessary resources such as people, operating budget, capital equipment, and so on.

The benefits of this process, aside from the obvious one of getting the plan written down, include buy-in of the ultimate *doers*, or the owners of the tactics, and early identification of timing and resource problems. These problems are frequently not apparent until a team of experts actually begins to try to put together a practical Implementation Plan *that they know they themselves will have to execute.*

This process seems simple, almost simple enough to leave as an afterthought, or worse yet, as an exercise for the team to thrash out on its own, without the strategy owner. We have found this to be a serious mistake, and would cite failure to complete this important step as one of the principal reasons for failure of plans.

CONTINGENCY PLANNING: PDPC

Planning creates the illusion that we are somehow "in control of things"; indeed, a powerful new process like Hoshin can intensify this illusion. The truth is, we can only do our best to chart a course of action that seems to be a promising one, hope for the best, and change course when the need seems

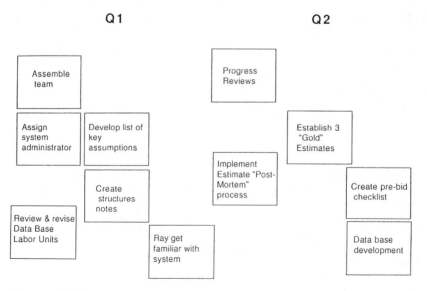

Figure 10.3 Arrangement of Completed Post-its™ on Timeline (Cowley & Associates 1996)

apparent. However, there is a method that can help improve the likelihood that our plan will succeed, and it is called the Process Decision Program Chart, described in detail in Chapter 13.

The basic idea of this method is to take an element of our plan that seems especially vulnerable, risky, or uncertain, and then to brainstorm in advance the things we can imagine going wrong with it. After that, we brainstorm ways of preventing or mitigating those problems. The process is illustrated in Figure 10.4. In the initial formation of the plan the Post-its™ that are generated by this method can be transferred directly to the timeline of Figure 10.3. This is shown in Figure 10.5.

Figure 10.6 shows how this process looks in a "tree" format. It is easy to see that the process can generate a lot of detail in the plan, even if only a few vulnerable areas are examined. The method is sometimes called a "Contingency Tree." Teams frequently find that many of the tasks necessary to implement the strategy come from the PDPC exercise, sometimes more than from the original brainstorming.

At a very high strategic level, PDPC is somewhat related to Scenario Planning, which asks, "What might happen in the future, and how can we be

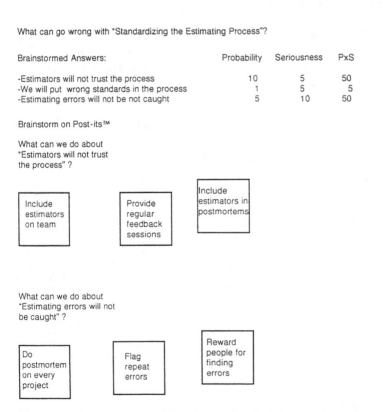

What can go wrong with "Standardizing the Estimating Process"?

Brainstormed Answers:	Probability	Seriousness	PxS
-Estimators will not trust the process	10	5	50
-We will put wrong standards in the process	1	5	5
-Estimating errors will not be not caught	5	10	50

Brainstorm on Post-its™

What can we do about "Estimators will not trust the process" ?

| Include estimators on team | | Provide regular feedback sessions | | Include estimators in postmortems |

What can we do about "Estimating errors will not be caught" ?

| Do postmortem on every project | | Flag repeat errors | | Reward people for finding errors |

Figure 10.4 Use of PDPC to Strengthen the Plan (Cowley & Associates 1996)

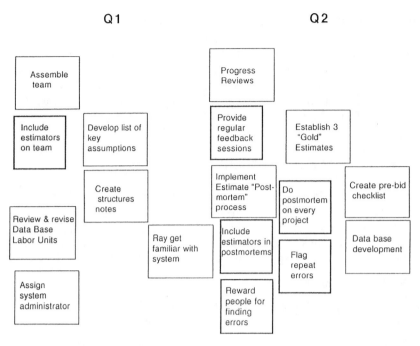

Figure 10.5 Addition of PDPC Post-its™ to Timeline (Cowley & Associates 1996)

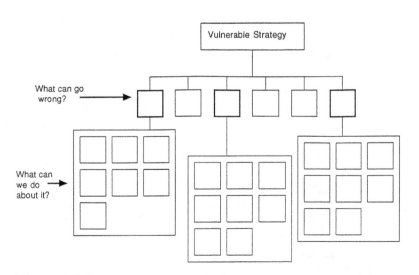

Figure 10.6 "Tree" representation of the PDPC process, showing the large number of ideas that can be generated for a single tactic or strategy (Cowley & Associates 1996)

prepared for the most likely or interesting scenarios?" Scenario Planning was given some notoriety by Royal Dutch Shell in the 1970s. It has been somewhat discredited since its initial success at Shell, because, in practice, it is too difficult for most organizations to predict and analyze a sufficient number of scenarios (Mintzberg 1994). However, PDPC does work, as long as it is used prudently. In fact, at the lower tactical levels, it can be used before the development of tactical plans to assist in that process.

USING IMPLEMENTATION PLANS AT HIGHER LEVELS

The Implementation Plan or Timeline format can be very useful for setting timing at the strategy level, even the Vision Element level. Strategies are frequently dependent on each other, even at the same level, so that their time sequence becomes important. The strategies for the Electrical Contractor example of Figure 7.9 are shown time-sequenced in Figure 10.7.

USING PROJECT PLANNING SOFTWARE AND SPREADSHEETS

In Figure 10.1, some the tactics shown are in reality small projects. It is common to use Project Management software to create the level of detail required within each of these tactics. A common system in use by many organizations is Microsoft® Project.

RESOURCE ALLOCATION

We've mentioned earlier that a major feature of Hoshin is that it facilitates focusing the organization on its most important objectives, by helping to

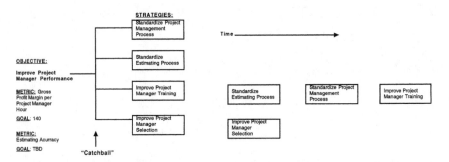

Figure 10.7   Time-sequencing of the First-Level Strategies using the Activity Network Diagram (Cowley & Associates 1995)

prioritize high-leverage areas of endeavor. Much of this happens in the process of developing and analyzing the organization's Vision, Chapters 6 and 7. However, the process is not automatic, and the executive staff of the organization must consciously limit the scope of plans at the highest level in the organization. While having a "feel" for how heavily loaded the organization's workforce is, particularly managers and professionals, is useful, it is far better to have a method of tracking human resource deployment. A simple method is illustrated in Figure 10.8, the Manpower Loading Chart. This example shows three months of activity for the executive staff of our Electrical Contractor; Power City Electric. The key executive tasks are listed down the left column, and the number of hours per month spent by each executive in the month of August, judged to be typical, is listed. This is usually a very interesting exercise for any workgroup, and some fairly typical problems are noticeable right away. Ray is evidently overloaded (and, as a result of this analysis, delegated some of his responsibilities to subordinates, and relinquished others to other executives), since a nominal month contains 160 possible work hours. Mitch has a similar problem. This exercise was started when Ray, a key contributor, announced that he didn't have time to participate in the Hoshin (and he was right!). The team was startled by the length of the list of tasks they were responsible for, and this motivated all of them to seek opportunities for delegating some of these duties. This opened up the subject of Business Processes, because without reasonably well-defined processes and procedures, it's difficult to delegate!

This approach to resource tracking and management lends itself very well to any common spreadsheet software, and it's use is essential for both tracking and forecasting manpower requirements. It is especially useful in professional manpower-intensive areas like Research and Development, engineering support, and others.

The important point of this is that organizations must know how their human resources are being spent, so that the balance depicted in Figure 5.7 can be approached, with workers and managers having time for Improvement, and Managers having time for Strategic Thinking and Planning.

FINAL PLAN REVIEW

After the plan has been completely deployed through Implementation Plans, the plans need to be "rolled" back up to do the final integrations, and to check again for duplications and inconsistencies, resource shortages, and possible financial constraints. From a high level, the plan ought to be carefully examined for opportunities for leveraging activities, that is, "killing more than one bird with a stone." This is made easier if the high-level Strategic and Operational plans are documented, as in Figure 8.7.

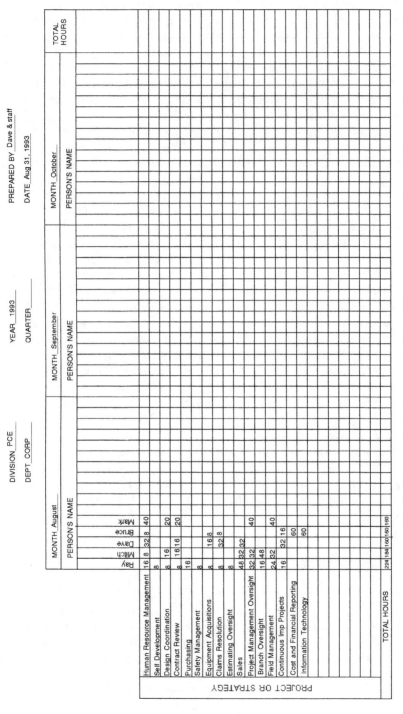

Figure 10.8 The Manpower Loading Chart (Cowley & Associates 1993)

After the Business Unit manager's approval, the plan should be published to all who are playing a role, and the plan can be implemented per the timing described in the Implementation Plans. The next chapter describes the Implementation and Review Process.

REFERENCE

Mintzberg, Henry. *The Rise and Fall of Strategic Planning.* New York: Free Press, Macmillan, 1994.

Chapter 11

Implementation and Review

It wouldn't appear that much can be said about implementation other than "Just do it!" However, there are some simple guidelines that will make implementation a richer source of insight to the organization, both short- and long-term, and we'll elaborate on them shortly.

We also want to emphasize in this chapter the vital importance of the Review Process. For most American workers and managers, the word "review" conjures up some pretty unpleasant thoughts. We want to stress the fact that the Hoshin Review Process is different, both in method and intent, from the classical review that most readers are familiar with. Our claim is that it is a much more effective and rewarding process. We also want to stress that "without the review, it ain't Hoshin." Hoshin just doesn't work without the Review Process.

IMPLEMENTATION

"Kickoff" Event

After the completed plan has been reviewed and approved by the Executive Management team, the organization is ready to implement it. Many organizations have an "event" to "kick off" the year's plans. This is usually combined with an overview of the past year's performance, and all employees attend. For organizations with multiple shifts and/or sites, this can be a major undertaking in itself. The purpose here is to communicate clearly the management's intent and commitment, and to gain the enthusiastic support of the entire organization. Memos, e-mail, and other forms of communication do not have nearly the impact of a "live" event for this purpose, so we strongly encourage management teams to put the time and energy into it.

Notes on Implementation

As team members execute the tasks and projects they have defined on their Implementation Plans, it is helpful if they keep a brief diary of their activities, particularly when problems arise, or when things go especially well. Two documents are useful for this purpose, the Fact Sheet, and the Abnormality Report. They can be used independently, or can be incorporated into the team member's diary. The Fact Sheet is shown in Figure 11.1. It is designed simply to record events that seem significant and related, such as problems with a business process or follow-up on feedback from a customer. Figure 11.1 uses an actual example of a shipment problem encountered by "ABC Semiconductor" company, one of our examples in Chapters 5 and 9. The Fact Sheet is designed to encourage recording only observable facts, not opinion or speculation ("Managing by fact"). Fact sheets can be used on an ongoing basis to record how a particular facet of the plan is working (like the planning process itself!), or can be used to track performance for a particular customer or process. Later, the information from various fact sheets can be integrated and analyzed to reveal important patterns or trends. This is especially useful in preparing for Reviews.

The Abnormality Report can take facts from a Fact Sheet, or from independent sources. It is intended to be a "closed loop" document, in that it calls for identification of a deviation in a process, and a description of what was done as a result. The example of Figure 11.1 is carried over to the Abnormality Report in Figure 11.2. The policy at this company was that the responsible supervisor was expected to follow up to be sure the corrective actions were carried out, and in the case where the process was the subject of

Strategy or Process_ Shipping		FACT SHEET	
Date	**Reported By**	**What Happened?**	**Interpretation/Analysis**
March 8, 1993	Joe	IBM called, irate. Shipment expected on their dock at 8 am not there. Customer production line shut down for lack of parts Shipment found on shelf in Shipping Dept. Was supposed to ship last Fri by overnight Fedex. I shipped parts by courier to customer. Cause of problem: Shipping papers from OP for some reason did not print out on Shipping Dept terminal.	There is no backup check Software or hardware malfunction? There should be no packages on shelf at end of day.

Figure 11.1 Example of a Fact Sheet (Cowley & Associates 1993)

1. Process or Item	Month/Day/Year
Shipping/Order Processing	March 8, 1993

2. What happened?

Missed Priority shipment to IBM.
See attached Fact Sheet

3. Analysis of causes

Paperwork didn't print out in Shipping
No check of priority shelf at end of day.
No check of OP paperwork sent vs. paperwork received

4. Emergency Countermeasures

Parts shipped by courier at 9 am 3/8/93

5. Evaluation of Results of Emergency Countermeasures

Confirmed receipt by customer 3 pm
Customer wants Corrective Action report

6. Measures for Prevention Against Recurrence (PAR)

1. Shipping supervisor to inspect Priority Shelf at end of every shipping day
2. Other operators informed of problem
3. OP paperwork sent to be reconciled with paperwork received at end of day

7. Plan for Removal of Root Cause

1. Simple automated reconciliation software to be in place by April 1
2. Software modified to prevent possibility of no printout . March 19
3. Modify shelves so top shelf at or below eye level for all operators. March 12.

Figure 11.2 Abnormality Report (Reprinted with permission of Hewlett-Packard.)

a Hoshin or Continuous Improvement effort, to see that the deviation was brought to the attention of the Hoshin or Improvement team so that it would be permanently "designed out" of the process.

Looking at the Abnormality Report, the reader may be able to discern three levels of response to any kind of problem or deviation: (1) An immediate action ("Immediate Countermeasures = ICM") to repair the damage (ship the parts by courier); (2) An immediate effort (Prevention Against Recurrence = PAR) to prevent further damage (inspect the Priority Shelf every day); and, (3) An effort to understand and remove the root cause of the problem so that it can't occur again. From the point of view of systematic improvement in organizational capability, item 3 is the most important, but in the normal course of events, frequently takes a backseat to the "firefighting" of items 1 and 2. In fact, many companies reward "heroic measures," rather than the systematic prevention of problems in the first place. It can be argued that organizations need to move toward yet another, fourth, response mode, in which they ask "Why didn't we predict and prevent this problem before it ever happened at all?" This is basically the concept of PDPC we introduced in the last chapter.

THE REVIEW PROCESS

"Real life is what happens when you've made other plans."—Dr. Joyce Brothers

The Hoshin Review Process has three important purposes: (1) It is intended to serve as the mechanism for keeping the Hoshin Plan as closely on track as possible; (2) It is the mechanism for identifying and acting upon opportunities to improve the organization's overall effectiveness by improving Management system and processes (including planning); and, (3) It is the basic element in the organization's learning process. We'll elaborate on each of these, but first let us present an overview of the Review Process.

Review Process Overview

The Hoshin Process, shown again in Figure 11.3, depicts the Review Process as part of at least two "PDCA loops." The reviews are the "Check" step in PDCA. Reviews need to be frequent enough to fulfill their purpose in keeping the Implementation of the plan "on track"—monthly for most levels in the organization, but possibly as often as weekly for some strategies and tactics.

Philosophically, the methodology of the Review Process is one of self-evaluation. In other words, the "reviewee" (the strategy or tactic owner) does not come to the review to be "evaluated." Rather, the reviewee comes to present the results of his or her self-evaluation of results on the strategy or tactic, using a defined process. Help is provided by the audience, some on content, but most on the reviewee's process of analyzing the results and preparing for the review.

The information required for the reviews is summarized on the Review Table shown in Figure 11.4. This form was introduced in Chapter 5. The "PDCA" cycle maps directly onto the Review Table, as shown in the figure. Even in the absence of a robust formal plan, the Review Table can be used to evaluate the effectiveness of actions, by simply asking the following questions:

- What did you intend to accomplish? (PLAN)
- What did you actually accomplish? (DO)
- How did the actual accomplishment compare with what you intended? (CHECK)

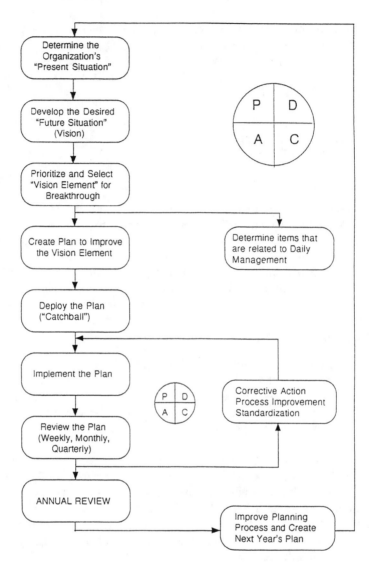

Figure 11.3 The Hoshin Planning Process (Cowley & Associates 1995)

- Analyze what happened and determine what you intend to do about it. For example, if the actual fell short of intent, analyze why and try again with an improved approach. Or, if the results were satisfactory, "standardize" the approach, that is, make it a part of the normal process, communicate the success, and train others, as appropriate. (ACT)

When client organizations begin planning, we frequently start with the Review of last year's plan and results. This generally produces a result similar to the example we described in Chapter 5, and puts the management team in a much more receptive frame of mind toward improving their planning.

The responsibility for preparing the Review Table is that of the strategy or tactic owner; he or she is also responsible for preparing the analysis of the outcomes, on backup sheets. The Review Table is intended to guide the thinking of the strategy or tactic owner, as well as to provide a convenient, uniform way of summarizing the results. The process is as follows. The first column is the statement of the objective, strategy, or tactic (OST), as recorded on the Annual Plan Table or Matrix, or Implementation Plan. The second column is the numeric goal for the OST. The third column is what was actually achieved, numerically. The fourth column is a "flag" to denote making or missing the goal. The fifth column is intended to be the summary of the reasons for a deviation (or reasons for success); the analysis leading to that conclusion should be attached on a separate sheet. Finally, the last column is intended to be a summary of the intended or ongoing corrective actions, and important implications for future plans; again, the analysis leading to these corrective actions should be appended to the Review Table.

The strategy or tactic owner is asked to think about what happened, why, and what has been determined to be the best course of action given those outcomes. In the case of a deviation, the owner is asked to think of the deviation as a problem to be solved, using the Seven Basic Tools described in Chapter 13, or any other suitable problem-solving framework. This work is preserved for presentation and posterity in the Review Table and its attachments. In the case of a success, the owner is asked to summarize how it was achieved, again for purposes of the presentation at the Review itself, but also for the organization's collection of "best practices." Some of the information

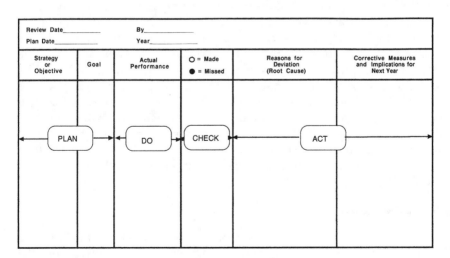

Figure 11.4 The Review Table (Cowley & Associates 1993)

that will be used in these efforts by the owners will be derived from the their diaries, Fact Sheets, and Abnormality Reports that have been prepared during the work period, but a reasonable level of analysis is also expected, in order to connect facts and events in a logical way to lead to root causes or best practices. The Problem Solving Process described in Chapter 13 is one proven way to do this; it also has the added benefit that it can be used in a "stand alone" mode to solve problems or improve processes.

Attendees at Review meetings are usually Strategy owners and their immediate teams. The agenda is prepared by the main strategy owner. It generally allows ten to fifteen minutes per strategy or tactic, with the team members in each case expected to present the results for their strategy or tactic very briefly, followed by a short discussion. The atmosphere needs to be congenial and supportive, keeping in mind that the principal purpose is to promote learning and progress. Notes should be posted on a flipchart by a designated recorder, who also has the responsibility to publish the notes and conclusions after the meeting.

We recommend taking ten minutes at the end of every review meeting to evaluate the meeting and propose improvements for the next meeting. Review meetings can become very efficient, and relatively brief, with practice and continuous improvement.

The Details

For successful Review Meetings, which continuously improve, the reader is encouraged to use the Review Checklist shown in Table 11.1.

This checklist will guide the strategy owners in their efforts to organize and run an effective meeting. We'll elaborate on each element of the checklist shortly, but let us make a few observations at this point. First, notice the relatively limited attendance at the review meeting; in fact it's the same team that created the strategies or tactics to achieve the strategy being reviewed. No other "high-level" managers. Second, although the prerogative always exists on the part of the strategy owner to "dictate" solutions and corrective actions, the real purpose here is for each owner to take ownership and be responsible for his or her promised results, and for the other team members to offer help and advice. Its a valuable self-development exercise for most people, and most really do eventually take responsibility for their planned outcomes. At the same time, the team really has an opportunity to learn to function effectively *as a team*. The toughest responsibility is on the strategy owner to make sure the reviews happen on schedule. We'll go into that in more detail now.

Scheduling Reviews

The best way to make sure reviews happen is to put them on the Planning Calendar before the start of the new year. That way everyone can put the event into their personal calendars. It is common practice to combine Hoshin

Table 11.1 Review Checklist

Before the Review	*Responsibility*
Schedule the Review	Strategy Owner
Prepare Review Tables (RT's)	Each Sub-strategy and Tactic Owner
Prepare Root-Cause Analysis	Each Sub-strategy and Tactic Owner
Publish Agenda	Strategy Owner
Assign Recorder	Strategy Owner
During the Review	*Responsibility*
Present Results (Review Tables, Root-Cause Analysis)	Each Sub-strategy and Tactic Owner
Q & A	Other Attendees
Maintain Supportive Atmosphere	All
Document Action Items	Recorder
After the Results Presentations (All)	
Review and agree to action items	
Discuss effects of deviations on the main Strategy	
Conduct 10 minute evaluation (+'s and −'s on flipchart)	
Adjourn	
After the Meeting	*Responsibility*
Publish all Results	Recorder
Update the Plan	Strategy Owner

reviews with normal business reviews, and, in fact, many organizations use the Hoshin Review methodology for their business results as well. We'll see an example later in the chapter (Figures 11.5 and 11.6).

A week or so before each review, the strategy owner should publish the agenda to the attendees, also denoting date, time, and place of the meeting. As an example, from Figure 10.1, Ray is the owner of "Standardize the Estimating Process," and would send the meeting announcement and agenda to "Buzz" and the System Administrator, who should already have that time and date blocked out on their calendars.

Preparation of the Review Tables (RTs)

We discussed briefly above how to fill in the Review Tables, but there are some additional points we'd like to make here:

1. It is mandatory for all columns to be filled in on the RT for Hoshin Objectives, Strategies, and Tactics, whether or not the goal was made. Keep in mind that it is just as interesting to hear about successes as it is "misses," and just as valuable to the organization.

2. Remember that column 5 is simply a summary of the analysis of the results. The analysis must be attached as a separate document.
3. In columns 5 and 6, be sure to include both process and results in the Analysis of Deviations and Implications for the Future.
4. When using the form for reporting normal business results (Critical Success Metrics and Critical Processes), put the name of the CSM or CP in the first column, and use the rest of the form exactly as was done for Hoshin OSTs.
5. CSMs and CPs are frequently reported on an exception basis on the Review Table, that is, only when the actual performance falls outside the specified Action or Control Limits.

Presentation of the Results

Each owner should prepare handouts and transparencies for their Review Tables and Analyses. At the designated time, the presentation is made briefly (5–10 minutes) using an Overhead Projector, and a brief discussion of the results is conducted (5–10 minutes), for a total of 10–20 minutes. The rest of the team is expected to maintain a supportive atmosphere, and questions and comments should be along these lines:

- "Please show us how you analyzed this deviation to Root Cause."
- "Please show how you made sure this Corrective Action will have the intended result."
- "Please be sure to complete the RT next time."
- "Please complete PDCA on misses next time."
- "Show us what was learned from that item that went so well."
- "Please tell us how we can help."

As each presentation is made, the Recorder should post action items and notes on a flipchart. It is the main Strategy Owner's job to keep the presentations on schedule.

After Presentation of the Results

Summarize and agree to the action items. Conduct further discussion if necessary.

Discuss the effect of any deviations of the sub-strategies or tactics on the main strategy.

Evaluate the Review Meeting by brainstorming on a flipchart positive (+) and negative (−) observations about the meeting from all the participants (Recorder).

After the Meeting

Publish all the results, including the evaluation and action items (Recorder).

Update all documents (Annual Plan Tables and Matrices, Implementation Plans, etc.), but don't lose the record of the plan as originally created (Strategy and Tactic owners).

Improving the Next Meeting

Use the evaluation to improve the agenda and conduct of the next meeting. At the next meeting, briefly review the evaluation and action items from the previous meeting.

Periodically (for example, quarterly), review the results of all Review Meetings and make appropriate recommendations for improvements in process, forms, and so forth. Implement the approved changes (Process Owners).

What to Look for in Diagnosis of Results

This is a checklist of the most common areas that need to analyzed by the reviewee before coming to the meeting:

1. Tasks scheduled, but not done (this is a "miss" and needs to be analyzed to its root cause).
2. Task completed, but wrong or unexpected outcome.
3. All strategies "OK," but Objective not met. (Basic flaw in planning, the "Necessary/Sufficient" analysis was possibly not done rigorously.)
4. Some strategies not accomplished as planned, but Objective met anyway. ("Necessary/Sufficient" analysis flawed, possibly. Goals set without sufficient data and/or analysis.)
5. Motivation waning. (Wrong objective, not worthy of breakthrough effort? Flaw in selection process?)
6. Look for objectives and strategies beyond the review time-frame that are certain to be affected by strategy or tactic misses reported in the current review. Flag these objectives and strategies now, and begin to plan corrective action.
7. Use "three-loop" PDCA to address misses—Immediate Countermeasures, Prevention Against Recurrence, Root Cause Removal—as discussed earlier in this chapter. The results should be detailed on attachments and summarized on the RT in the last two columns.
8. Make sure that "things gone right" are highlighted and, where appropriate, standardized (meaning, adopted by the organization as Standard Practice).

Example

We'll use the review of the plan shown in Figure 10.1 as an example to illustrate the process. The Review Table is shown in Figure 11.5. Note that since we are reviewing the tactical plan, the only "Goals" are the scheduled completion dates for all the items. In the case of Strategies, there should be numeric goals from at least one of the other "QDCE" categories we discussed in Chapter 7 (Quality, Delivery, Cost, Employees).

Note that there are some problems with this Review. The major difficulty seems to be that Ray, the project leader, does not have time to manage the project. The efforts to "offload" him were not entirely successful, and more needs to be done to delegate or remove some of his current workload. The other major problem is that this situation didn't get visibility until April, because Reviews weren't held on schedule.

The patterns observed in Ray's review were repeated in the rest of the organization, but to a lesser extent. Having these results and observations in "black and white" had a profound effect on the management team. They internalized the observation that they all had somewhat of a problem with time management, and redoubled their efforts to systematize their business processes so that effective delegation could take place. They also learned that they tried to do too much in the Hoshin, and made an effort to focus their efforts more effectively. This management team took the position that *failure is sometimes the best teacher*, and tried to make it easy for their employees to report failures and problems honestly. This is what we meant at the beginning of the chapter by organizational learning and the effect that reviews have on improving organization effectiveness.

Figure 11.6 shows the Review Table the same team used to review their Operational results—Daily Management. This team did Hoshin and Daily Management reviews in the same monthly meeting, and used the same basic approach in analyzing successes and failures. Some organizations prefer to

Review Date April 4, 1994		By Ray			
Plan Date Sept 16, 1993		Year 1994			

Strategy or Objective	Goal	Actual Performance	O = Made ● = Missed	Reasons for Deviation (Root Cause)	Corrective Measures and Implications for Next Year
1. Assemble team	January	January	O		
2. Assign system administrator (SA)	January	March	●	Ray too busy to interview	Immediate: Further unload Ray so he has time to mange project.
3. Develop list of key assumptions	February	February	O		
4. Create structures notes	February	February	O		Future: Revisit Business Processes and delegate more to next level of management.
5. Ray get familiar with system	March	Not done yet	●	Ray too busy	
Progress Reviews	Every Month	First review in April	●	Ray too busy	Dave follow-up and make sure reviews are conducted monthly; if reviews had been conducted on schedule we could have prevented part of the slippage.
6. Implement Estimate "Post-mortem" process	April				
7. Review & revise Data Base Labor Units	January	January	O		
8. Establish 3 "Gold" Estimates	May	Will slip to July	●	Ray too busy	
9. Create pre-bid checklist	June				
10. Data base development	Start March	Not started yet	●	SA not hired on schedule, Ray too busy	

Figure 11.5 The Review Table for "Standardize the Estimating Process" (Figure 10.1) (Cowley & Associates 1993)

Review Date April 4, 1994 Plan Date Sept 16, 1993		By Ray Year 1994			
Strategy or Objective	Goal	Actual Performance	O = Made ● = Missed	Reasons for Deviation (Root Cause)	Corrective Measures and Implications for Next Year
Year to Date Revenue	$6.1M	$4.5M	●	Late start on KEH project. Unrealistic Target	Use past experience to get better estimate of project start dates
Gross Profit-$	$937K	$523K	●		
-%	11%	11.8%	O		
Net Profit-$	$478K	$161K	●		
-%	4.9%	4.9%	O		
Breakeven Point-$	$4.5M	$4.4M	O		
Total Backlog-$	$2.5M	$3.5M	O		

Figure 11.6 Review Table for Daily Management (Cowley & Associates 1993)

review Daily Management items on an "exception" basis, that is, only discuss and analyze "misses."

ORGANIZATION LEARNING AND IMPROVEMENT

The simple example just shown illustrates the powerful effect that the Hoshin process can have on organization learning and improvement. In fact, this is why the PDCA cycle is called the "learning cycle." Genuine learning is the process of generating new capability or capacity in the organization. It is accomplished only by *doing*! Attending training sessions and studying are a part of this process, but no learning takes place until the new principles have been put into practice, mistakes are made and corrected, and the practice is repeated until the hoped-for results are obtained. Profound learning takes place when breakthrough goals are set, because the individuals and teams frequently have to challenge and move on from what they already know to explore new, untried methods. And, of course, the more challenging the goals, the higher the likelihood for setbacks.

It is probably evident that there is value in sharing or transferring the knowledge gained by an individual or team with the rest of the organization. For a small organization like our Electrical Contractor, frequent reviews are perhaps the best mechanism for this. But, as organizations get larger, there really needs to be a process for systematically sharing and capturing knowledge. Some large organizations have "expert systems" based on computer "groupware," databases, and e-mail systems. For all organizations, "share-fairs," conferences, and poster sessions can be effective "events" to stimulate sharing and knowledge transfer. An effective and easily-accessed library function can be helpful.

An additional facet of organizational learning was mentioned in Chapter 5, namely, that as implementation of the plan proceeds, more and more is learned about organizational capability, so the assessment process is really a continuous one. As new learning occurs in the process of implementation, it can be summarized on the Review Tables and described in more depth in backup attachments. As an alternative, a document like Table 5.2 in Chapter 5 ("What did we learn from this review?) could become a formal part of every review, after the presentations and discussions. The "learnings" don't have to be confined to internal organizational issues; there will generally be important external factors that ought to be included (competitor actions, customer behaviors, and so on).

The reader interested in organizational learning is encouraged to spend the time it takes to read Senge's *The Fifth Discipline* (1990). Another valuable reference is *The Knowledge-Creating Company* (Nonaka and Takeuchi 1995).

"Rolling the Reviews Up"

After the reviews of the lowest-level strategies are complete, the next level strategies are reviewed, and so on, until the Hoshin objective and the first-level strategies are reviewed. For maximum effectiveness the reviews should all be conducted within a fairly tight time-frame, such as a week.

THE ANNUAL REVIEW

The most important review of the year is the Annual Review, which normally occurs early in the fourth quarter. The purpose here is to get an assessment of the year's progress early enough to incorporate the results in the next year's planning cycle. The results expected at the end of the year are reviewed, and all the results of earlier reviews are recapped. Significant "learnings" are incorporated into the organization's management system, as well as into the planning process for the next year. Review Tables are used just as before. The Planning Calendar should be revisited and modified if necessary. The Annual Review meeting is sometimes held concurrently with the initial planning meeting for the next year. Some organizations hold semi-annual reviews, and regenerate plans every six months.

DISCUSSION

This book so far is intended to represent the "how to" details of the Hoshin process. It is intended to help managers and facilitators who are committed to learning and institutionalizing this powerful process in their organizations. However, the Hoshin process is one that is really only learned by practice and repetition, so managers are encouraged to get started, even if they are not confident that they fully understand all the principles in detail.

Hoshin is one of the most effective ways for higher-level managers to focus their leadership efforts and, indeed, to improve their leadership skills. It is based on the PDCA concept and incorporates the added feature of "breakthrough" thinking, which will help organizations to attain new plateaus of achievement—but only if the process is followed in its entirety, including the Review Process.

The next chapter discusses what you can do to get Hoshin started in your organization, recognizing that use of this methodology may run counter to the prevailing culture. Remember that if you want dramatically better results, you have to do something dramatically different!

REFERENCES

Nonaka, Ikujiro and Takeuchi, Hirotaka. *The Knowledge-Creating Company.* New York: Oxford University Press, 1995.

Senge, Peter M. *The Fifth Discipline.* New York: Doubleday, 1990.

Chapter 12

*How to Introduce the Strategic Management System into Your Organization**

"**J**ust do it!" is a popular and appealing advertising slogan.[1] It has some appeal, as well, as a process for introducing a new system in an organization: don't get caught in "analysis paralysis," just do it!

But organizational change is far more complex than starting an exercise program. The number of publications on change and change management is exceeded only by those on leadership—and many current leadership books identify "change management" or "change leadership" as the leader's primary obligation.

"Well, it all depends . . ." is the universal answer to the question, "How should we introduce the strategic management system into the organization?" It depends on:

- The organization's culture
- Leadership style
- Communication style
- Amount of other change going on simultaneously
- Readiness

    Perceived need for changes in strategic management
    Understanding of Total Quality Management (TQM)

---

*Thanks to Geri Dillingham and Mike Maslak for contributing the case study of North Island Federal Credit Union (NIFCU) at the end of this chapter.

[1]Nike, 1995. The "it" is exercise; the advertisements promote athletic shoes.

Knowledge and skill with problem-solving (Plan-Do-Check-Act—see Chapter 13)

Knowledge and skill with tools (see Chapter 13)

Process management sophistication (see Chapter 14)

Level of trust

The implementation of the new system is usually carried out by a team. Depending on the size and complexity of the organization, team members may include the CEO, the COO, strategic planning specialists, human resource specialists, quality management specialists, change management specialist, operations managers, market research or demographics staff, and so forth. Frequently, the team will start with an assessment of the organization's readiness for Hoshin-style strategic planning, such as those found in *Breakthrough Leadership* (Melum 1995) or *Hoshin Planning* (GOAL/QPC 1989), or they will construct their own evaluation based on this list.

If the implementation team finds serious gaps in the readiness for Hoshin-style planning, they need to start with a plan to reach an appropriate level of readiness. The authors have referred to this phase as the "Zero'th year of Hoshin planning"; that is, the year of preparation before the first year of actually using the new system (Melum 1995).

This follows the general plan for transition to high performance organizations presented by Resnick-West in the Association for Quality and Participation landmark study (1995). The general plan steps are as follows:

1. Identify the need for change.
2. Lay the foundation for change.
3. Develop the skills and begin redesigning the work.
4. Implement the redesigned work.
5. Continuous improvement of the new system; organizational learning.

There is an exact parallel here to the Hoshin system itself: stages 1 and 2 parallel strategy generation; stages 3 and 4 parallel strategy deployment; and stage 5 parallels strategy review and feedback (see Figure 3.1). These five stages will be used in this chapter to outline the process of implementing the new strategic management system.

Blanton Godfrey of the Juran Institute (1996) reports that the elements of Hoshin are being adopted by many leading companies and that there is a high correlation between the quality of their planning systems and their business success. Many of the companies have not heard of the Hoshin process—they created or modified their own system when they needed it, because they needed it. A case study of "natural" Hoshin concludes this chapter. The North Island Federal Credit Union tells its own story of how they decided to change, how they changed, and, if they had the opportunity to do it over, what they would do differently.

IDENTIFY THE NEED FOR CHANGE

Identification of the need for change will involve both technical analysis and leadership. The technical analysis is the comparison of your current planning system to the new Hoshin or Hoshin-like system. Create an assessment chart, listing the features of your current system, the features of the new system, the gaps, and the plan for filling the gaps (see Table 12.1).

It may be necessary to create a second chart or table to plan the actions, using your own project management system and specifying:

- Who will do the work.
- What are the criteria for success.
- What resources (human, financial, organizational, etc.) are required.
- What other activities are depending on this.
- What schedule is required.
- Any other information needed in your project management system.

But, if existing systems are good, use them. It will shorten your "zero'th" year and accelerate acceptance if people see that the strengths of the existing system are being enhanced, not ignored.

The leadership component of this step, identifying the need for change, itself has two parts:

- The leadership vision of the future with a strategic system that aligns the organization to achieve certain objectives.
- The communication of that vision.

In identification of the need for change, many leaders find it useful to engage groups of employees in discussion of the current and future planning systems, as a way of combining the technical analysis of the change and the communication of the future desired state. This leads very naturally into the next stage.

Table 12.1 Assessment of Changes to Planning System. This is an Example for an Organization that Needs a Lot of Preparation

Element	Current System	New System	Gap?	Plan
Data				
Customer demographics	Current customers	Potential & current	yes	Purchase data
Customer satisfaction	Complaints only	Multiple factors	yes	Start July in NE district
Process capabilities	Each department	Customer-focused	yes	Training complete, results expected 3d Q
...				
Communications				
Vision & Mission	Top-down	Participatory	yes	Cascade dialog
Strategies	Top-down	Catchball	yes	Education/training/practice
Opportunities	Solicited from all	Catchball	no	Education/training/practice
Trust	Variable in hierarchy	High throughout	yes	Continuous "walk the talk"
...				

LAY THE FOUNDATION FOR CHANGE

In this stage the small group that did the initial planning widens its scope. It is common to iterate these first two steps: as you expand the group involved in transition to the new way of working, you may learn more about how to make it effective, and you may then change the plan that was drafted in stage 1.

Laying the foundation for change involves both technical and human issues. The technical issues are those that change the systems of your organization. For example, if you will need a more effective way to communicate the relationship between strategies and tactics, and the relationships among various strategies, a technical approach might be the use of groupware (Lotus Notes, or something similar), or an "Intranet" (internal version of the world wide web), or even a bulletin board (electronic? cork?). The choice depends on the size, geographical dispersion, and culture of your company, as well as the level of existing infrastructure.

The human issues in this example are those of the *willingness* to communicate, once the technical issues of the *ability* to communicate are overcome. It is easy to underestimate the resistance to data and information sharing. Once people have agreed that alignment is good, and that informed employees will be able to contribute to the alignment and to the accomplishment of the goals, then everyone will contribute, right? Wrong! In one medium-sized food products company recently, it took *many* months for all the technical specialists to learn how to share their data. Reasons for withholding it ran a whole gamut of rationalizations:

- The customer trusted me with this data—another employee might be careless with it.
- I'm a technical expert—generalists might not understand it.
- If I'm the only one who understands this, it will be harder for them to lay me off.
- If everyone understands the strategic issues, then I won't be the person they come to for explanations of what's happening.

These are issues of power and prestige—and are very hard to articulate. Most of the participants in a change effort are publicly committed to the need for change, the need for shared information, the benefits of the change, and so on. When their personal biases are in conflict with the public policy, the personal biases usually win!

Two techniques will help your organization through this stage of change:

- Involve the people whose work is being changed in designing the change.
- Use pilot projects to test the new concepts at every point, and incorporate the results of the pilot project in the company-wide implementation concept.

During the pilot projects you will gather many kinds of information on how to make the changes effective in your organization. The need to explicitly promote "buy-in" to the new structures will be diminished if you put your efforts into developing and learning from pilot projects. The participants will become messengers and missionaries to the rest of the organization. Much of the emphasis in Steven Covey's work (1996) is on achieving clarity of vision and commonality of mission throughout the organization. The success of Covey's books in the 1990s is an indicator that many people in many organizations welcome the opportunity to contribute to change, if they know what it is and why they are being asked to participate.

TEACH THE IMPORTANT CONCEPTS OF HOSHIN TO ALL EMPLOYEES

In this phase, the conversion of the old planning system to the Hoshin system is carried out. Some training is required for people to learn the concepts of strategy development, strategy deployment, and strategy review, and to learn the tools of analysis and creativity (especially the seven management and planning tools—see Chapter 13).

"Redesigning the work" is carrying out the plan developed in stage 1 and refined in stage 2. It may be as simple as issuing a calendar with the schedule for various stages of gathering data, conducting analysis, or holding meetings. Or, it may be as complex as developing new data-gathering and communication methods, installing e-mail or groupware, or conducting competitive and world-class benchmarking studies (see Chapter 14).

Many organizations have tried to skip education on the strategic system and only do tools training. The usual motivation for skipping training is a combination of the desire to get started quickly with a lack of understanding of how strongly people resist change—even changes that sound beneficial.

Skipping this element of education is usually a mistake. The classroom environment is a safe place for people to try out new ideas. People who have had a chance to practice using new concepts are far more likely to apply them creatively when placed in high-risk circumstances, than people who are learning both the concepts and the tools at the same time. (This doesn't just apply to the corporate world—it is the whole concept behind simulator training for pilots and astronauts, and simulation games for everything from war to city management.)

The classroom environment gives people an opportunity to voice their concerns and get their questions answered *before* being asked to take the risk of publicly participating in the strategy generation and deployment activities. Senior executives may not perceive that there *is* risk, but in many organizations the "pre-TQM" culture of blaming people for problems has been in place a lot longer than the TQM culture of improving processes.

Residual fears from the pre-TQM culture can make people reluctant to participate in creating strategies that they see as risky.

Consider "just-in-time" training, rather than mass training, for maximum effectiveness. Adults in typical corporate training classes forget eighty percent of what they have learned within two weeks, if they don't use it! You will probably do two kinds of training:

- Tools and techniques
- The strategy system

The tools and techniques should be taught shortly before use, to avoid the eighty percent loss factor, and the system should be taught shortly before the person's first participation in a strategy generation or deployment session. Their rehearsals will be fresh in mind, they will have had the opportunity to gather appropriate data, and they will (in the best of cases) be motivated to participate.

PICK AN IMPORTANT ISSUE AND FOCUS ON IT

Be prepared for the chaos of the first year of the new system. The good news is that your second year will be easier. The bad news is that you can't get to the second year without experiencing the first year!

The "catchball" process is most likely to be imperfect in the first year. Typical problems include the following:

- Some managers will be very reluctant to involve their work groups in strategic issues, and will try to limit participation to implementation issues.
- Some managers will be very reluctant to let other departments know that they have deficiencies.
- Some managers will be very reluctant to let other departments know that they depend on their help.
- Some will try so hard for perfection that they will never be ready to contribute their information to the overall plan. Then, when priorities and budgets are set, they will feel slighted.

Check-Act-Plan-Do-Check-Act is the method that will make the system work. Each time you implement one of the elements of your Hoshin system, check the effectiveness, check the understanding, check the usefulness of the forms or whatever communication system you are using, and improve as you go. This is the practice of the three elements of the review system. In the first year, you'll use it much more than in subsequent years.

As a reminder, the three questions of strategic review are:

1. How does the work compare to the plan? If it is on plan, great! If not, how can the review team help the action team?

2. Is the plan still valid? Should the work continue?
3. Is the planning system in need of improvement?

Use changes in the system as an opportunity to model the PDCA system, and to demonstrate process improvement on the most important systems and processes in the organization.

The other major source of failure is yielding to the temptation to use the system to accomplish all the work of the organization. Selecting one "Hoshin" objective will focus the organization's energy on the selection process, initially, then on the accomplishment of the selected strategy. In the initial years you will be learning how to manage the system, and will quickly be overwhelmed by detail if you try to apply it to all the work of the system. Companies that started this approach in the early 1980s typically worked with a highly prioritized system for ten years before expanding the Hoshin-like system to multiple objectives (Johnson and Daniel 1993).

CONTINUOUS IMPROVEMENT

By the end of the second year, most organizations have functioning Hoshin systems. The challenge from that time on is to stay fresh. The review process and the data collection stage of the strategy-generation process are the keys to freshness.

The review process is the element that is built into the system to encourage you to challenge yourselves. You use it to avoid working on plans that have become outmoded, and you use it to collect the lessons learned throughout the organization on common problems of implementation, so that these problems can be overcome.

An extreme example of a failure to stop working on obsolete plans was presented by an Air Force officer at a strategic planning workshop. He had been responsible for the Total Quality Management education and process improvement support at Homestead Air Force Base when it was destroyed by Hurricane Andrew. He told an impressive story of dedication to duty and of heroism: the Air Force maintained their mission readiness by moving the aircraft to safe locations and applied their resources to rescuing people and reestablishing safe water, power, and shelter for their own people and for the surrounding communities. But, when the dust settled, he found that he was required to continue to file weekly reports on the TQM teams and the TQM training program, each week reporting that he was underspending his budget and providing a corrective action plan.

Their system lacked question 2 of the review system. The energy and creativity that were demonstrated during the crisis were being eroded by the bureaucratic nature of the reporting system.

How can data gathering keep the system fresh? Challenge yourselves to ask new questions about the data that you need to create strategies:

- Add *new techniques* for understanding who your customers are, who potential customers are, and what they can tell you about the future directions of the business (see Chapter 14).
- Add *technology evolution studies* to predict your own future path and possible paths for your competitors. Include possible alternate technologies, which may bring new competitors into the field (Domb 1996; Slywotzky 1996).
- *Benchmark* the data-gathering and analytic methods of your best competitors and of world-class companies—this can provide the stimulus you need (see Chapter 14).

The customer-focused continuous improvement philosophy of total quality management should not be a ritual. It should be the source of the creative energy that aligns the organization to achieve the vision that you have set forth.

CASE STUDY: NORTH ISLAND FEDERAL CREDIT UNION

In this section, North Island Federal Credit Union's CEO Mike Maslak and Senior Vice President of Planning and Marketing Geri Dillingham tell the story of the current Plan-Do-Check-Act process that they use. They developed the process because, in their search for ways to become an excellent organization, they found that they needed it. You will see that without using any of the jargon of Hoshin planning, they developed the same sequence of plan generation, plan deployment, and plan review, with a kickoff event, catchball, and deployment matrices.

We met NIFCU through participation in the California Council on Quality and Service. Mike had been an examiner for the Malcolm Baldrige National Quality Award, and was one of the founders of the CCQS. Mike had become a Baldrige examiner as part of his process of learning about transformation of organizations. Although NIFCU, as a non-profit organization, could not apply for the Baldrige award, Mike modeled NIFCUs internal evaluation process on the Baldrige.

We have asked Mike and Geri to write their own case, emphasizing how they got where they are, what advice they would give others, and what, if anything, they would do differently if they had the opportunity to start over.

NIFCU Overview

North Island Federal Credit Union (NIFCU) is a member-owned financial cooperative which was federally chartered in California in 1940, and serves over 120,000 members, primarily in San Diego county. NIFCU provides consumer financial services much like a bank, including savings and checking accounts, certificates of deposit, auto and credit card loans, real estate services, and expanded delivery access through a comprehensive automated teller machine network and a 24-hour automated telephone teller system.

Credit unions differ from banks by nature of their ownership; they are owned by members rather than stockholders. Every member has an equal vote and the opportunity to elect their board of directors, which is comprised of volunteers from the membership. Credit unions, as not-for-profit cooperatives, embrace the national vision of "People Helping People," and return their earnings in the form of higher savings rates and lower fees than banks. The credit union industry is federally regulated under the Treasury Department through the National Credit Union Administration, with restrictions on who can be served, the products that can be offered, and the type of investments that can be made with members' money.

North Island Federal Credit Union is one of the three largest, locally-owned financial institutions in San Diego, with ten branches and $660 million in assets. NIFCU has 330 employees, all geographically located in San Diego county.

President/CEO Michael Maslak joined NIFCU in 1987 and, together with the board, formalized a strategic approach around an employee-focused culture. The credit union's *Formula for Success* states that "employee satisfaction (with accountability) drives member satisfaction, which, in turn, drives long-term financial success." This focus on the human side of quality is the supporting "cultural column" in the Architecture for Continuous Quality Improvement, which is the name for NIFCU's annual planning process.

A Cyclical Planning Process

In 1988, NIFCU implemented a cyclical planning process which includes all levels of the organization in strategic planning. The process entails executive pre-planning to complete a current situational analysis and propose key business priorities.

Each branch and department in the credit union subsequently holds a team planning session to discuss the business priorities as they relate to the specific areas, and complete their own situational analysis and assessment of their ability to support the organizational priorities. A typical team session will last about two hours, and include the refinement of the branch or department mission statement, plus a strengths, weakness, opportunities, and threats (SWOT) review based on their staffing, technology, competition, and other factors at the business unit level. The results of these planning sessions, with priority placed on weaknesses and threats, are centralized with the senior vice president of planning and marketing to provide as input to the board of directors' strategic planning event with the senior executive team. The board then validates or refines the credit union mission, objectives, and direction, based on the team input. Upon agreement regarding the strategic plan, the plan document—the Architecture—is completed and distributed (Figure 12.1).

Communicating the Strategic Plan

Once the long-term plan is finalized, focus is placed on the key business priorities for the upcoming year. Each division completes a tactical plan from the corporate strategic direction. These plans are compiled into a single document, the Architecture for Continuous Quality Improvement, and shared during a full management workshop at the beginning of the year. Major cross-functional projects are identified and prioritized in the written plan to assist with communication.

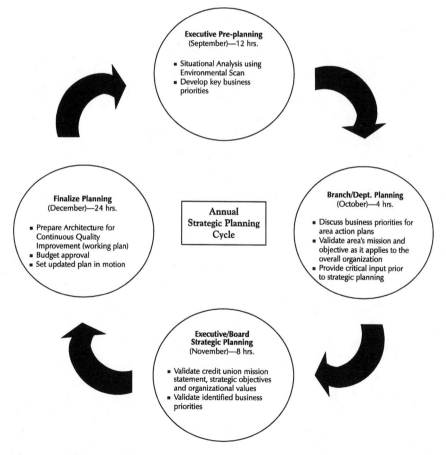

Executive Pre-planning
(September)—12 hrs.

- Situational Analysis using Environmental Scan
- Develop key business priorities

Finalize Planning
(December)—24 hrs.

- Prepare Architecture for Continuous Quality Improvement (working plan)
- Budget approval
- Set updated plan in motion

Annual Strategic Planning Cycle

Branch/Dept. Planning
(October)—4 hrs.

- Discuss business priorities for area action plans
- Validate area's mission and objective as it applies to the overall organization
- Provide critical input prior to strategic planning

Executive/Board Strategic Planning
(November)—8 hrs.

- Validate credit union mission statement, strategic objectives and organizational values
- Validate identified business priorities

Figure 12.1 NIFCU's Annual Strategic Planning Cycle

A Staff Operation Meeting is held annually with all employees. This celebratory event is held on a Friday evening at the beginning of the year, and serves as a key communications forum with all staff to highlight the accomplishments of the previous year and focus the entire team on the priorities for the coming year. NIFCU produces a staff annual report specifically for the evening, with a report structure mirroring the *Formula for Success*, segmented by results of the employee opinion surveys, member service ratings, and financial performance.

NIFCU also communicates the strategic vision through credo cards, which are updated annually and provided to every employee. The card includes NIFCU's Vision and Mission Statements, the corporate Values, the Formula for Success, the Quality Criteria for member service metrics, the External Member Service Guarantee, and supporting Internal Service Guarantee. Most employees keep these bi-fold cards by their desk or in their wallets (Figure 12.2).

Translating Strategies into Actions

Strategic-to-tactical plan integration is highlighted in Figure 12.3. Action plan items are functional projects and on-going responsibilities within a division. Quality improvement projects (QIP) are cross-functional between divisions. NIFCU developed custom QIP software for branches and departments to register their cross-functional projects, and requires the ranking of each proposed project by percentage of support for specific strategic objectives and business priorities, which is used for determining resource allocation.

The individual tracking mechanism for plan deployment is the Accountability Map developed by the Cardwell Group of Cleveland, Ohio. The Accountability Map is a mutually-negotiated annual performance plan, developed by the employee and his or her supervisor, which outlines detailed expectations and "measureables" for the year. Monthly dialog sessions are held on the maps as checkpoints for plan progress and to make any necessary adjustments as the plan unfolds. Senior executive management audits the mapping process on a quarterly basis to ensure that the adjustments are integrated into a coordinated organizational plan update.

Planning Refinements—Using the Baldrige Template

One of the major refinements to NIFCU's organizational plan was the formalized "adoption" of the Malcolm Baldrige Award quality template as the credit union's quality template in 1991. This template was complementary to NIFCU's culture for two reasons: first of all, the award criteria also emphasized the value of the human side of quality based on the point distribution in Sections 4.0 and 7.0; and secondly, the template was non-prescriptive, allowing the credit union to use the criteria to identify areas for improvement, but develop custom solutions internally.

Vision Statement

We deliver member-driven service that is unparalleled by any institution in the financial industry. We are committed to providing superior products and service to our members by exceeding their expectations, resolving their problems, and delivering financial peace of mind. Our organization is employee-focused, caring, innovative, and Family Friendly, empowering us to excel in delighting our members. Our goal, through continuous quality improvement is to attain superior efficiency which translates to improved service, productivity and financial success.

Mission Statement

North Island Federal Credit Union is a member-owned, employee-focused financial cooperative committed to providing and continually improving quality member service and superior financial products and services that promote personal and fiscal responsibility and organizational safety and soundness.

NIFCU's Formula for Success

Employee Accountability
and Satisfaction
+
Member Satisfaction
=
Financial Success

Printed on recycled paper.

SAN DIEGO'S OWN

Corporate Values

NIFCU's corporate values are embodied in the acronym CLASSIQ, which stands for:

C **Communications–** Providing open channels, top-down/bottom-up strategic planning.

L **Leadership–** Promoting teamwork and assuming responsibility. Drives inspired loyalty and trust among team members.

A **Accountability–** Supporting the organizational commitment of service, safety and soundness by individually accepting a personal role in quality improvement.

S **Symbolism–** Visible celebrations and manifestations of the culture.

S **Service–** A relationship focused on sharing our values and satisfying the members' expectations through internal/external service guarantees.

I **Integrity–** The "heart" of the organization. Delivering what you've promised to others.

Q **Quality–** Continuous improvement, employee involvement and ongoing member feedback.

Service Guarantee

Employees of North Island Federal Credit Union guarantee commitment of service excellence to our members. To provide the best environment for handling your financial needs, we will strive to reach the highest levels of performance using the attributes which you have identified as essential for total quality service:

1 **Timeliness–** Responsiveness in completing your request.

2 **Accuracy–** Reliability of the transaction.

3 **Friendliness–** Courteous and attentive service.

4 **Clarity–** Complete and understandable information provided.

5 **Competence–** Knowledgeable and well-trained staff to handle your request.

6 **Features–** Consistent and competitive rates and superior features on a full array of financial products.

7 **Accessibility–** Convenience and ease in conducting your transaction.

8 **Appearance–** Safe, clean and professional business environment.

Each NIFCU employee is empowered to ensure that our response to your request consistently meets, and ideally exceeds, your service expectations.

Internal Guarantee

If you're not serving a member, you're serving someone who is serving a member.

Figure 12.2 NIFCU Credo Card

NIFCU has completed both informal and formal assessments using the Baldrige criteria. Most recently, NIFCU has applied three times for the Eureka Award for Quality and Service, a statewide "baby" Baldrige. (NIFCU has received the "best-in-class" designation both years in the Non-Profit Category.) The formal feedback report has provided invaluable support and validation of management's assessment of areas for improvement, and the gap areas are reviewed and prioritized in the annual planning process.

The value of self-assessment was expanded throughout the credit union with the establishment of the President's Award for Quality in 1994. Branch and department teams have the opportunity to apply for the award

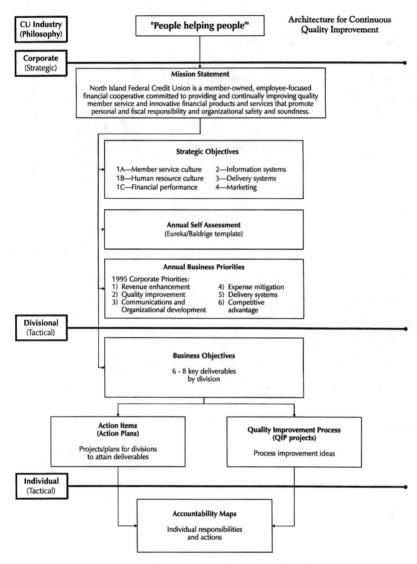

Figure 12.3 Architecture for Continuous Quality Improvement

by completing a ten-page application that mirrors the seven sections of the Baldrige Award in an abbreviated fashion. Outside examiners from other San Diego companies serve as judges and provide written feedback reports. The gap areas from these reports are used in the team annual planning to make improvements in individual areas, much like the overall assessment is used organizationally.

Planning for Results—Key Metrics

The planning process is futile without key metrics to monitor long-term progress toward goals. Through NIFCU's planning process, the credit union identified its positioning goal to be the "premier San Diego community financial institution" within five years, and identified membership growth goals and delivery system channel mix to achieve the desired positioning. Key metrics in six categories, with goals set for one, three, and five years, are measured on an on-going basis:

Category	Key Metric
Customer Service	Net Membership Growth
	Eight Quality Criteria
	Timeliness
	Accuracy
	Friendliness
	Clarity
	Competency
	Features
	Accessibility
	Appearance
Products and Services	Loan to Savings Ratio
	Accounts per Household
	Average Savings Balance
	Average Loan Balance
Employees	Employee Turnover Rate
	Employee Opinion Survey Results
	Return on Training Investment
Business Support	Internal Service Survey Results
	Electronic Systems Availability Rate
Financial and Operations	Return on Assets
	Capital Ratio
	Members per Full Time Employee
Supplier Quality	Supplier Performance Rating Index

All metrics are trending positively, but they can best be summarized by returning to NIFCU's *Formula for Success:* Employee Satisfaction + Member Satisfaction = Long Term Financial Success.

In terms of employee satisfaction, the outside facilitator of NIFCU's employee opinion survey, who works with sixty companies nationally, concluded, "Overall, the positive opinions of North Island Federal Credit Union employees are collectively the highest that this consulting organization has received from any organization surveyed."

Member satisfaction scores have been monitored weekly for the past seven years and are well above peer comparisons. In 1995, NIFCU did a proxy simulation of the model used in the national American Customer Satisfaction Index (ACSI) and received an overall 85 rating from their members, compared to the national index of 74 for Banks and 74.8 for Financial Institutions as determined in the ACSI Baseline Report, 1994.

Financially, the credit union has seen solid financial growth. It receives the top rating in capital from the federal regulators, which indicates safety and soundness. Return on assets has steadily risen, with average savings balances doubling since 1988, and average loan balances setting the benchmark for peers.

Using the Long-Term Plan in Decision-Making

Many times, a mission statement and strategic plan are memorialized in a binder and placed on a shelf till the following year. An effective plan must be easy to understand and frequently referenced in the decision-making process to have value. Often times, it is the vision from the plan that allows the organization to be creative and change paradigms for doing business.

A prime example of taking a strategic focus and putting it into action was NIFCU's decision to expand into indirect lending, that is, lending done directly at auto dealerships rather than through credit union branches. NIFCU's strategic positioning as a world class organization had already identified the tenet of maximizing *virtual partnerships* to expand business lines.

For credit unions, the paradigm had been long-established to grant auto loan pre-approvals to members prior to shopping for autos at the dealership. Credit unions had done everything in their power to keep members from the "clutches" of auto-dealer financing. Yet, the facts were working against the paradigm: members had little time and demanded greater convenience, thus eighty-five percent of all auto loans made were done directly at the auto dealership. NIFCU was one of the first credit unions in the country to work cooperatively with the 100 auto dealerships in the marketplace and grant NIFCU financing as an option on the dealer list. It meant having to pay a fee to the dealers for the loans, which ultimately was a small price to gain 100 additional "loan centers" or virtual partners with no overhead. The decision was difficult, because it was not popular with other credit unions. However, loan volume has tripled since the program was established, and member satisfaction scores strongly support the move toward increased convenience.

More recently, the credit union had to do a review of its credit card portfolio. That review indicated that members who did not keep savings in the credit union, and had no other services, caused higher losses. In determining how to address this tier of the membership, the board and management returned to the mission statement, which, in effect, promised "superior products with superior service" to all members. The credit card analysis prompted a focused discussion at the strategic level, which resulted in an adjustment to the mission that, realistically, NIFCU could provide *competitive* products with superior service to all members, and superior products to those members who maintained a relationship (other accounts) with the credit union.

NIFCU's Next Steps

Each year, refinements to the planning process are identified. This year, the board of directors will be brought in at the initial pre-planning step to complete the situational analysis. Plan metrics have been fine-tuned at the organizational level, but need further refinement as they cascade through the organization to the team and individual level.

NIFCU plans to use more of the formal Hoshin planning tools to drive even greater creativity in the planning process and to guard against any unintentional "group think," since the key members of the management team have been working together for a number of years.

Lessons Learned

There are several key planning issues that, if accelerated, would have improved NIFCU's organizational effectiveness. While the planning structure was correct from the beginning, and included all areas of the credit union in the process, each area used to publish its own plan document supporting the organizational direction. The results were 26 different business-unit plans from the branches and departments. The Architecture for Continuous Quality Improvement, published annually for the past three years, now links all of the plans into a concise document, one which has improved organizational communication of the plans by covering the business objectives of every unit in the credit union.

Another improvement would have included integrating "best practices" from other companies at an earlier stage. It wasn't until the Baldrige template was adopted that NIFCU fully understood the need to look for benchmark comparisons to improve internal processes. The credit union just recently participated with nine other national financial institutions in a best practices study for "Customer Inquiry and Complaint Resolution" in the service sector, using the facilitation coordinated by the APQC/ International Benchmark Clearinghouse services. Studies such as these provide tremendous input regarding optimal staffing structure, support systems, and world class response goals. Reviewing best practices outside the credit union industry has given NIFCU a strategic advantage in leveraging future investments in staffing and technology.

Concluding Remarks

North Island Federal Credit Union has successfully implemented an organization-wide planning process and communicates it through a plan document called the Architecture for Continuous Quality Improvement. The credit union has refined its planning process to incorporate the Malcolm Baldrige Quality Award criteria as its template for self-assessment to assist in defining the strategic gaps to address during planning. This is further enhanced, through the company deployment of the internal President's Award program, at the business unit team level (branches and departments).

The key to successful long-term planning has been the establishment of short-, mid-, and long-term goals to measure progress. Responsibility for the plan lies with every individual in the organization, and progress is tracked by using the Accountability Mapping process with employees and by maintaining monthly checkpoint discussions with supervisors.

REFERENCES

Bennis, Warren. *Why Leaders Can't Lead*. San Francisco: Jossey-Bass, 1989.

Covey, Steven R. "Organizational Alignment." *Quality Digest*, March 1996.

Domb, Ellen, Karen Tate, and Bob King. "Systematic Innovation." *Journal of Innovative Management* (1996) 1:2, pp. 65-70.

GOAL/QPC Research Committee. *Hoshin Planning: A Planning System for Implementing Total Quality Management*. Methuen, MA: GOAL/QPC, 1989.

Godfrey, A. Blanton. "Integrating Quality and Strategic Planning." *Quality Digest*, March 1996, p. 23.

Johnson, Catherine G. and Daniel, Mark J. *Setting the Direction: Management by Planning*. Ottawa: Conference Board of Canada, 1993.

Kouzes, James M. and Posner, Barry Z. *The Leadership Challenge: How to Get Extraordinary Things Done in Organizations*. San Francisco, CA: Jossey-Bass, 1987.

Melum, Mara and Collett, Casey. *Breakthrough Leadership: Achieving Organizational Alignment through Hoshin Planning*. Chicago: American Hospital Publishing, 1995.

Resnick-West, Susan. *High Performing Work Organizations*. Cincinnati: Association for Quality and Participation, 1995.

Sylwotzky, Adrian J. *Value Migration*. Boston: Harvard Business School Press, 1996.

Chapter 13

The Tools of Hoshin*

BASIC TOOLS

The basic tools of quality improvement are used to improve processes. These tools are frequently known as the Seven Quality Control Tools, or the Seven SPC Tools, because of the way they were grouped together when popularized in quality circles in the 1960s in Japan and in the late 1970s in the US. They are a combination of creativity tools (brainstorming, the fishbone diagram) and analytic tools (flowcharts, checksheets and Pareto charts, run charts, variable and attribute control charts, histograms, scatter plots) that are typically used by teams of people who perform the processes to find and implement the improvements.

Process improvement is most frequently taught using the "Deming cycle" or "Shewhart cycle" of Plan-Do-Check-Act (PDCA) (Brassard and Ritter 1994). See Figure 13.1. The process is analyzed in terms of its capability to do what the customer needs in a way that is effective for the company, and a plan is created to correct deficiencies. The plan is tested (*Do*) and evaluated (*Check*, also called *Study*). If the test was successful, the team *acts* to make the new method the standard, while continuing the measurements to decide when a new Plan-Do-Check-Act cycle is needed.

Because of the natural human tendency to start making a plan if the first step in the improvement process is labeled "plan," numerous variations on Plan-Do-Check-Act have been coined to serve as reminders that several steps of analysis are needed to develop the plan. Figure 13.2 shows the USA-PDCA model. The plan phase explicitly includes Understand, Select, Ana-

---

* Thanks to Weston Milliken for contributing the *Management and Planning Tools* section of this chapter.

151

The basics:

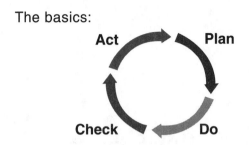

Figure 13.1   Process Improvement & Problem Solving: PDCA

The details:

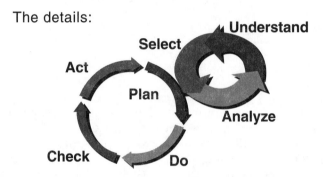

Figure 13.2   Process Improvement & Problem Solving: USA-PDCA

Table 13.1   Process Improvement Tool Matrix

	Stage	Plan				Do	Check	Act		Type		
Tool		*U*	*S*	*A*	*P*	*D*	*C*	*A*		*Creative*	*Analytic*	*Decision*
Brainstorming		×			×			×	×			
Flow Chart		×			×		×	×			×	
Cause/Effect (Fishbone)		×	×					×	×	×	×	
Checksheet				×		×	×				×	
Pareto Chart			×	×		×	×				×	×
Run (Trend) Chart		×		×		×	×				×	
Control Charts		×		×		×	×				×	
Histogram		×		×		×	×				×	
Scatter Plot		×	×	×							×	×

lyze, which may cycle several times before the team creates the Plan for the improved process (Shores 1987).

The tools themselves are listed in Table 13.1, Process Improvement Tool Matrix, which also shows the tool type (creative, analytic, decision-making), and the stage of problem solving in which the tool is typically used.

WHY ARE THE BASIC TOOLS IN A BOOK ON STRATEGY?

There are two reasons for including a brief review of the basic tools in a discussion of strategy:

1. Knowledge of the current state of business processes is necessary as a precursor to the strategy-generation stage and to guide the decisions about which processes need to change. The knowledge of which processes have been improved, and how successful the improvements have been, can also be useful when generating new strategies.
2. Many strategic action plans will be deployed as improvement projects. The basic tools will be combined with the management and planning tools later in this chapter to perform the analysis and implementation of the first improvement, and to initiate continuous improvement of the processes.

Consider a situation in which a company sets a strategic objective to improve customer telephone service, as part of an overall strategy to triple the satisfaction of existing customers and attract an equal number of new customers due to its reputation for service.

The part of the project that is deployed to the Customer Service Representatives (called "reps" in the figures) is the challenge of improving service for existing customers who make inquiries by phone. They start their USA-PDCA process by using a flow chart, Figure 13.3, to understand (U) the process. A small piece of the process is shown, for a single call.

They then conduct a brainstorming session to consider what could cause inadequate service. In brainstorming, a facilitator records everyone's suggestions visibly (typically on a chalk board or flip chart) so that the early ideas in the session can influence later contributions. The "rules" of brainstorming appear in many texts on problem solving, and usually include the following:

- Write the topic explicitly.
- Let the ideas flow.
- Record all ideas.
- No criticism (positive or negative) during idea generation.
- Build on other ideas.
- After all contributions have been recorded, evaluate the list. Remove duplicates, combine related ideas, and decide how to use the list.

In this case, they noticed that all their ideas fell into the categories typical of a Fishbone Diagram (also called an Ishikawa Diagram, after its chief popularizer, or a cause-and-effect diagram). Figure 13.4 shows the Fishbone Diagram, in which "Telephone Service is Inadequate" is the "head" of the fish, and issues related to processes, people, machines, and material make up the "bones" of the fish. Each of the concepts from the brainstorming session is

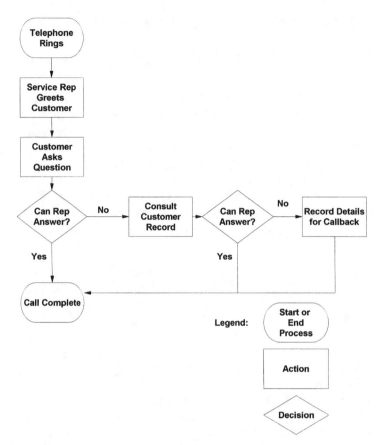

Figure 13.3   Flow Chart for Example: Answering a Customer Inquiry

placed on a "bone." In some cases, new ideas are stimulated by the discussion. For example, in deciding if "Transfers get lost" belongs on the "Machines" bone, because it might be due to either switch problems or software problems, the team also decides to put it on the "People" bone, because it could also happen if a rep makes an error. The importance of the fishbone diagram is the discussion of possible causes, and the speculation on the relationships between causes. The fishbone diagram is a creativity tool; it stimulates discussion.

The team then needs to gather data to decide which of the issues on the fishbone diagram is actually causing problems. Figure 13.5 is a checksheet that the reps themselves kept. This helps the improvement team move from the "Understand" stage of process improvement to the "Select" stage. It is clear from this chart that problem 5, customer record not available, is the most frequent problem. A Pareto chart, Figure 13.6, is an alternate display of the same data.

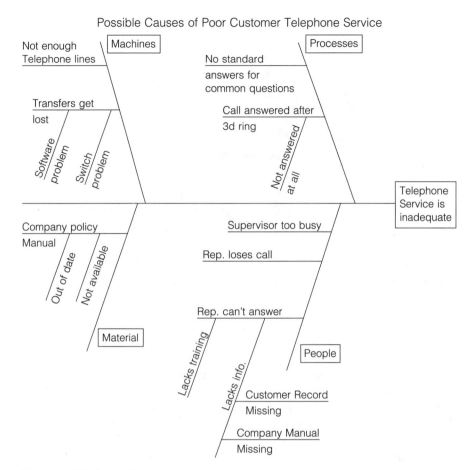

Figure 13.4 Fishbone Diagram for Example: Possible Causes of Poor Customer Telephone Service

	Day 1	Day 2	Day 3	Day 4	Day 5	Total
Possible service problems						
1 Answer after 3 rings	//	///	/	ⅣⅣ/	//	14
2 First person can't answer customer questions	///		/	//	/	7
3 Call never answered	///	ⅣⅣ	//	/	/	12
4 Call gets lost when transferred	/		//			3
5 Customer record not available for reference	/	ⅣⅣ ⅣⅣ	ⅣⅣ ///	ⅣⅣ //	///	29
6 Customer gets different answers each call	//	/		//	//	7

Figure 13.5 Checksheet for the Example Strategic Problem: Improve Telephone Service to Customers

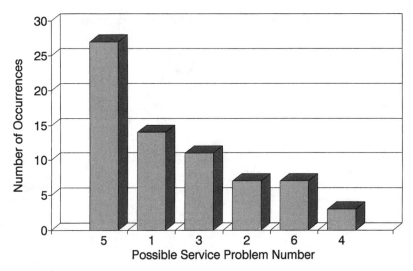

Figure 13.6 Pareto Chart for Example: Improve Telephone Service to Customers

If frequency is an appropriate criterion for selection of the improvement target, then the choice is obvious. It is frequently necessary, however, to collect additional data and construct additional Pareto charts. It might be more appropriate, for this example, to collect data on the level of customer impact of particular errors, rather than just the number.

Moving into the analysis stage of problem solving, the team uses a run chart, Figure 13.7, to look at the number of occasions that problem 5, missing customer records, occurred during the course of the last year. No obvious pattern was found in this case, but run charts frequently reveal patterns of business scheduling—changes in trends at shift change if the chart is plotted by the hour, or changes on the last day of the week, or last few days of the month, if the process is affected by overloads elsewhere in the system.

The control chart, Figure 13.8, looks like the run chart, with the addition of upper and lower control limits. These limits are not the customer specifications. They are calculated from the statistics of the data and conventionally represent three standard deviations (three sigma). The probability that any data points fall outside the upper or lower control limits because of chance is 0.3% (three tenths of one percent.) In other words, if points are outside the control limits, there is a very high probability that something has disturbed the normal process—the process is out of control.

Control charts are used to determine if a process is in control or out of control. Another useful way of expressing this is whether special causes of variation (out of control), or common causes of variation (in control), are present (Scholtes 1988). Process improvement works best if special causes are removed first, getting the process under control, then common causes are removed, reducing variation.

This can be seen in an alternate way by using histograms of the process (Domb 1994). Figure 13.9 is a histogram for this telephone service example. Comparing histograms from several measurement periods would let us see if the process is under control (same shape histograms), or out of control (different shapes), see Figure 13.10. Once the process is under control, the common process problems can be removed.

The process is out of control, in the common sense of being unpredict-

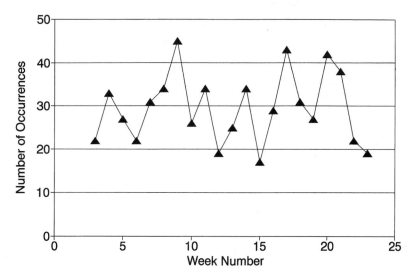

Figure 13.7 Run Chart for Example: Missing Customer Records

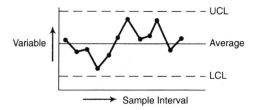

Figure 13.8 A Typical Variable Control Chart. Significant features of the control chart are: Vertical axis, the value of the variable; Horizontal axis, time or sample number; Upper and lower control limits. (Figure from *Readings in Total Quality Management* by Harry Ivan Costin, copyright © 1994 by Harcourt Brace & Company, reproduced by permission of the publisher.)

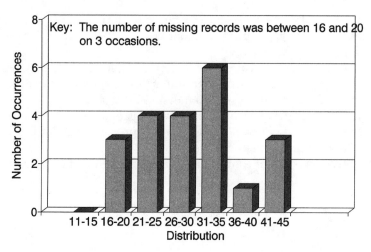

Figure 13.9   Histogram for Example: Missing Customer Records

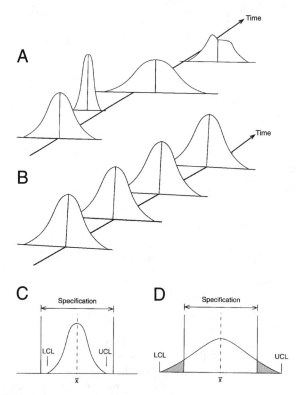

Figure 13.10   Panels A and B show a time series of histograms. In panel A, each histogram is different (shape, midpoint, width, height)

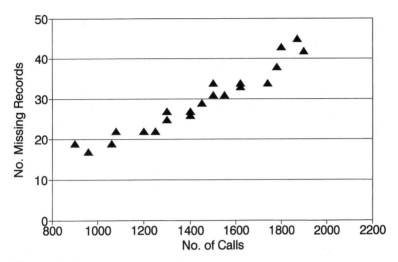

Figure 13.11 Scatter Plot for Example: Missing Records vs. Number of Calls

able. In panel B, the histograms are all the same shape. The process is predictable, so improvement work can begin. In most cases, improvement will aim at reducing the width (variation), and at moving the midpoint (higher, if this is a desirable parameter, lower if it is undesirable). Panel C shows a process which is *capable*; that is, the control limits fall within the specification, and panel D shows a process which is not capable. The shaded areas represent production that is within the control limits, but not useful. When a process is not capable, much effort must be spent to separate useful from non-useful products.

The last of the basic quality improvement tools is the scatter plot, Figure 13.11. It is used to test hypotheses in developing the plan for improvement. In this case, the team has questioned whether the missing records are a more frequent problem during weeks when they have a lot of calls. The straight line relationship between the two variables shows that there is, indeed, a correlation. The team will have to make more observations in the workplace, and flow chart the details of the process to discover if there is a cause-and-effect relationship, what it is, and how to remove the problems.

A typical process improvement project will involve several iterations of whichever subset of these tools apply to the specific situation. Typically, in the "check" and "act" stages of Understand-Select-Analyze-Plan-Do-Check-Act, the team selects the tools to be used for ongoing process monitoring and the indications for future cycles of improvement. The strategy team will use these ongoing business measures, too, as part of the data for deciding which business processes to maintain, and require improvement at either the breakthrough level or through incremental improvement.

THE MANAGEMENT AND PLANNING TOOLS: SIX CREATIVE TOOLS FOR DEVELOPING CONSENSUS, VISION, AND A SHARED OPERATIONAL DEFINITION OF SUCCESS*

This section provides teams with six creative tools and techniques to enable them, in combination with other processes in this book, to develop shared vision, consensus, and a common definition of success. These tools help to enable the concrete actions and measurable results critical to the success of Hoshin Planning.

TOOLS HELP TEAMS

The implementation of Hoshin Planning requires a consistency of focus on the part of everyone in the organization towards accomplishing the key result objectives, or Hoshins, which come to be adopted by the organization.

The tools employ techniques that encourage and facilitate many of the cooperative behaviors that are essential to the operational success of Hoshin Planning. Readers can depend on the tools, when implemented with the tips provided, to support cooperation and the creative sharing of ideas among team members. In this chapter we provide readers with a number of tips to make tool use flow smoothly and ensure cooperation among team members.

THE TOOLS THEMSELVES

The Tools

- Matrix Diagram
- Affinity Diagram
- Radar Chart
- Relations Diagram
- Tree Diagram
- Process Decision Program Chart
- Activity Network Diagram

All tools are described as being used by groups. While some of these tools can be used to good effect by individuals, their greatest impact results from using the collective wisdom of teams with diverse functional and personal

---

*This section was contributed by Weston Milliken, CUE Consulting.

backgrounds. While exceptional individuals might possess the uncommon ability to craft appropriate Hoshins for an entire company, most mortals will benefit from the thinking provided by teams. Therefore, all of these tools will be described as used by teams.

This is a set of qualitative "tools" geared to be used by teams. The qualitative tools described in this chapter differ from the quantitative Statistical Process Control (SPC) tools in that they work with ideas and not numbers. They may be known to some readers as some of the "Seven Management and Planning Tools" or "Seven New Tools."

Quality tools are far more useful when they are used as part of a larger, integrated process. Hoshin is the structure which will make these tools more effective. As teams become more familiar with the use of the tools and how they fit with Hoshin Planning, other applications will become apparent. This chapter details some of the tools that experience has shown to be effective in support of Hoshin Planning and Implementation.

It has been said that, "If you have only a hammer, all of your problems look like nails." Just as a hammer is not used to plane a door, the affinity diagram is not used when the desire is to prioritize a set of ideas. The Relations Diagram may be more appropriate in that instance. It is important to know your tools.

An understanding of the various uses of the tools will come in time— as the user becomes familiar with the contents of the toolbox. It is very important to the effective use of these tools that (1) the group practice the use of the tools to become proficient, and that (2) the group facilitator study the tips in this chapter to ensure their effective use.

WHY THE USE OF TOOLS IS IMPORTANT

Problem Teams

There are a number of teams that fail to accomplish the objectives they want to reach. There are a multitude of problems afflicting teams, a few of which are discussed below. These tools help to overcome these problems.

All of us have participated in meetings that are unfocussed and seem to accomplish nothing. Participants ramble on, tied to their own point of view in the belief that theirs is the only relevant perspective. It becomes a battle of tongues, rather than an effort to collaborate. In such a scene, people tend to become defensive about their own ideas and attack opposing ideas—and occasionally their proponents. This is hardly the way to make an informed decision. People have shared their ideas, but there is no consensus and no solution.

Another problem which groups often face is how to support introverts, twenty-five percent of the population, who are more reflective than extroverts. Introverts tend to speak only when they are sure of themselves. They are often intimidated by the more assertive, sometimes thinking that the extroverts open their mouths and start speaking even before they have figured out what to say! Without special attention, the team can fail to get the thoughtful input of the reflective introverts, and they can leave a meeting feeling unappreciated and unneeded. Their resentment about lack of inclusion can subvert the whole group's "ownership" of decisions and provoke disharmony at a later time.

Other groups rely on false assumptions to make decisions. Instead of using the scientific process to gather data and analyze it, they rely on assumptions of what has gone wrong or is likely to go wrong. Not surprisingly, this approach can lead to the wrong solutions, or solutions that solve only a part of the problem at hand. Incorrect or sub-optimal solutions are applied to problems and, therefore, the problems remain unsolved.

One last example of a problem group is one which seemingly gets along and, to all appearances, solves a problem having analyzed the data and spoken generally about a solution. After a time, however, it seems that the problem that was identified still exists, only slightly modified by any actions taken as a result of the meeting. The problem here is follow-through.

FIVE NEGATIVE BEHAVIORS AND HOW TO AVOID THEM

1. Treating the Hoshin Tools process as a "flavor of the month."
2. Jumping to conclusions and prejudging the outcomes.
3. Abandoning the use of tools after one or two tries.
4. Shunning conflict and disagreement.
5. Treating opinion as fact.

In order to get the most out of the tools in this chapter, it is important to avoid these common behaviors that plague teams and create scenarios such as those outlined above. Here are some causes of such problems and a few paragraphs with ideas to help you avoid them:

Treating the Hoshin Tools Process as the "Flavor of the Month"

In many large organizations, new initiatives come, attract senior management interest, and then fade away leaving hardly any trace. In order for Hoshin planning to avoid this fate, it is *critical* to have the hands-on support of senior management in its implementation. Meetings of company leaders should consistently include updates and reports on implementation and effectiveness. Only by constantly "walking their talk" will the leaders gain the confidence of employees that Hoshin is here to stay.

As a corollary to this leadership support for the overall process is the need for leaders to learn how to use these tools and thus trust their outcome. Only if the leadership values and respects the work and effort that goes into using these tools will they inspire the same kind of respect for the tools and valuing of the results from their subordinates. It is therefore essential for the leaders to understand these tools and know how to use them, in order to inspire others to use the tools and create an organization-wide appreciation for the process of Hoshin Kanri.

Jumping to Conclusions and Prejudging the Outcomes

One of the problems that many users will have to overcome is our education! Virtually all of the people who have advanced into leadership positions in companies have years of analysis and problem-solving behind them. For what other reasons would they have advanced in their corporations? In some sense, much of that training needs to be held in abeyance while the tools are learned and tried. In this way, the tools are given the opportunity to work.

When appropriately facilitated and used, the tools assist in the tasks of analysis and problem-solving for you. The Affinity Diagram helps to generate ideas and group them. The Relations Diagram provides a rough map of the system in question and shows the relationships among drivers and dependents. The Tree and Process Decision Program Chart help one to think through a process and ensure that (1) all steps are considered, and (2) potential problems are unearthed.

In this sense, the tools do the analysis for you; they provide the discipline. The disciplined approach teaches team members to develop insights more quickly over time, by utilizing their intuitions, data, and experience. Teams can wait until the tool prompts them for various input, rather than rushing to a solution that may or may not be the best.

Abandoning the Use of the Tools After One or Two Tries

In addition to letting the tools do the work for you, it is essential that the tools be used. This may seem obvious, but many organizations, while seeing benefits from using the tools, regress back into the old "seat-of-the-pants" decision-making processes that feels comfortable.

"It is hard to teach old dogs new tricks," as the saying goes, but "practice, practice, practice" is the antidote to this tendency. Try the tools consistently when approaching all kinds of problems. Then, when you apply them to Hoshin Planning, they will seem familiar and easy to use. The tools may initially seem difficult and time-consuming. But the additional efficiency achieved over the long-term by finding the right solutions and making sure that everything is covered far outweighs the short-term costs in time and energy. Trust the tools and treat them with respect and you will get tremendous payback for your efforts.

Shunning Conflict and Disagreement

In various ways during our lifetimes, most of us have learned that conflict is bad. From complaints around the dinner table, to arguments over what television show to watch, it became clear that verbal dissent was inappropriate or, at the very least, unappreciated.

As with our various cultural or gender-based perspectives, each of us brings lessons from our past into the workplace. Many cower at conflict or dissent, trying to "make it all better." Even so, when our positions are questioned, we may take it as a personal attack, rather than a well-meant effort to get at the truth.

Unfortunately, these learned tendencies limit our abilities to make the best business decisions. Rather than confront a belligerent and noisy colleague with our perspective on the truth, we sometimes paper over the conflict. The result can be an organization or department unwilling to confront problems that exist, and encouraging a vague atmosphere of discomfort that saps everyone's energy and leads to poor results.

Fortunately, there are ways to combat this problem "What is the data behind your position?" is a good question to ask, for instance. Instead of perpetuating the "I'm right and you're wrong" vicious cycle of attack and defensiveness, this question forces people to ask others for the hard, factual data behind their opinions, and models a willingness to listen that, in turn, opens everyone up for a discussion of the actual merits of an idea. This question is very effective in the use of tools and should always be modeled by the facilitator when personalized disagreements or unfounded assumptions surface.

Also, being willing to engage in constructive conflict is a paradigm shift that some organizations, notably Motorola, have managed to effect. As long as the conflict is moderate, not personalized, and based on fact, it can have a stimulating effect on the decision-making process and ensure that all important ideas are heard. Effectively creating such a paradigm shift is not easy, and may require outside intervention, but the tools do encourage the surfacing of all ideas and discussions based on fact, and are a good first step in this direction.

Treating Opinion as Fact

As promoted by scientific decision-makers from Kepner-Tregoe, J.M. Juran, and W.E. Deming, to Gerald Nadler and Shozo Hibino, it is important to work from data, not assumptions. When data is not available, it may be necessary to work from assumptions, but this should *always* be avoided wherever possible.

In cases where the future will differ from the past, data is of limited use. It will be necessary to use scenarios, models, projected future realities, and the like to gain an understanding of the situation. The tools will then help to merge these assumptions with the data that is available and on-hand.

It may be helpful to use this set of rules when faced with a lack of knowledge:

- Always argue from facts.
- When you can't argue from facts, get them!
- When you can't get them, try to verify your assumptions.
- Question accepted "fact" (also known as "assumptions") during brainstorming processes (Affinity Diagram, Process Decision Program Chart).
- Only reopen discussions when absolutely necessary when working with the judging/narrowing steps (Relations Digraph, Tree Diagram).

BENEFITS OF USING THE TOOLS EFFECTIVELY

For the best use of the tools, it is important to approach their use with specific attitudes. Many of the people who will be using these tools in the Hoshin Planning process are well-trained professionals with years of experience and a significant set of opinions about what works and what does not work. These set paradigms can pose a significant challenge to seeing situations in new and more accurate ways that may be the difference between success and failure in Hoshin Planning. Particularly in the unstable environment that characterizes the modern business world, it is important to be able to see situations in new ways when times demand it. Andrew Grove, CEO of Intel, calls this the "strategic inflection point" (Grove 1996).

It is important for team members to allow the tools to do the work for them. Resist the impulse to jump to conclusions. Resist the desire to "know it all" and anticipate or "out-think" the tools. Trust that the tools will deliver the results they promise. If you have not used these tools before, you may be understandably skeptical of these claims. However, after years of experience, the authors can attest to their value and usefulness.

At times, using the tools may seem tedious, but there are many benefits:

1. Audit trail for decision making.
2. A clear way to communicate with non-team members.
3. Conflict management.
4. Collaboration and team spirit.
5. Empowerment.

Audit Trail for Decision-Making

If a team decision is proven wrong in the future, it is possible to examine the process to see where the mistake was made and revise your approach or false assumptions in the future.

A Clear Way to Communicate with Non-Team Members

Wherever a team is in an organization's hierarchy, the tools provide evidence of a team's disciplined efforts. For senior management, the tools enable a clear communication of what is to be accomplished and why. For teams closer to operational processes, the output of the tools enables managers to review the work and provide additional input that may have been outside of the scope or expertise of team members.

The output of the tools is not a vague "sense of the meeting," but rather a black and white consensus, on paper, that everyone has agreed to. This enables clear communication in the catchball process of Hoshin Planning—the negotiating step between levels of stretch objectives for each unit in order to accomplish the "Hoshins" set out by the organization.

Conflict Management

As people work with the tools, personalities tend to take a secondary role to ideas and their merits. While some assertive individuals can and will find ways to promote themselves and their ideas through the process, it becomes obvious. However, the tools make it easier to embrace another's ideas, or abandon one's own, for two reasons: (1) the tools take the discussion from around the table and focus it on an object—the paper on the wall, and (2) as the group learns to listen and comes to trust each other's wisdom and experience, it becomes easier to trust the group process.

As the various tools help the team to evaluate ideas, embracing some and discarding others, team members come to realize the values of the tools. One of the things that is most exciting in facilitating the work of teams with these tools is the way that people can so quickly come together around new ideas, evaluate them fairly, and jointly agree to a decision that they all "own" and support.

Collaboration and Team Spirit

As team members come to respect each other, there is a sense of rapport and enthusiasm that comes from setting and accomplishing team objectives. Part of this comes from the fact that the tools enable the team to become self-managing, providing the structure to police themselves regarding completion of the work and consideration of important aspects of problem solving, such as thinking through what might go wrong.

It is important to get the team to agree *collectively* to a *group* solution to a problem—accomplishing an Hoshin objective, for example. The tools make agreeing to solutions easier by providing an objective process by which to generate, prioritize, and categorize ideas.

Such collective "ownership" is critical to the collaborative process. As Joseph Juran has said, "People support best that which they develop." As Hoshin Planning strives to align the organization around a small number of objectives, such ownership by employees is essential. "Catchball," described in Chapter 3, is one way to effect this ownership. Using these tools in teams is yet another.

Empowerment

As organization charts become flatter and organizations become leaner, employee empowerment becomes increasingly important. Employees *empowered* to make decisions and *enabled* with the right training are best able to respond to customers quickly and effectively.

But blind empowerment without training, accountability, and supervision of some sort can be tantamount to organizational suicide. Managers therefore need to provide appropriate training in various tools (these and others) to ensure the continuing success of organizations.

The tools in this chapter provide an important way for employees to manage their own processes. The tools provide the kind of self-discipline that the ranks of middle management formerly ensured. As employees use the tools intelligently, they also do the groundwork to support appropriate decisions.

TEAM COMPOSITION

Before we present the mechanics of the tools, it is appropriate to say something about who should comprise the teams that will use the tools.

As stated elsewhere in this chapter, it is very helpful to include a diversity of functions among the team members doing Hoshin Planning. For example, it makes sense for representatives from finance, marketing, design, administration, manufacturing, and service to serve on the teams charting the organization's future.

It may be appropriate to change the membership in the teams depending on their function. For example, individuals working on the Activity Network Diagram should know very well the tasks that they are sequencing in the use of the tool.

People with practical applications knowledge should be involved in this tool. When using broader and more conceptual tools, such as the Affinity Diagram, it may be more useful to have people with wide-ranging experiences who are creative and conceptual (Kao 1996). In every case, think about the tool's function in your process and include people who can be most helpful to that function.

In addition, research has shown that having people with diverse backgrounds also improves the creative process of a team. People from different cultural, racial, or gender backgrounds often bring differing perceptions into the process. Likewise, incorporating customers and suppliers, both internal and external, to the organization bring diverse points of view. These differences stimulate discussions and often provide just the kind of breakthrough thinking that propels organizations into successful futures.

In short, teams who are considering "Hoshins" for an organization should be comprised of a diversity of individuals. It is important to include those closest to the process and those closest to the customers when brainstorming new ideas or making decisions that will affect the process.

While some of this process can be delayed to the catchball process discussed in Chapter 3, it is important to include as many of those affected as soon as possible, for it will help to gain their ownership of the various decisions made, as well as their creativity.

THE TOOLS THEMSELVES

MATRIX DIAGRAM

What the tool accomplishes:

Visual Representation of Data   The Matrix Diagram provides the user with a visual representation of the strength and/or direction (positive or negative) of the relationship between two or more sets of ideas. The Matrix Diagram is a familiar tool to everyone and is often used. Anyone who has worked with a spreadsheet has used the Matrix Diagram. The numbers on a financial statement, for example, indicate the relationship between a time category (months or fiscal years) and an income or expense category.

Another example is a checkbook register, or the place in your checkbook where you note the payee and the amount of the check. The information presented indicates the strength of relationship between the check number, the payee, the amount, and the balance in the account. There is also a column in this matrix to indicate whether a check has cleared. The check register provides us with an example of a matrix that uses words, numbers, and symbols to convey information about relationships. By looking at the check register, one can determine if a check has cleared, the amount of the check, and so on.

Steps

1.   *Determine which sets of data are to be compared*: Consider the outcome of the tool that you desire. What does the team expect to accomplish by plotting the relationship between two sets of information? Is it to express the accurate measurement of the relationship, as in a checkbook balance or a company's income statement? Or does the team want to indicate whether one set of actions will support or work at cross-purposes to another? Or, as a third option, does the team want to indicate the presence and/or strength of a relationship?

2. *Determine symbols to be used*: Depending on what the team wants to show with their matrix, different numbers or symbols can be chosen. If a quantifiable relationship is to be plotted, numbers can be used. If the positive or negative influence of one action on another is to be mapped, plus and minus symbols can be used. If indicating the presence or rough strength of a relationship is the goal, there are many options. A team could use "x" or "xx" to indicate the strength of a relationship, or chose another set of symbols that evokes meaning for them.

3. *Determine if an L-shaped or T-shaped matrix should be used*: An L-shaped matrix is the typical matrix format. In a checkbook register, it is common to have the check numbers along the vertical axis and the other categories to be recorded (payee, amount, balance, etc.) recorded across the top on a horizontal axis. The T-shaped matrix simply moves one of the axes into the center of the matrix (see Figure 13.12), creating a "T" shape. This approach may be helpful if the team wishes to denote some information by symbols and some by numbers, for example, or if it will otherwise enhance the readability and comprehension of the tool.

4. *Create the matrix and insert the information*: In this step, the diagram is set up according to the selected format. The items which are to be compared are

What to do	How to do it	Review	Tool	Creativity	Analysis	Consensus	Action Planning
X	X	X	Matrix Diagram		X	X	XX
X	X		Affinity Diagram	XX		XX	
X			Relations Diagram		XX	XX	
X		X	Radar Chart		XX	X	
	X	X	Tree Diagram		X	X	XX
	X		PDPC	X		X	XX
	X		Activity Network Diagram		X	X	XX

Figure 13.12 Matrix of Tools. In this example, the authors have created a T-shaped matrix diagram relating to the tools described in this chapter. In this case, the tools are compared with the stages of the process (left matrix) and the intent of the process (right matrix). We have used "x" to indicate moderate use and "xx" to indicate frequent use.

listed in rows or columns in a T- or L-shaped format. Next, symbols or numbers are inserted to illustrate the presence and/or strength of the relationship between items.

How the tool helps you (outcomes):

Visual Representation of Information   The tool provides teams and team supervisors with an easy to read representation of the existence and strength of relationship between items listed. Teams report that having this visual information available on flipcharts provides a ready-reference and is easier and faster to comprehend than text descriptions.

AFFINITY DIAGRAM

What the tool accomplishes:

Generates Many Ideas   The Affinity Diagram quickly generates a large number of ideas without the use of precious airtime, as occurs in the standard, verbal brainstorming process. It is a very efficient approach and also provides partial anonymity if the questions being addressed are at all contentious or difficult.

Group Agreement on Groupings of Ideas   The Affinity Diagram is a group process in which, if everyone participates, there is agreement by the group on the outcome of the tool. This provides a collective "ownership" of the results beneficial to any implementation steps requiring team-member support.

Three Levels of Creativity   As you use the Affinity Diagram, a large number of ideas are generated—the first level of creativity. Next, as the affinity cards are grouped by like ideas, a second level of creativity is utilized. Third, the header cards are written, summarizing all of the richness and flavor of the subordinate cards. This is the third creative step of the tool.

Avoids Arguments over Whether Ideas are Right or Wrong   The process permits all ideas the light of day. As ideas are grouped and header cards are written, the less important ideas fade away without anyone having to say anything negative about someone else's idea. This makes for a collective agreement on the important groupings, without making anyone less important or demeaned in the process.

Breakthrough Thinking   As the group works the Affinity Diagram, especially in the phase where the header cards are being written, new associations and "Ah-ha's" can occur, leading teams in new directions. For example, some member of the team may see in the affinity something that has eluded the organization for a long time. Pay special attention when writing the header cards so that none of the important subtleties of the grouping are hidden from view.

Steps

1. *Agree on general question to be answered:* This is a good place to brainstorm strategy questions, such as, (a) "It is 1999 and we are a success. How did we get here?" or (b) "What are all the issues that we need to address in managed health care?" or (c) "How does the competition, ABC Corp., get new products out in half the time?"

2. *Brainstorm ideas, one idea per Post-it™ note:* There are a couple of different approaches to this process. Individuals can write their ideas on sticky-back notes in silence, with the understanding that they will answer questions about the meaning at a later time, if necessary. Alternately, people can speak their ideas out loud and they (or a scribe) can write the sentences on the Post-it™ notes. The former technique has the advantages of speed and anonymity. The latter can stimulate participants' thinking as they hear the ideas of others in the group.

3. *Arrange completed notes at random:* The notes are placed on the butcher paper at random (no pre-grouping). People are certainly welcome to write additional ideas on note cards as their thinking is stimulated by what others have written.

Alternate approach: One of the authors of this volume sometimes uses a different approach: the simultaneous writing, posting, viewing, and sorting of ideas. As with all of the options listed, bear in mind what outcome you desire from the tool, and use common sense to tailor the tool to that desired outcome.

4. *Sort quickly into groupings in silence:* Groupings are done in silence so that others can concentrate on what they are reading. Also, some feel that this permits both sides of the brain to be used, rather than just the left side, which is dominant when words are spoken. If the notes are moved with the non-dominant hand (righties use the left hand, and vice versa), it also encourages use of both logical and symbolic brain functions.

It is important not to stick the notes to each other as you are grouping. This makes it less easy for someone else to move them if she or he disagrees with the placement.

If you disagree with someone else's placement of a card, simply move it. If there is a persistent disagreement on placement, simply copy the card and place it in both categories.

It is important in this step to sort based on the *ideas* contained in the statements on the cards, not just the words. For example, "Improve employee health benefits," is very different from "Downsize the organization by separating fifteen percent of the work force."

5. *Write the Header Cards:* In this step, the team members write a summary card reflecting the contents of each individual grouping of idea cards. The summary card must reflect all of the richness, flavor, and variety of the cards beneath it. This can be a daunting task.

It can be helpful to some teams to find the single, unifying word or concept related to each grouping, write that word or phrase as a temporary header, and return later to write the whole sentence.

Resist moving cards that initially seem not to fit. Unless there is a clear and unambiguous mistake, one member of your team may have seen a connection between items that is eluding the other members. Ask yourself, and your team members, if there is a nugget of wisdom in the grouping, and attempt to convey that in your header card.

The header cards should be as detailed and thorough as required for your processes. If you are taking the header cards into another process after the Affinity is completed, such as the Relations Diagram, you will need to create the best header cards your team is capable of. If the subsequent use of the Affinity is less exacting, your efforts can be more casual. As with all of the tools, always keep in mind what you are trying to accomplish with their use, and vary your approach to the tool in order to accomplish your aims.

Generico Example

The company used in our example, Generico, is a producer of high-end, technologically advanced television equipment. Its customers include retail, the early adapters of emerging technology, and industrial, cable television stations and other media producers who require the high-quality product Generico manufactures. In addition to their off-the-shelf product, the company has a service arm, installing equipment, and a consulting arm, performing needs assessments and customizing software.

Generico has been active in implementing Total Quality Management principles in their organization, including employee empowerment supplemented by a generous Employee Stock Ownership Plan (ESOP). Generico has also developed partnerships with their suppliers, such as chip suppliers and writers of their technical manual, among others.

Generico has enjoyed a strong reputation in the field, but has some concerns about its closest competitor, Specifico, to which it will compare itself in using the Spider Chart.

In addition to the Generico example, shown in sequence to illustrate how the tools can be used with one another, are some examples taken from other sectors of the economy. These are intended to show that the tools can be used effectively to help various industries face significantly different problems.

In this example, team participants are answering the following question: "It is four years from now. Generico is the leading supplier of new video technologies for retail and industrial companies. How did Generico get there?"

Using the Affinity, they have projected themselves into the future, imagining their potential success and posing the question of what it takes to become the preferred supplier. From the answers, readers can get some sense of the issues facing the company.

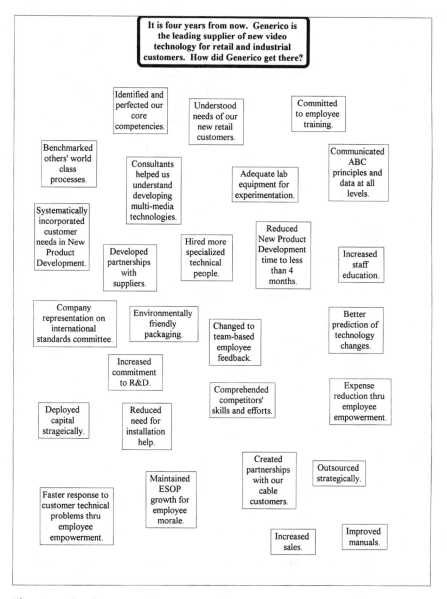

Figure 13.13 In this first diagram, the sticky-back cards are posted at random on the sheet of paper. There is no order to their arrangement. Once all participants have placed their cards on the wall, it is time for the sorting to begin.

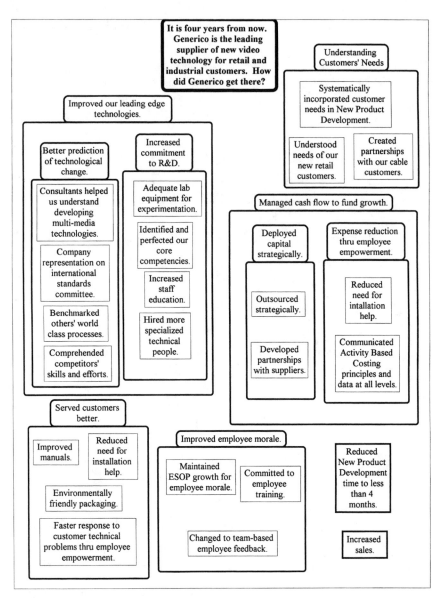

Figure 13.14 The second diagram shows the cards sorted by affinity. It is important at this step to be sure that the similarities in the groupings reflect actual content, rather than simply similar words. As you look at the groupings (within the heavy-lined boxes) note whether you agree with the placement of the cards. Can you find the one card that was repeated when participants argued over the proper placement of the card?

In the boxes above the groupings are the **Header Cards**. These cards summarize the flavor of all the cards within the grouping. Some, as you will see, are simply cards from the previous random sorting that the team judged to be good summaries of the cards beneath. Two of the groupings have three header cards. The one on top of all of the groupings is known as the **Superheader**. The other two cards above the affinity groupings are known as **Subheaders**.

174

Other questions which might profitably have been asked are: "How can we learn more about the anticipated needs of customers X years from now?" and "What are the issues involved in company employee morale?"

How the tool helps you (outcomes):

Data and Ideas are Generated or Collected   The tool provides a very quick way to generate a large number of ideas sorted into categories by affinity for use in other tools, or as an output with its own uses.

Ideas are Grouped by Category   The tool effectively permits the group, without verbal argument, to group ideas into categories linked by ideas. The silent process encourages more thoughtful sorting and may result in breakthrough associations or inspirations for the team.

The Groupings are Summarized   As the header cards are written, the group works to summarize all of the richness and flavor of the cards in the groupings, so that the cards may be used in later tools, such as the Relations Diagram, the Spider Chart, and the Tree.

The Work of the Team can Easily be Reviewed   One advantage of the tool is that the brainstorming of the team can later be reviewed by others not in the group who may have additional ideas and perspectives. These managers and co-workers can add their own ideas and contribute to the process.

Helpful Hints

Honor Your Colleagues' Bifocals   Write big and clearly in marker (for all tools)

Ideas and Headers should be Complete Sentences   It is important to be as clear as possible in recording your ideas. Imagine that the reader is someone who is intelligent, but knows nothing about your process. Make your ideas clear enough for her to understand.

At a minimum, use a verb and an object in a sentence. "Sell" is not as good an idea card as "Sell widgets" or "Sell the company," for example. It is best to use the active tense, where possible.

If There is Persistent Disagreement   If participants cannot agree on the placement of a card, copy it over and place it in two categories: Don't argue about it. Placement in both categories may be valid. Focus instead on finishing the process of grouping the remaining cards.

After Grouping, Resist Moving Cards   When writing the headers, resist the impulse to move a card into another category, unless it is clearly and unambiguously wrong. Instead, ask yourselves *why* the card was placed there—there may be a good reason that is not immediately apparent. This is where breakthrough associations can happen.

When to Use An Affinity Diagram during the Hoshin Planning Process:

Development of the Vision   The Affinity Diagram is extraordinarily helpful in creating a vision of the future. A set of particpants can let their imaginations roam with the expectation that the Affinity process will structure the output and vision.

Initial Strategies, Company-Wide   When creating the overall strategies of the company, one of which will later become the Hoshin.

Developing Targets   Once a Hoshin has been selected, Affinity Diagrams can be used to develop a grouping of targets that need to be met in order to have a successful implementation of the Hoshin.

Team Creativity   The Affinity can be used to brainstorm and group the means necessary to accomplish the targets.

RADAR CHART (Sometimes called the *Spider Chart.*)

What the tool accomplishes:

Visual Representation of Information   The graphic is a reminder of how a company rates to its competition, or to itself at a different time. It reminds team members of the reasons for the project and can be a useful reference for a project team.

Requires Metrics   The tool requires the team to quanitfy measurements that indicate success in approaching particular goals. Scores can be numerical or qualitative, but they must be defined. This part of the process can be the most creative and important that the team undertakes.

Encourages the Sharing of Perspectives Among Cross-Functional Members of the Team   While assembling the Radar Chart there is an opportunity for learning: "You mean you really think we are perceived like that in the marketplace?" "What makes you think the competition will be that good in three years?" "How does manufacturing see this issue?" "How can we get data on this?" And so forth.

Helps the Team Come to Consensus As the team works together to score where the company is in relation to the competition, or to a company that it is benchmarking, discussion and learning takes place by determining the various categories to score, as well as the metrics of the scoring.

Steps

1. *Determine the axes of the Radar Chart:* Brainstorm the list of appropriate axes, or take them from a list already available. For example, profitability and product or service quality are often on the axes.

2. *Determine the scale of the axes:* By convention, the tip of each axis denotes scores higher or better than those at the origin.

   It is always best to use clear measures rather than general ideas. You might want to define "5" as responding to customers complaints within a week, while "10" is responding immediately.

3. *Label axis, show scale:* Write legibly.

4. *Determine competition x's (and y's) score:* Come to collective agreement on where your competition is, or where you know they will be. Mark their score on the axis. Use a different color for each competitor.

5. *Determine your score today:* Come to collective agreement on where your competition is, or where you know they will be. Mark this score on the axis using a unique color.

6. *Determine where you need to be at time t:* Given the previous determinations, and your sense of the customers and the marketplace, determine where you need to be at the end of your Hoshin period, be it three years, five, or ten. Mark this on the axis using a bold color.

How the tool helps you (outcomes):

Comparison Chart Participants and non-team members can clearly see where the organization is today versus (1) where it needs to be, and (2) where the competition is or will be. This ensures that you are dealing with reality rather than an overly optimistic (or pessimistic) view of how your organization measures up to its competition.

Later Review This tool can act as a reminder to participants at later steps why it is so important to create progress on various gaps.

Helpful Hints

Always Use Data It is helpful to insist on using real data (customer surveys, employee surveys, etc.) to support your measurements.

Post Sheet   Having your work on the wall during later processes helps to remind team participants of the big picture.

Vary Colors   Use different colors to make the chart more easily readable.

Connect the Dots   It is often helpful to connect the dots of competitors' ratings, as well as those of where your organization is today and where it needs to be. This improves readability.

RELATIONS DIAGRAM

What the tool accomplishes (general):

Displays Relationships Among a Set of Ideas   The source of these ideas are often Affinity header cards, that is, the summary cards for the Affinity groupings developed in an earlier process.

Systems Thinking—Arrows of Influence   Books such as *The Fifth Discipline* have impressed on readers the importance of looking at business systems in their entirety. This serves to avoid the suboptimization resulting from the "functional silos" or rigid boundaries that traditionally have existed between departments.

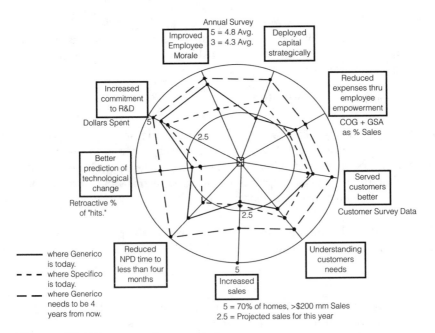

Figure 13.15   Radar Chart example.

The Relations Diagram helps users to see how different participants view the relationship among the various components studied. As one systematically asks of two items which of them has the greater impact or influence on the other, the complex web of relationships in a system is examined by the entire team.

The resulting diagram is a rough model of the system in question. As the dominant items in the system (the "drivers") become apparent through the systematic use of the tool, participants have, in effect, identified the levers they can use to efficiently control the system in question.

Figure 13.15 In this chart, there are three lines and two circles. The lines indicate the ratings of various companies at various times. The circles denote a measurement of 2.5 and 5, with 5 being the best possible.

The words next to the Header Cards indicate the metrics to be used in the gap analysis (such as, "dollars spent" and "customer survey data"). The solid line links points on the various axes that indicate the team's best estimate of where Generico rates today. The dotted line indicates where the major competitor, Specifico, is today. The third dashed line indicates the team's consensus about where Generico needs to be for success four years from now.

In selecting the two time-frames in analyzing Generico's position, we bring the team back from speculation about the future ("We are successful four years from now—How did we get here?") and ground them in the present. The team is asked today's ranking, and where they need to be in four years, based on their knowledge of the technology's potential, their competition, and the marketplace. After the blue-sky, future-oriented thinking, this provides a useful grounding step in the present. The tool also requires teams to think in terms of metrics: How will they know their goal has been accomplished? What are the measures of success?

The example shows some of the types of metrics or measures that the team will use to determine success. For example, to measure "Employee Morale," the team has opted to use the average rating of the annual employee survey. A 4.8 average was considered the best possible, taking the 5 level of the axis. A 4.3 average will equal a 3 on the axis.

"Increased Sales" will rate a 5 if seventy percent of the market has purchased our equipment *and* we exceed $200 million in sales. A 2.5 ranking will be given for achieving the sales level Generico projects for this coming year. This approach to scoring—having compound factors that must be achieved for success—is often the case when the objective is abstract or high-level.

For reasons of space, we have not given examples of measurement for all of the axes. Nevertheless, it is a critical part of the tool to give each axis metrics and clearly state what the ranking score means: for example, as a 5, 4, 3, 2, or 1. In all cases, measures should be made that are better for the company at the 5 level and less beneficial at the 1 level.

As a result, this tool can be very powerful in application. Dr. Juran speaks of separating "the vital few from the trivial many." The Relations Diagram permits participants to create a model of the system using qualitative data. The model points towards the vital few—the efficient ways to guide systems towards desired ends.

Graphical, Visual, Easy to Explain   As one draws the arrows indicating the relationship between the various pairs of cards, patterns begin to emerge. As with many of these tools, the graphical result enables easy explanation to managers, or other outsiders, that document the decision-making process.

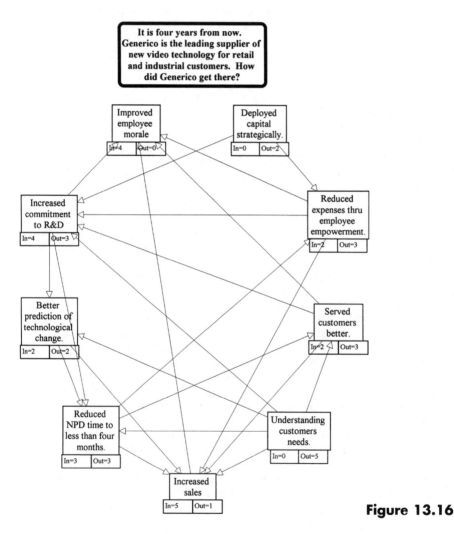

Figure 13.16

Steps

1. *Determine source (headers, other):* Header cards from the affinity are often used to help team members understand the relationships among the categories determined using that tool. Also, a list of ideas can simply be brainstormed by the team. If the team is dealing with other ideas or concepts that are well known, these can be used as well.

2. *Post the issue cards in a circle on the flip chart:* Leave enough room between cards to draw arrows. If you have a large number of cards, you may wish to use a fine point pen to draw the arrows. This will ensure that you have enough space to avoid confusion.

3. *Pick an anchor card and compare it to each of the other cards, going in a clockwise direction:* By "anchor card," we mean one card that will be compared with all of the other cards. Just as the anchor allows a boat to move

---

Figure 13.16 This is a completed Relations Diagram. The header cards from the previous Affinity Diagram are arranged in a circle, as shown. Next, a question about the relationship between one set of two cards is asked. "Does 'Understanding customers' needs' (card X) cause or influence 'Increased commitment to R&D' (card Y), or is it the reverse, or is there no relationship?"

Using similar questions, each card is compared in sequence with *all* of the others. The result is a diagram showing patterns of influence. The arrow is drawn from the influencing card to the influenced card. Arrows can only run in one direction. No arrow is drawn if there is no relationship.

Once all cards have been compared with all other cards, the incoming and outgoing arrows of each card are tallied, and marked nearby. In this example, the driver issue (with the most outgoing arrows) is "Understanding Customers Needs."

The use of the tool indicates the relationships among the factors that bear on Generico's progress to becoming the preferred supplier in four years' time. If the team's understanding is correct, the most important thing Generico needs to do is "Understanding customers' needs." However, this is a provisional conclusion. Before focusing entirely on this driver, it is necessary to compare Generico with its competition and to set goals as to where it needs to be in four years. This is done next in the Radar Chart.

Please note here that it is not appropriate to ignore cards that are not selected as drivers in the Relations Diagram. Just because the team doesn't select them as a driver doesn't mean they don't need to get done! Take note of the other elements of becoming the preferred supplier. You may wish to include them in the Tree Diagram (Figure 3.17), as actions taken to accomplish the company goal are mapped out in detail.

freely about it, an anchor card allows the team to be sure it has compared one card with each of the others before moving on.

Reading the two cards, ask, "Does [card A] cause, impact, or influence [card B]? Or is it the reverse? Or is there no relationship?"

If a causal influence exists, draw an arrow from the influencing card to that which is influenced. Proceed in this fashion around the "clock" until the relationship between the anchor card and all others has been considered.

4. *Move the "anchor" to the next card in a clockwise direction and compare it with the other cards in the circle: Continue* this process of moving the anchor to successive cards until all possible pairs have been considered. (It is not necessary to compare cards that have already been considered a second time.)

5. *Count the number of incoming arrows and outgoing arrows from each issue card:* Cards with no, or very few, incoming arrows are "Drivers." These are the issues that drive or influence the entire system or process being considered.

Cards with no, or very few, outgoing arrows are "Dependents." They depend on, or are the outcome of, other parts of the process.

6. *Sum the number of incoming and outgoing arrows for each card:* Cards with high sums are intimately involved in the system represented on the page. Cards with lower numbers have a more peripheral impact on the system. If issues considered to be critical fall into this category, it may be useful to brainstorm other influencers of these cards to better understand how they can be influenced.

How the tool helps your team (outcomes):

Provides a Rough Prioritization of Importance   As team members complete the use of the tool, participants are able to identify the "drivers"—the issues that dominate the system and can be manipulated most effectively to get the outcomes desired. Although the process is not rigidly scientific, the tool provides a defensible model until better data is available.

Demonstrates Interrelationships   At the completion of the exercise, there is a visual map of how items relate to one another. If problems develop later, it is possible to revisit the diagram to determine (1) the categories that may have caused the problem, or (2) any diagram corrections that may be needed.

Provides Perspective on the System   The tool provides participants with a map of the system and the team's best understanding of where the dominant influence lies, as well as the more dependent subsystems.

Easy to Share with Others for Input, Buy-in   As with many of these tools, the output can be posted or otherwise shared to ensure that managers, or others who were not part of the group, agree with the chart, or, if not, can provide input into the decision-making process as it goes forward.

Driver May Point the Way to Appropriate Hoshins   If team members are looking at an organization-wide set of systems, the driver issue may help point to appropriate Hoshins. Since the driver issues, by definition, have a controlling or dominant effect on the system, Hoshins should be developed to impact the driver issues to assure the most effective use of energy or money.

Helpful Hints

Limit Yourself to One Idea Per Card   Combined ideas in a card (often appearing in the form of compound sentences) can create confusion later in the process.

Clearly Define Your Terms   Different people may mean different things by profitability, acceptable quality, clear communication.

TREE DIAGRAM

What the tool accomplishes (general):

Maps a Logical Hierarchy of Tasks and Means—a Process Tree
The Tree Diagram can show a breakdown of tasks into their component parts. It systematically and logically maps out the lists of tasks and sub-tasks (the means) to accomplishing a task or goal.

Given the task of building a house, for example, builders must finish the following broad processes: (1) build the foundation, (2) frame the house, (3) build the roof, and (4) finish the interior. Each of these steps, in turn, has a set of smaller process steps that need to be accomplished in order for the higher level step to be completed.

Can Also Show Components of a Physical Object—a Component Tree   Another type of tree, the Component Tree, lists the components or elements of a process or object. In a variation on the example given above, the idea of a house is broken into its component parts by category rather than by process steps. In the building of a house's concrete foundation, for example, the materials could be listed: framework, rebar, concrete, as well as the plumbing and electrical components inset into the foundation.

Note that while the previous example was time-based (steps need to be coordinated with each other to ensure completion of the task), the list of components in this example is merely a list, not a process, and does not require a focus on timing or the sequencing of tasks.

Logic Check   The Tree helps to be sure that all steps are considered that are required to accomplish a goal. The Tree Diagram process includes a check and act step that encourages team members to bring a critical eye to their work and ensures that all tasks envisioned actually can be completed by the means outlined in the Tree Diagram.

Target/Means Cascade   The Tree diagramming process helps the team systematically break down goals or targets into their component parts, that is, what needs to be done to accomplish the objectives. The cascade effect can be seen as one realizes that the each of the means becomes a target to be accomplished by various subsets, creating a logical hierarchy of tasks and means.

Steps

1. *Determine the form of the tree: vertical or horizontal:* Place the root question or objective in the appropriate location.

2. *Determine the root question or objective:* In this step, team members are asked to state their objective in the form of a task or goal. Sources can include (1) a driver issue of the relations diagram, (2) the dependent issue of relations diagram, or (3) an objective such as a Hoshin.

   If the choice is (2) a dependent issue of the Relations Diagram, you may find it helpful to consider the driver issues of the same Relations Diagram as tasks that need to be completed in order to accomplish the objective.

3. *Ask the question, "How do we accomplish this objective?" or "If you had to break out this step into sub-steps, what would they be?"* Write the sub-steps out, one per card, and place at the first level.

   If the team has trouble generating sub-steps, it may be helpful to ask this variation of the question: "If you had to break this root or branch into only three sub-steps, what should they be?"

4. *Ask the same question again for each of the branches:* There should be a minimum of two branches from each card.

   Stop at actionable items level (or other level appropriate to the outcome that you desire).

5. *Review step:* Start at the lowest level of the tree and work backwards to determine if you have left out important steps. Just as the "How" question was asked as the tree branched out ("How do we accomplish this task or objective?"), recognize that when going back towards the root the question is "why," as in, "Why are we doing this step?" The answer to this should be to accomplish the next higher-level task. (*It may be helpful to refer to the tool example here.*)

   To make certain that the objectives are actually accomplished by the steps that are outlined, consider all of the branches off of each objective card. Ask

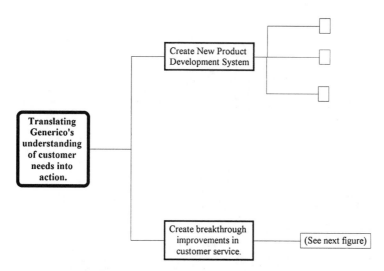

Figure 13.17 Tree Diagram. The root objective has been divided into two main branches: Create New Product Development System and Create Breakthrough Improvements in Customer Service. For the sake of this example, only one of the sub-tasks will be "treed out" into its component parts.

of those branches, "If we do all of these steps, have we actually accomplished our objective?

If the answer is yes, proceed to the next branch. If the answer is no, add the appropriate branches that will make sure that the objectives are accomplished.

How the tool helps you (outcomes):

Shows Breakdown of Steps of a Process or Product As can be seen in the examples of Process and Component Trees (above and below), the main objective or task is broken out into a series of sub-tasks that need to be accomplished in order to accomplish the main task. Each sub-task, in turn, is broken out into a series of tasks or means by which the sub-task is accomplished, and so on.

Enables the Identification of Missing Parts in the Review Step Given the logical hierarchy of tasks and means outlined above, a check step of the thinking process can be incorporated. Ask of each set of sub-tasks or means if, when they are all accomplished, the main goal or task is accomplished. If not, it becomes necessary to think of additional steps that may be required to accomplish the goals.

In this way, team members can review and revise their thinking. It is far better to make mistakes on paper than in misspent activity.

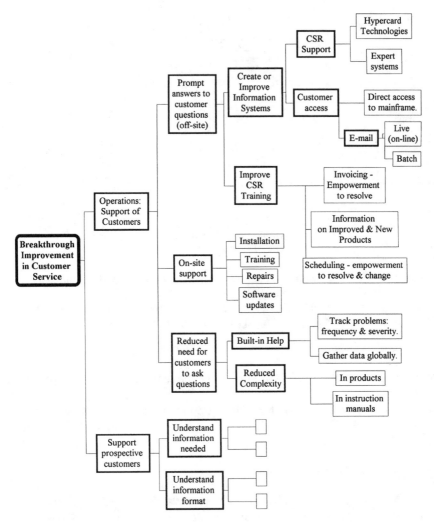

Figure 13.18   The team has broken down the breakthroughs in the customer service branch into several levels of detail. At each level, the question is asked, "If this is my objective, what are the major sub-tasks that, if done, will enable accomplishing the objective?" The answer to this question, or the means to accomplish the objective, are written onto sticky-back notes and placed on the paper. This facilitates the moving of the various steps if a mistake is later recognized.

The branches are extended into levels of detail until the team has reached the level of assignable tasks. In the example, the small blank boxes indicate that there are sub-tasks or means that have been omitted for space considerations.

Helpful Hints

Trees—Portrait or Landscape?   The example shown is a horizontal tree. A vertical graphical convention is also perfectly appropriate.

Keep the Branches and Twigs at Roughly the Same Level of Detail Across the Tree Diagram   If you are having trouble identifying the appropriate level at which a process or sub-process falls, compare it with the levels of detail on another branch and maintain rough parity among branch levels.

Always Have More than Two Branches Coming Off of a Higher-Level Item   It is a convention of the tool to have at least two branches coming out of each higher level branch or limb. Having fewer than two suggests that the extension in question is just a restatement of the higher-level branch.

Branch Out to an Appropriate Level of Detail   When you reach the level of actionable items (for example, have marketing ask our customers X), this is a good place to stop. Others suggest that stopping at a level just above actionable items keeps the tree at an appropriately abstract level. Go to the level that satisfies your project objective.

Do NOT Draw the Branches of the Tree Until It Is Complete   Avoid rework by being sure you have the branches in the appropriate places and that you have completed the logic check before drawing the lines to connect the cards. This will help someone on your team from having to redraw the diagram and reset the cards if a line is drawn in error.

Limb the Tree If Overgrown   If the tree is particularly complex, it may make sense to "limb the tree" so that the various branches or sub-branches are each located on its own sheet.

This Is Not an Activity Network Diagram   Remember when creating a tree that it is not a PERT chart, or a flowchart of activities to be accomplished. It is not intended to show what needs to be done when. Rather, it merely outlines the task to be accomplished, along with the means to accomplish it.

PROCESS DECISION PROGRAM CHART (PDPC)

What the tool accomplishes (general):

Preventing Problems   The Process Decision Program Chart (PDPC, also sometimes known as the Contingency Tree) enables teams to consider the likely problems that may occur and to brainstorm countermeasures to prevent likely problems from coming to pass. This is its chief purpose and has proven to be very helpful for many strategic planning teams.

Contingency Planning   Although preventing problems is preferred, it is also possible to use the tool to develop contingency plans for things that can go wrong, but are not preventable.

Grounds Pollyannas   In some companies there is over-optimism when it comes to planning. Teams agree on the tasks, but they are rarely implemented successfully. This tool can help by grounding the Pollyannas in reality—the likely problems that may disrupt plans—and help the planners to achieve successful implementation.

It Can Stimulate Cross-Functional Cooperation   Asking cross-functional teams to brainstorm possible problems and countermeasures or contingency plans, gives the group an opportunity to hear the questions and problems that others encounter in the course of their work, enabling all to understand the impact that their actions may have on other departments or individuals.

Steps

1. *Place Tree Diagram with steps to be accomplished on one side of your page:* Place the root or goal statement (what you are planning to accomplish) to the edge of the page. Show the means steps (the "hows") next to the goal statement. Show the "branches" to the level you want to proof against potential problems.

If the completion of the entire project on time and without error is essential—that is, human or corporate life is in danger—it may be necessary to apply this thinking to all levels of the branches.

Usually, however, such thoroughness is not required, and a broad list of steps is all that is examined. Use your own judgment and experience to determine the appropriate degree of detail.

2. *Brainstorm and research probable problems:* Go through the items at the lowest level of each of the branches, brainstorming and researching possible and likely problems that might prevent the successful completion of each step. Write each problem on a card or Post-it™ note and link it with a line to the step it relates to.

For example, in the erection of a building, one might want to consider a delay in the delivery of building materials, but not an uncontrollable or unlikely major earthquake, nuclear explosion, or other "act of God."

When the team is unqualified to know the possible or likely problems that could prevent or slow success, it may be necessary to interrupt the process

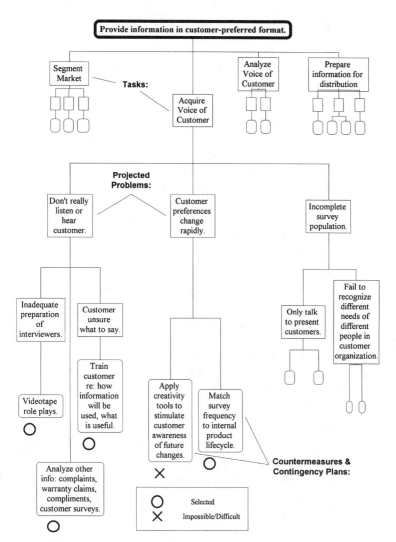

Figure 13.19 Process Decision Program Chart. In this figure, a different branch of the tree is outlined. "Understand information format," in Figure 13.18, has been rephrased as "Provide information in customer-preferred format." That goal or objective has been broken out into four means or sub-tasks: segment market, acquire voice of the customer, analyze voice of the customer, and prepare information for distribution.

One of these, acquire voice of the customer, has been broken out. The question was asked, "What are reasonable or likely problems that might occur to thwart accomplishment of the objective?" In two cases, the potential problems were broken down into more specific problems, using the Tree format.

Next, recorded in the boxes with rounded corners, are the reasonable countermeasures, or contingency plans, that might be used to prevent or fix problems that occur. The team develops a series of possible countermeasures or contingency plans before going back and marking, with an X for "no" and an O for "yes," whether or not the solutions should be built into the planning process. In our example, four solutions have been selected, and one has been rejected.

and research what could go wrong, or bring members onto the team who have implementation knowledge.

3. *Brainstorm countermeasures:* Next, look at the possible problems and collectively brainstorm countermeasures for the likely problems.

If countermeasures are impossible (it may be impossible to prevent a strike by a supplier's personnel), consider contingency plans (such as alternative suppliers) who can get you out of your bind if it happens.

Write each countermeasure or contingency plan adjacent to the listed problem, and link it with a line to the problem it addresses.

4. *Select appropriate countermeasures:* Review the preventative steps or contingency plans devised to address the potential problems that have been identified. Select the ones that you want to incorporate into your planning with an "O." Reject the ones you deem inappropriate, or overkill, with an "X." Tools such as Return on Investment Analysis, Probability of Occurrence, and Risk Analysis may be needed.

5. *Build the countermeasures into your process:* Finally, incorporate the countermeasures or contingency plans that you have selected into your planning process. This will help to ensure that the people who will carry out your plan carry out the steps that are judged to be vital to your plan's implementation.

For instance, it may be appropriate to find substitute suppliers to ensure uninterrupted building construction in the example above.

How the tool helps you (outcomes):

The Process Decision Program Chart is particularly effective in the deployment and review stages of Hoshin Planning. At these points in the Hoshin Process, one can think through the implementation steps and what might get in the way of successful deployment of the organization's Hoshins. As likely problems are discerned, countermeasures and contingency plans can be developed to increase the likelihood of success.

Develops Preventative Measures   As described above, the tool helps the planning team to develop measures to prevent likely problems. It helps to ground teams in the reality that the world is uncertain and even the best laid plans can go astray.

Develops Contingency Plans   If problems cannot be prevented, contingency plans can be developed and built into implementation plans to assure successful completion of a project.

Forces Team Members to Think Through the Implementation of Plans and the Steps Required   Many organizations have a history of crafting solutions that fail to solve problems. For these, this tool can be a great help. If people do not have experience in planning and implementing a project—and thus knowing the likely problems to bedevil a project—this tool is very helpful in bringing planners' attention to these problems. In this way, the tools applies discipline to the planning process.

Helpful Hints

Keep the Brainstormed Problems in the Reasonable and Likely Categories   While it may be fun (and creative) to think of absurd or fun problems—and may become essential if the brainstorming gets too tedious or boring!—it is not helpful to spend a great deal of time brainstorming problems and countermeasures that are out of your sphere of influence (such as earthquakes or unlikely wars or riots), unless those events might have a deadly impact (as in a nuclear power plant located on an earthquake fault).

Do the Brainstorming in a Group   It is a false economy to think that this can be done by one person only. There is a valuable synergy that can come from groups brainstorming together. A great deal of learning can be had from this process, and additional steps or brainstorming can be beneficial to all participants.

Encourage Actual Problem-Solving   It may be tempting to use this process simply to build in extra time to ensure completion of the project—a process known as "padding." Instead of padding, use the PDPC to improve your process. Solve problems before they happen. Set realistic goals. Should an unanticipated problem delay your completion, use that as helpful data to improve your process next time.

No one is helped by deluding himself. If there is a propensity to do this in your organization, it may be necessary to do more work in driving fear out of your organization. Encourage people to look towards improving processes rather than laying blame for mistakes.

ACTIVITY NETWORK DIAGRAM (AND)

The Activity Network Diagram (AND) is a tool that enables planners to consider the required implementation steps for a project. Tools that are substantially similar to the AND are the PERT Chart, the Gantt Chart, and the Critical Path Method. If the reader is more comfortable with these methods, it is not necessary to learn the AND. The techniques you know will serve you equally well.

What the tool accomplishes (general):

Maps Out the Tasks to Be Accomplished   The Activity Network Diagram is a tool that enables a team to get a clear picture of the series of tasks to be accomplished, as well as mapping those that are parallel with one another (can be done simultaneously), and those that must be done in sequence (one before the next).

Sequences Tasks   The tool enables a team to see clearly the sequencing of tasks. Putting these tasks on paper may help to discover concerns or problems with staffing of the project that would otherwise go unnoticed. For example, as a team is planning the use of human resources, it can determine if there is personnel available to do the tasks that are laid out in the order required. This can be a significant benefit of the planning process.

Shows Parallel Tracks Where They Exist   Likewise, mapping of the tasks that are parallel to one other, that is, can be done at the same time as one another, can also help with the planning of human resources and the understanding of a project. If tasks can be done at the same time, it may free up people or time in ways that are unforeseen. Also, as problems are identified, it may be possible to create additional parallel paths (by paying others to do work traditionally done internally, for example) that will free up time or other resources.

Records the Duration Time of Each Task and of the Entire Project   By forcing those who use the tool to assign times to tasks, the Arrow Diagram enables team members and planners to calculate the entire length of the project and the lengths of time required to complete a range of subtasks.

Creating this information on paper enables the implementers to reference the scheduled start and stop times of each task or set of tasks and to determine if they are on schedule. If they are behind schedule, they can alert those who will be affected. If they are ahead of schedule, they will know and can plan for the consequences.

Also, by determining the required time anticipated to complete the project, planners can investigate alternative approaches if the projected time schedule exceeds the time available. This is known as "crashing" the project or its longest chain of tasks, by paying more, reengineering the project, or otherwise altering the current plan.

Determines the Critical Path   The "Critical Path" is that set of tasks that, linked together, force the project to its longest duration. Tasks that lie on the Critical Path must be completed on time in order for the project to be completed on time. This is why they are termed "Critical" to the completion of the project.

By knowing the tasks that lie on the critical path, implementers can pay special attention to these items to ensure completion of the project according to schedule. Without knowing which tasks are on the critical path and which are not, implementers might waste time completing a task in a great hurry that will have no impact on the ultimate outcome. Knowing the critical path helps to focus limited resources on tasks that require them, in order to finish a project successfully.

Steps

1. *Determine tasks:* The first step requires the users to determine all of the tasks that need to be accomplished in order to finish a given project. Each task is written on a piece of paper or a Post-it™, leaving enough room to add time durations and other calculations to be described.

As with all of the tools, the tool should be tailored by the user to accomplish the task at hand. If planners are working on a critical project, it may be important to consider every task that needs to be done. If the project is less critical, a broader listing of tasks may be adequate. In either event, the tasks are written one per card.

2. *Sequence tasks:* Next, the tasks are sequenced. If one of the listed tasks needs to be completed before one (or more) subsequent tasks can be begun, it is placed in front of the succeeding tasks and an arrow is drawn from the preceding task to the subsequent one.

Likewise, if two (or more) tasks need to be completed before a subsequent task can be begun, an arrow is drawn from both tasks to the subsequent card. This indicates that the two tasks must be completed before the third can be begun.

At the same time, planners should consider if there are tasks or sets of tasks that can be done at the same time as one another. These are known as "parallel tasks" and they are indicated by aligning each task or set of tasks with those that can be done simultaneously. If some combination of these sets of tasks need to be completed before another can be begun, the arrow notation is handled, as noted in the paragraph above.

3. *Record time duration of each task:* On each card, note the time duration of each task. Ideally, the time marked should be known data. If it is unknown, it should be researched to find the actual time it will take. If this is impossible, planners should use their best estimate. Take care to ensure that the units of time are consistent throughout this process.

4. *Calculate early start (ES) and early finish (EF) times:* Starting with the first task of the project, write a "0" (for time = zero) in the upper left pane of a four-pane "window" that you create on the card. This is the earliest time (Early Start or "ES") that the first task can start—time zero. In the upper right pane of the window, write the time duration of the first task (zero + the duration of the first task). This is the earliest time that the task can finish (Early Finish or "EF").

Follow the arrow(s) emanating from the first task card. On each card attached to the first, the upper left pane (ES) should be filled with the Early Finish (EF) number from the first or immediately preceding card. To this number is added the duration of the task on the card in question, and the upper right pane is filled with this sum. This process is carried forward until all of the top panes of the windows on all cards are filled.

In the instance where two (or more) cards precede a following card, indicating that both tasks must be completed before the subsequent task can begin, take the *largest* early finish (EF) number from the preceding card and insert that into the ES pane of the subsequent card.

The meaning of these numbers is simple. They indicate the earliest time (ES) that a task can be begun, given the sequencing of tasks, and the earliest time that a task can be completed (EF), given the sequencing of tasks.

5. *Calculate late start (LS) and late finish (LF) times:* Having completed step 4 in its entirely, it is now time to calculate the Late Finish (LF) and Late Start (LS) times. In essence, the process is the same as calculating ES and EF, only the calculation is done from the final card and the mathematical process is subtraction rather than addition.

Starting with the last task of the project write the EF of the same card in the lower right pane of the four-pane "window" you have created in step 4. This is the latest time that this task can be completed (Latest Finish or "LF") and still have the project completed on time. In the lower left pane of the window, write the difference between LF and the duration time of the task (LF–task duration). This is the latest time the project can begin (Latest Start or "LS") and still permit the project to be completed on time.

Follow the arrow(s) in reverse direction from the last task card. On each card preceding the last card, the lower right pane (LF) should be filled with the Latest Start (LS) number from the last or the card immediately following. From this number is subtracted the duration of the task on the card in question, and the lower left pane is filled with this difference. This process is carried backwards until all of the lower panes of the windows on all cards are filled.

In the instance where two (or more) cards follow a preceding card, indicating that both tasks can only be begun after the prior tasks are completed, take the *smallest* Latest Start (LS) number from the subsequent cards and insert that into the lower right (LF) pane of the preceding card.

6. *Identify the critical path:* The Critical Path is defined as that set of tasks that must all be done in the time-frame alotted in order for the project to be completed on time. Tasks on the critical path can be easily identified from the calculations in steps 4 and 5—the ES and LS numbers are identical with each other. So are the EF and LF numbers. Put another way, the earliest start and the latest start times that the task can be begun to have the project finish on time are the same.

Implementers need to pay particular attention to the items on the Critical Path. It is critical that they be completed on time in order for the project to be completed on time.

7. *Identify areas of slack:* Tasks that provide slack time (or leeway) to a project are those that do not lie on the Critical Path. These items have ES and LS numbers that differ from one another. This difference is the amount of slack time that is available to that task. While it remains critical that the task be begun before the LS ("latest start") time, the task does not have to be begun before that time and the project will still be completed on time.

8. *If required, identify crash opportunities:* If it is determined that the EF and LF numbers (times) on the last card exceed the time that is available for the project, and if the project still must be completed, it is time to look at items on the critical path to see which of them can be shortened (if any), and at what cost.

Often, alternative processes or personnel are available for a price that can quicken the completion of a given task. Each of these is likely to have a different cost per unit of time saved, and the objective of the planner is to shorten the duration of the task with the least possible additional cost.

Having followed steps 1 to 7, the planner knows which items lie on the Critical Path and the sequencing of the tasks. The planner's attention will be drawn to those items on the Critical Path that, if shortened, will by definition shorten the entire length of the project (except in cases where there are parallel Critical Paths, or where shortening tasks is limited by task durations on parallel paths).

The planner will compare her options to find the least costly options for shortening the project as required. She will select those most appropriate. Having found those items, the Activity Network Diagram is redrawn and recalculated to determine project duration and the new Critical Path.

How the tool helps you (outcomes):

Records Sequencing of Tasks   Knowing the sequence of tasks enables planners to better understand their projects and the constraints and demands that the projects will place on their implementation systems. Having a handle on these requirements and limitations, the planner can easily communicate his concerns to colleagues and managers and has a clear map of what is required to be done.

Calculates Time Required for Completion of Project   In many new or substantially revised projects, planners do not already know the cumulative duration of tasks involved in the project. This tool enables planners to make these calculations and grasp the requirements of time and resources to complete a project successfully.

Identifies Opportunities for Shortening Project Time   As noted above (step 8), the tool enables planners to revisit a project and determine if it is possible to shorten its cumulative duration and which tasks are best considered to be shortened or "crashed." The Activity Network Diagram assists planners by allowing them to consider different tasks for crashing, evaluating their options in terms of cost.

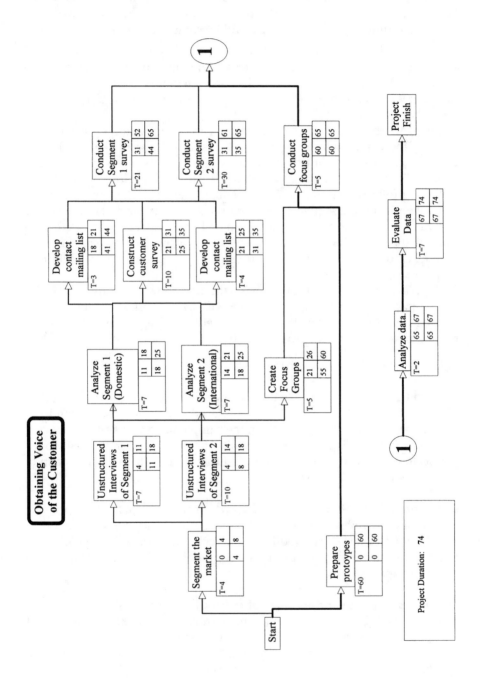

Obtaining Voice of the Customer

Figure 13.20 Activity Network Diagram. In this figure, there is an example of a completed Activity Network Diagram (AND). The project described is that of collecting **the Voice of the Customer, as described elsewhere in this book**. The two main items that are accomplished in this project are (1) the testing of prototypes with focus groups, and (2) arranging for, conducting, and analyzing potential customer responses.

Wherever there is an arrow, the arrow originates at the task(s) that precede(s) the task(s) located next to the arrow's head(s). For example, the start of the project, by definition, precedes the parallel paths of "Segment the market" and "Prepare protoypes." Similarly, "Segment the market" must be completed before "Unstructured Interviews" of either segment is possible. Likewise, the "Unstructured Interviews" of both segments must be completed before any of the following steps can begin: "Analyze Segment 1," "Analyze Segment 2," and "Create Focus Groups." And so on.

The number "1" in a circle indicates a break in the Activity Network Diagram that begins again at the other "1" in a circle. This break is made for formatting reasons. It has no duration in time and therefore no impact on the total project duration time.

The "T = ___" indicates the amount of time, in days, that the project will take. When creating ANDs, it is important to ensure that the units of time marked in these boxes are consistent with one another. Do the numbers in days represent work days, for example, or calendar days?

As described in Steps 5 and 6 of the AND description above, the numbers in the "windowpanes" at the lower right portion of each task card indicate the Earliest Start and Earliest Finish (top left and top right panes, respectively), and the Latest Start and Latest Finish (bottom left and bottom right, respectively) for the particular task. When the Earliest Start and Latest Start for an individual task are identical, this indicates the item is on the Critical Path.

The Critical Path in this diagram is noted by the bold line that runs through four tasks. These tasks must be begun and ended on time in the project to be completed in seventy-four days. All of the other tasks have some slack time. They need not be started at the Earliest Start time for the entire project to be completed on time. However, they must be started by the Latest Start time, or the project will not be completed on time.

Helpful Hints

Do Not Try to Calculate Late Start and Late Finish before Calculating All Early Start and Early Finish Times   Experts in this process know that LS and ES, and LF and EF times on the critical path are identical. Experts also know other ways to shortcut the mathematical calculations described in steps 5 and 6. We recommend, however, that novices avoid trying to take shortcuts until the process and concepts are clear and well-understood.

Work with Implementers or People with Implementation Knowledge   When assigning time durations to tasks, and sequencing the tasks to be accomplished, it is very helpful to have people on your team with implementation knowledge. If these people are not immediately available, be sure to check your sequencing and task-duration assumptions for accuracy. Alternately, it may save time to ask them for information before proceeding with your mapping and calculation.

Use Post-it™ Notes for Easy Revision of Task Sequencing   People who are experienced in this process appreciate the convenience of paper with reusable adhesive, commonly known as Post-it™ Notes. These technologies help when planners recognize they have forgotten a step or need to break a step into two components for clarity or precision.

Also, it is useful to avoid drawing the sequencing arrows in pen until the team members are convinced that the sequencing step has been completed correctly.

A Layout Tip on the Task Cards   Leave space on task cards to mark time duration, as well as ES and EF, and LS and LF. You will need space to mark the time duration of the task. Also, you need to have space to write in the results of your ES and EF (Early Start and Early Finish) and LS and LF (Late Start and Late Finish) calculations. The convention is to place these numbers within a set of four "windowpanes," as can be seen in the example. Be sure to have enough room for multiple digits, as the cumulative time increases to the total time duration of the project.

Computer Software   If you will be creating large numbers of Activity Network Diagrams and want to automate the calculation process, consider that there are many software packages available to help you and your team. The author has had good experience working with MicroSoft Project Planner™. You may also wish to check with other planners and implementers to find their favorites.

You now have been introduced to all of the tools, as well as examples of each. In addition to the benefits of effectively using the tools (outlined above) we have identified some positive attributes of the tools for your consideration. Our experience is that the tools are extremely beneficial to teams because of these characteristics. We believe that you will find the same with practice.

POSITIVE ATTRIBUTES OF THE TOOLS

1. *Visual quality of tools:* The visual quality of the tools helps teams to look at problems in new ways. Research in psychology has shown that individuals use a different part of their brains when focusing on graphic images rather than words. The tools help to bring more brain-power and creativity to the problem-solving process.

2. *Focusing on the tool instead of on the other person:* As a problem or issue gets analyzed on flipcharts using the techniques of these tools, it becomes depersonalized. This is quite different from having a free-ranging discussion that promotes a focus on each person, then their ideas. This helps teams to follow Dr. Deming's dictum to focus on the process, not the people, when examining problems.

3. *Disciplined process rather than free-flowing conversation:* The tools focus the problem-solving into a few categories, such as idea generation, prioritization, logical breakdown of tasks, and contingency planning. Rather than having to corral a free-ranging discussion into practical decisions, the tools enable the facilitator to focus on other matters, such as whether assumptions or facts are influencing the decisions. This improves the quality and focus on the work.

4. *Helps to get the collective mind on paper:* The tools automatically get thoughts and decisions on paper in ways that all people can see and agree to. There is not the time delay while a minute-taker puts his impressions into the computer for all to see at the next meeting. When using the tools, there is less opportunity for manipulation and mistaken perceptions to pollute the recording process.

5. *Output that can be reviewed later by the group, as well as others interested in the implementation process:* Finally, the tools enable outsiders, such as managers or implementers, to see and comment on the work process. The output provides an opportunity for those with more knowledge in a particular area to question assumptions or facts and improve the decision making process.

BEHAVIOR APPROPRIATE FOR THE TOOLS

Careful Listening A willingness to respect others' opinions is critical to the successful application of the tools. It is human nature to imagine that your ideas are superior to others, but studies of group process suggest that it is the rare person who is brighter than the collaboration of many minds.

Respect for Others   The tools do not stop domineering individuals from being domineering, but the tools provide an excellent set of rules that, if played by in good faith, will create a sense of collaboration where all partici- pants are on an equal footing. It is our belief that this democracy of decision- making vastly improves the process of Hoshin Planning.

Willingness to Let the Tools Do the Work   As mentioned earlier in this chapter, the tools exist to help teams and individuals in their decision- making processes. When used properly, and with discipline, the tools will do what they promise. Do not subvert their work by jumping to conclusions, or arbitratily deciding after the fact that the output of the tools was wrong.

Allows Tools to "Self-Facilitate"   Another aspect of these tools is that, to a large degree, they facilitate themselves. Teams that are just beginning to use the tools may benefit from facilitation tips from those more experienced, but after a few times working with the tools, they become quite comfortable to use. The discipline of the steps followed to create the diagrams and charts, along with the helpful hints provided herein, will provide the team with all the structure they need to accomplish their objectives. The tools facilitate themselves.

Act on Data, Not on Assumptions   Gather data wherever possible. "In God we trust, all others bring data."

Value Respectful Conflict   When disagreements occur, don't insist on your point of view, ask the other person for their source of data, and evaluate your own position with this new information added.

Proficiency Comes with Practice   Best use of the tools comes from practice. Be sure of your objective before using the tools; make sure that tool supports your objective.

A CLOSING RECOMMENDATION

Practice, Practice, Practice   The most important action the reader can take to become more proficient in using the tools is to practice them. The novice user may find himself frustrated by the amount of time the tools require. He will discover in time, however, that the planning assistance provided by the tools solves many implementation problems in advance. The results are well worth the time invested.

REFERENCES

Brassard, Michael and Ritter, Diane. *The Memory Jogger II*. Methuen, MA: GOAL/QPC, 1994.

Brassard, Michael. *Memory Jogger Plus*. Methuen, MA: GOAL/QPC, 1989.

Domb, Ellen. "Statistical Process Control: Sophisticated but Simple." In *Readings in Total Quality Management*. Orlando, FL: Dryden, Harcourt Brace College Publishers, 1994, pp. 277–283.

Grove, Andrew S. *Only the Paranoid Survive*. New York: Doubleday, 1996, pp. 1–23.

Kao, John. *Jamming*. New York: Harper Collins, 1996, pp. 1–19.

Mizuno, Shigeru. *Management for Quality Improvement: The 7 New QC Tools*. Cambridge, MA: Productivity Press, 1988.

Nadler, Gerald and Hibino, Shozo. *Breakthrough Thinking*. Rocklin, CA: Prima Publishing, 1990.

Scholtes, Peter R., et al. *The Team Handbook*. Madison, WI: Joiner Associates, 1988.

Senge, Peter M. *The Fifth Discipline*. New York: Doubleday, 1990.

Shores, A. Richard. *Survival of the Fittest*. Milwaukee, WI: ASQC Quality Press, 1987.

Chapter 14

Essential Techniques for Strategic Planning*

"**A**ssess the strategic environment" is the step *before* generating strategies. Two key elements are knowledge of the outside and knowledge of the inside. The *outside* consists of your competitors and your customers, and the *inside* is your people and your processes.

This chapter on techniques mixes elements of the inside and outside in each section, since the techniques benefit your understanding in both areas. The first section is an overview of the techniques of competitive benchmarking, to understand your competitors' methods of doing business, and of world-class benchmarking, to evaluate your internal processes with reference to the best, in order to improve. Then, the Process Management section reviews the concepts of measurement, control, and improvement. Finally, the section on the Voice of the Customer covers several of the techniques of contextual interview, field studies, and focus groups. The case studies for the Voice of the Customer are drawn from a local school district and a small service business, so that you can see that these techniques are of general applicability to organizations that produce commercial products and services, or social benefit.

BENCHMARKING

The term "Benchmarking" as a strategic and tactical research technique was popularized by Robert Camp (1989) in his book that presented the techniques that were codified by the strategic benchmarking group at Xerox.

---

* Thanks to Carolyn Day for contributing the *Voice of the Customer* section of this chapter.

The term suggests the establishment of relative measures, as in surveying, where altitudes, latitudes, and longitudes of each point are established relative to a benchmark point. "Benchmarking" in its current usage is far more than the establishment of relative measures; it includes the analysis of your own processes, the benchmark comparison of another company's processes, and analysis of the differences. Some companies also include the plan for improving your own processes as part of the benchmark system, while others consider the improvement plan to be a result of the strategic decisions based on the benchmark data.

The general process of benchmark research is shown in Figure 14.1.

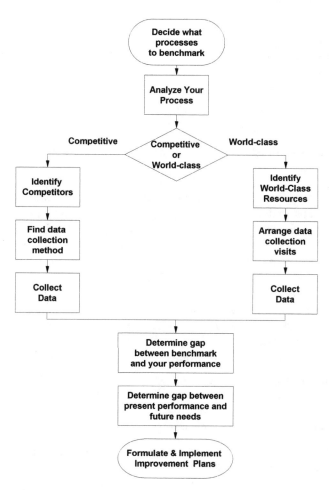

Figure 14.1   Benchmarking Process

The two most frequent roadblocks to starting a benchmark study are:

1. Reluctance to do the work of analyzing your own processes.
2. Lack of knowledge of which companies to use for comparison studies.

Overcoming roadblock #1 will be a necessity for all aspects of embracing a continuous improvement culture. Overcoming roadblock #2 requires systematic research, but far less cultural challenge. In addition to many sources listed in Camp's *Benchmarking* (1989), there are more comprehensive guides to resources in *The Benchmarking Workbook* (Watson 1992), *Competitor Intelligence* (Fuld 1985), and through the International Institute for Benchmarking (APQC 1996).

Resources include the following:

References from suppliers

References from customers

Trade associations
    Trade association studies
    Trade association libraries

University research services

Department of Commerce

US Navy Best Manufacturing Practices

US Food and Drug Administration "Good Manufacturing Practices"

Industry consultants

Using consultants and trade associations for benchmarking studies can accelerate the process of getting data from other companies, and it may be the only way to get data from competitors. Take care, however, that the data is in a form that is useful to your company for *improving* processes; you want descriptions of the comparison firms' processes and methods, not just the measurements of the results.

Benchmarking's power as an advanced tool for quality improvement has been recognized in many ways. Benchmarking appears throughout the Baldrige Award Criteria (1996) in the form of questions to address. In sections on business processes, operational processes, operational results, and customer satisfaction, these four questions appear in various versions:

"Do you know what your competitors are doing?"
"How do you compare to the competitors?"
"Do you know what world-class standards are?"
"How do you compare to world-class organizations?"

The Ernst and Young study (1994) of world-wide quality improvement found that benchmarking was most helpful to companies that were in intermediate to advanced stages of quality improvement (beginners made more progress based on internal studies and response to their customers).

The Baldrige Award-winning companies are frequent benchmarking targets in the areas of strategic planning and, especially, for data-gathering and analysis. The 1995 winners, Corning Telecommunications Products Division and Armstrong World Industries' Building Products Operations, have very different systems (Bemowski 1996) that share the Hoshin properties of customer focus, measurement, coherent vision, and frequent review. AT&T's Universal Card Division and Texas Instruments Defense Products Group give frequent seminars on their strategic management and measurement systems.

Benchmarking is a precursor to strategic plan generation. A continuous program of competitive and world-class benchmarking will keep you supplied with fresh data on options and opportunities for improvement with high levels of impact on your strategies.

PROCESS MANAGEMENT

Process management is included in the list of essential techniques for strategic planning, because it provides the strategy team with the knowledge of the functioning of their own business processes. The strategy team can make decisions about which processes support new strategies, which require radical change, and which will be continuously improved.

Management of any kind is a feedback system:

Define what is to be done.

Define the measurement that determines whether it is done successfully.

Use the measurements to maintain or improve the performance.

All people, regardless of job title, perform management actions. In the move toward self-managed ("supervisor-less") work teams, the fact that all people manage work is becoming more obvious.

At the same time, many organizations are finding that not all of their processes have been managed using a disciplined system. Work was defined in terms of the person doing it, rather than in terms of the customer benefit, the organizational benefit, or any other model. This has evolved into a tremendous interest in "metrics"—the measurement of business system performance (Hronek 1993; Juran 1989; Camp 1989; APQC 1993).

Adding to the controversy are authors as diverse as Deming (1986) and Drucker (1995). Deming is well known for his fourteen points for leadership. The two that bear on process management are:

11.   Eliminate work standards (Quotas). Eliminate management by numbers, numerical goals. Substitute leadership.
12.   Remove barriers that rob people of their right to pride of

workmanship. Eliminate management by objective and annual merit ratings.

Drucker, on the other hand, identifies three categories of management measures needed to run any enterprise:

Foundation Information

Productivity Information

Competence Information

These apparent contradictions will not be removed here. The issue of whether people find it more motivating to work toward fixed numerical goals, or toward goals that they have set for themselves, or toward a standard of excellence that is described multidimensionally, will not be resolved any time soon. These issues are very specific to the culture of each organization, and need to be handled within that culture.

What applies to *all* management of all work is the need for feedback.

- It could be the analog feedback from your eyes to your brain, so that you can direct your hands and feet to control your car to keep it on the road at the right speed.
- It could be the numerical information from a gauge that tells the operator of a paper-coating machine that the thickness of coating is staying within tolerance, or straying out of tolerance, so she needs to adjust the machine. Or it could be the statistical process control charts that make it easier to understand the system, and avoid tampering with it.
- It could be the customer satisfaction data that is gathered directly by customer interview, or indirectly by analysis of warranty claims, and is used to improve the product or the process of delivering the product. (Legend has it that one of the "big three" automotive companies had no linkage between the warranty data, which was collected by the legal department, and the engineering department, which authorized design changes, until 1985.)

How Often Should We Measure the Process?

The speed of feedback depends on the speed of the process, and the frequency of the opportunities for improvement. If you are making thousands of items per hour, and your process is delicate, you might need to measure continually. The economics of continuous measurement and continuous adjustment will drive you to Dr. Demings' Point 3, build quality into the system in the first place. Decisions on frequency of measurement should be based on a combination of statistical analysis and common sense.

The frequency of measurement also depends on the risk of not measuring. Risk should be evaluated in the largest sense and can include:

Legal liability

Customer relationship damage

Cost of correction of problems

Damage to society

Risk to health of workers

Risk of loss of information

and many more.

What Is the Right Thing to Measure for This Process?

Measurement isn't magic. There is no one "right" measurement. Look at the decisions that are being made, and measure what you need to know to make the decisions. In most process management scenarios, measurements are used to stabilize a process, or to improve a process. In both cases, the measurement of most interest is the measurement of what the customer needs.

If you perform a service for another employee, he is your customer. So the measurement that would help you manage the process of delivering that service, either to perform it the same way each time, or to improve it, is the measurement of the factors that lead to your customer's satisfaction. To determine that measure, it may be necessary to observe the other employee using your result. This could be as simple as observing your customer, or as complicated as instituting activity-based cost accounting.

The growing popularity of open-book management (Stack 1994) reflects both the need for, and the complexity of, measurement. Taking the idea of measurement and the idea of pride of workmanship to their logical conclusion, the president of Springfield Remanufacturing Co. decided to open the books to all employees every month, so that they could help improve the company. It took three years, and a lot of education and a lot of process analysis, to realize that dream. What the managers found was that the traditional measures, mostly retrospective financial measures, did not tell anyone enough to help her improve her work. It took education on the traditional financial numbers—what they are, and how they are calculated—combined with an extensive analysis by all workers of their own work, to enable everyone to use the numbers to make contributions to the overall success of the company.

How Are Measurements Used for Improvement?

The basic improvement cycle, Plan-Do-Check-Act, was described in Chapter 13, in the section dealing with basic tools of quality improvement. Table 14.1

Table 14.1   Continuous Improvement and Measurement. The Stages of the USA-PDCA Model (Fig. 13.1) for Continuous Improvement and Process Management Measurements That Are Useful in Each Stage.

Continuous Improvement Stage	Measurement	Tools
Understand	Past history, Customer impact, Financial impact	Flow chart, Control charts, Run chart Financial measures
Select	Customer impact Employee impact	Pareto charts, prioritization matrix Risk/reward analysis
Analyze	Problem frequency & type, trends	Control charts, Run chart, check-sheets, Histograms
Plan	Time, Customer impact problem frequency	Flow Charts, Control charts Histogram, Scatter plots
Do	Customer impact Problem frequency	Run and Control charts, checksheet Pareto charts, Histogram
Check	Change in Customer impact	Survey, questionnaires, interviews Checksheet, Run charts
Act	Customer impact Employee impact Financial impact	Run and Control charts, checksheet Pareto charts, Histogram Financial measures

shows an overall flow of the process of process improvement, explicitly showing the measurement points.

The information about your processes that are used to manage the processes are important input to the strategy development process. The strategy team can make decisions about which processes support new strategies, which require radical change, and which will be continuously improved.

VOICE OF THE CUSTOMER*

What's needed in strategic plans is the same diligence that we have heard about for years on the front line. And what we've heard for years is that a key element to success is customer satisfaction. What we need to know, up front, is the wants and needs the customer has that our organization, with its mission, can provide, and what would enable us to provide it, in the eyes of the customer, better than anyone else. But to bring that "voice of the customer" into the planning process means that we have to truly listen to the voice, and let it help direct us towards the strategic imperatives on which the

---

* This section was contributed by Carolyn Day, Quality Solutions.

business must focus to be successful and grow. We must learn to listen before we act, to use the voice of our future success, our current and future customers, to create our strategic direction and plans.

Companies have invested substantially in customer surveys on products and services. A day doesn't pass without business establishments, be it restaurants, hotels, auto mechanics, or veterinarians, asking you to fill out cards answering their questions about your satisfaction with their products and services. Customer satisfaction surveys are valuable tools, providing useful information about customers' satisfaction, but as a sole source of customer information they are not likely to get the voice of the truly dissatisfied customer. They also ask the customer questions of interest to the business, not necessarily what's important to the customer. And, surveys are performed *after the fact*. Surveys should be balanced with the customers' needs, in their own words, up front, in order to create the strategies. Only in this way can the planning process assure that the business is focusing its plans and strategies on meeting, or exceeding, customer needs, rather than discovering, often too late, that it has failed to do so, and has thereby lost that customer, and more.

Methodologies are available that:

- Capture the voice of the customer in their own words to avoid biasing the information by summarizing or interpreting what you think the customer is saying. Recording the voice of the customer and then transcribing it verbatim will assure that nothing is lost in interpretation or note-taking.
- Group these needs, prioritize them, and evaluate your current performance in meeting them (Figure 14.2).
- A hierarchy of needs (primary-strategic, secondary-tactical, and tertiary-operational) are identified (Figure 14.3).
- An analysis of the customers' priorities and gaps in performance provides the capability to focus the planning on key breakthrough opportunities for the company. Customer needs are carried throughout the design process, to insure that they do not become lost or subordinated to design, engineering, production, or other processes. Specific measures are established in the House of Quality (Figure 14.4), the first of the Quality Function Deployment matrices, to assess the ability of the product or service to meet customer needs.

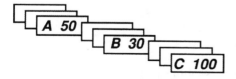

Figure 14.2   Needs are arranged into logical groupings, with no predetermined number of groups or categories. Priorities are established on a scale of 100 and current performance is assessed with a letter grade assigned.

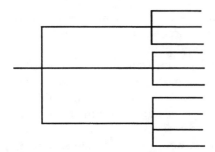

Figure 14.3 The hierarchy of needs resembles a tree diagram and depicts levels of detail in the customers' needs from primary or strategic (left,) to secondary or tactical (middle), to tertiary or operational (right).

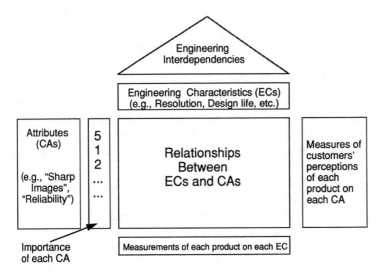

Figure 14.4 The House of Quality

These customer needs can then be balanced with research on future trends to create an enlightened strategic plan for the company. In the following seven-step approach, we will explore how that can be done:

1. Identifying who you are.
2. Identifying your customers.
3. Gathering the customers' needs.
4. Synthesizing the data.
5. Understanding what the customer is telling you.
6. Introducing the Voice of the Customer into the planning process.
7. Providing the infrastructure to use the plans and keep it current.

STEP ONE: Identifying Who You Are

Throughout our ongoing strategic planning process, listening to and understanding our customers starts with understanding who we are and what our business is—in other words, our Mission.

Linking Customers to Your Mission . . .

The need to develop a clear and definitive mission and vision is one of the things we learn as we embark on a quality journey. But, why is it so important, and how does it fit in to the voice of the customer? Clearly, if we have elucidated our mission, or why we are in business, we will have a clearer picture for ourselves, which means that we will be more likely to deliver what we are in business to deliver. And, as we think about that further, if our employees know why we are in business, and what we are in business to deliver, they can deliver it better. We can even carry this process one step further and suggest that if our customers know what our mission is, they might be able to contribute to helping us understand whether that mission is meeting a need they perceive. Thus, in addition to traditional customer satisfaction measures, we could actually get input from customers as to whether our business is providing a product or service that meets a real need, as well as how well we're meeting that need. That might sound like a subtle difference, but too often we seek to understand whether we are doing things right, when we might better try to understand if we are doing the right things first, and then if we are doing them right.

A number of organizations have sought to involve customers in their mission and, thereby, establish a "partnership" with their customers to insure that they are doing the right things, as well as the right things right.

The City of San Ramon, California discussed and developed, in an open meeting with the public present, the mission of that city's government and council, inviting the public to participate. News coverage provided a forum to share that mission with those not in attendance at the meeting. This was then followed by building into the budget and planning process a link between the budgets and the services provided, as well as the mission, and providing for further public feedback opportunities as budgets and service plans were presented to the council in open meetings.

AutoXcellence, an auto-body repair shop in San Ramon, California, shares its mission with its customers both in its shop and on a folder in which repair receipts and warranties are provided, clearly asking its customers to let them know if their expectations are not being "exceeded," so that they can make improvements. By sharing their mission *and* seeking feedback in the context of that mission, they will get more valuable data, because the customers know in what context they are being asked to comment on the services.

The San Ramon Valley Unified School District has shared its mission with the public and invited individuals from throughout the community to participate in understanding and contributing to the planning process for delivering on that mission. Groups of citizens worked with educators from all areas of the district (staff, faculty, administration) to focus on key strategic initiatives, as well as to develop and hone the means for the district to deliver on their mission and to address the concerns of all parties in the development of the systems supporting the education of the youth in this district.

... And the Vision

If we carry that concept of involvement on through to the vision, think of the power!

The vision is a picture of a future state, a picture of where we want our business or organization to be in three, five, ten years. Some will say that's not practical. Things are changing too rapidly in today's environment to project where you want to be three years from now, let alone five or ten.

We have speculated on how valuable it might be for our customers to know, and even contribute, to our mission. It would now seem even more beneficial if our customers could contribute to our vision of the future. They represent, in large part, our ability to grow and realize that vision. So why not involve them in its conception and evolution, as well as its fruition? Think of the power of having your vision be a shared vision with your customers, and as a result, your customers having some sense of ownership in your successful attainment of it.

When the City of San Ramon involved its citizens with their mission, it provided a forum for discussion on a number of levels to understand where that citizenry sees the city being in the future, and for developing a shared vision of growth, support, involvement, and partnerships with residents and businesses to meet those expectations.

AutoXcellence had a vision to grow its business and build a model environmental facility to better meet its expanding business needs, while at the same time addressing customer and community needs for ever-improving quality of work and environmental protection. It was this "shared vision" of a new environment that led, over a three-year time-frame, to the construction of a new facility with extensive use of architectural innovations brought about by listening to both internal and external customers, and partnering with the local utility company to incorporate the environmental efficiencies.

Patelco Credit Union in San Francisco, California listened to its customers as it planned its growth and modified its vision for the future, increasing its emphasis on new technologies to meet the growing needs of its current and future customer base for flexibility and "anywhere banking."

Inherent in this process of linking customers to the mission and involving them in the creation, and thereby the realization, of the vision is the ability to identify who those customers are, which brings us to step two.

STEP TWO: Identifying Your Customers

Much has been written in recent years about customer focus in today's businesses, as well as in today's government and education. Little has been said about how to identify those customers and differentiate one from another. It seems rather simple, doesn't it? Doesn't everyone know who their customers are? They're the ones who buy our products. True, or maybe not.

Let's look at a fairly simple example: a car. You and I know that we are the customers, because we are the ones who buy the car. Right? Sure, but from Detroit's standpoint, are we the customer, or is the car dealer who buys from Detroit and sells to us the customer. For many years, Detroit saw the car dealer as the customer, and that spelled disaster, while the Japanese listened to the ultimate customer, you and me, and took advantage of what they heard.

In the case of our auto-body shop, it seems even more clear that we, the car owners, are the customer. We must keep in mind, however, that in most cases of auto-body repair, it is the insurance company that writes the check for the bulk of the repair (beyond the deductible). The insurance company can approve or disapprove the cost of the repair, based on their "standard." So, does that make the insurance company the customer? Like the dealership above, the insurance company is certainly a key stakeholder, but in terms of satisfaction with the quality of the repair and the repair experience, it plays a secondary role to the car owner.

Looking at a more complex situation, it becomes even more difficult to separate customers from stakeholders—or intermediate customers. Let's look at a hospital. Health care is one of the premier issues consuming both our government and ourselves. Examine for a minute the customer of a hospital. Is it us, or is it the doctors?

Also complex is identifying the customers in our education system. Is it the parent? The student? Society? Higher education? Business? Who is the customer in our education system?

How Do We Identify Our Customers?

One way that attempts have been made to bring this whole concept into focus is to explain that all of us are both customers and suppliers to each other, and that there are internal and external customers we have to think about. This is all true, and provides us with a "chain" of customers and requirements as we develop our products and services (Figure 14.5).

However, it doesn't really help us in trying to focus on what we need at this point to embed the Voice of the Customer in our Planning Process. In fact, thinking about all the myriad of customers, the links in the chain to the ultimate customer may distract us from our primary target, our reason for being in business. Think about it in terms of who makes the difference in

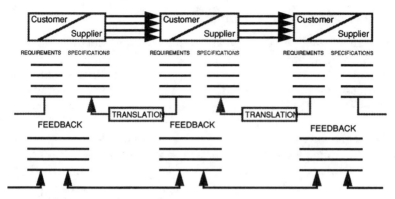

Figure 14.5   Customer Supplier Model

whether you stay in business or not. That is the end-user, the person who uses the product or service you provide, or the customer.

Going back to our auto manufacturer, clearly the end-user is the auto driver. And for the hospital? It's still not as clear, for the doctor is the one who "uses" the facilities of the hospital, but it is still the patient who is the end-user, or recipient and "beneficiary" of the services provided *by* the doctor *at* the hospital. And in education? If the product of the education system is an educated student, then who is the end-user of that product?

STEP THREE: Gathering the Customers' Needs

To achieve your business' mission and vision, to meet and exceed customer needs, we must have an effective way to gather and understand those needs. This, of course, presumes that your organization has leaped or removed the first great barrier to accomplishing this—admitting that you don't know what your customers' real needs are. In a world focused on the information super highway, where "knowledge" is considered a strategic imperative, it is sometimes difficult to admit one doesn't know something as basic as one's customers' needs. And yet, in reality, many organizations rely predominantly on their perceptions of their customers' needs and wants, and believe they are accurate. The more perceptive organizations, on the other hand, ask the customer.

Traditional approaches to gathering customer information and feedback has been through a variety of techniques, including customer-satisfaction surveys, "exit" interviews, and new product focus groups. However, most of these approaches are after the fact, or at least after the initial prototyping. In order for us to make the most effective use of customer information (their wants and needs), we need it up front in the planning process, not after the product or service has been delivered, or designed, or the customer is "exiting." That is too late. We have already wasted time, effort and money, or lost that customer.

What we need to know, up front, is the wants and needs the customer has that our organization, with its mission, can provide, and what would enable us to provide it, in the eyes of the customer, better than anyone else.

We need to identify the different types of customers (or segments) to whom we provide products or service, and then assess their specific wants and needs. Why is segmentation important? And how do we go about segmenting our customers? Segmentation enables us to explore and appreciate the differences in wants and needs of the various customer types, types being defined as having different purchase or use criteria, and having unique needs that they expect your product or service to meet. In the auto manufacturing arena, customer segments may vary by income level, family status, age, intended use, or geography. With local government, segments may include residents, business, income level, family status, and age. In education, by school system affiliation, segments may include age, level of education, business, and higher education. Needs might be collected for a specific product or service, collecting a complete voice for each segment, or by organization, if only the importance customers place on specific needs vary by segments.

If different segments have diverse needs, it is important that we carefully assess the various customer segments from which we gather that voice. Limiting ourselves to one key segment may give us a distorted view of our customer needs and cause us to miss potentially valuable new opportunities or niches. The auto manufacturer who only looks to build cars for the high income, large family, primarily for highway use may be missing out on a superior market by ignoring the fact that family sizes are diminishing, and with those diminishing sizes, alternate travel means may be more practical than driving. The city that looks only at its residents' needs may find themselves unable to support those needs if business, and their contribution to the tax base, leave for cities that better support their needs. The educational system that looks only to parents, or to higher education, or even to students planning to attend higher education, may be limiting their views, and thereby their planning, to serve their complete customer base.

There is no simple "plug-in" formula for identifying market segments, but there are some perspectives or questions we can use to help identify differences in our customer bases. There are different needs, each with its own life cycle, and different needs may drive different segment behaviors. First, we look for those who are the lead users of our products and services, that is, lead users in terms of frequency of use, dollars invested, repurchasing, and volume purchasing. There also may be differences in the lead users based on how they use the product or service, causing them to be separated into different segments. Then we identify who else "touches" our products or services, understanding their role and their needs in the success of those products and services. Third, we see who else must be satisfied with our product or service to maintain customer satisfaction today and in the future. This segment might include dealers, brokers, regulators, value-added resellers, and so on. And, finally, we identify non-customers, or competitors' customers, that would fall within our market, the people we would like to have as customers. All of these might represent different segments that could provide insightful information on customer needs, now and in the future.

GATHERING THE VOICE OF THE CUSTOMER

Identifying customer needs is primarily qualitative research, as opposed to the quantitative nature of customer-satisfaction surveys.

Surveys are a critical part of the customer-satisfaction formula and of the ongoing improvement of the product or service, but until you have the qualitative data to help you derive the products and services you are providing the customer, it is moot to ask them if they are satisfied with how you are providing it. First, we must understand what the right things to do, build, or provide are, and then the right way to provide or service them. Gather the voice of the customer first. Use that voice to design and build the product or service. Then survey for satisfaction, or to look more finitely at particular product or service improvements.

Hearing the Voice of the Individual Customer

At this point, we have identified that our customers, the segments from which we are seeking customer needs, and that we are seeking qualitative information in order to understand what our customers' needs and wants are. We also recognize that our customers know what they want and need, although they may express them in different terms than we do, and that our "solutions" may not fit our customers' needs *unless* we ask them what they are. Next, we need to develop our ability to listen to the voice of the customer. Listening is often embraced as a passive activity, but to be effectively employed, it must be a very active and involved engagement with the speaker. We also need some guidelines on what information we are trying to glean from our customers, so we get consistent and comparative data. An interview guide needs to be prepared as a framework for the interviews. While this does not need to be a list of verbatim questions, and indeed should not be, it does need to identify some questions and areas of information to explore with the customer. We want to get all the information we need and, basically, have the same areas addressed by all the customers. If completely different topics have been covered with different customers, we will not be able to collate results.

Decide what information you need to find out, structure an interview or discussion guide, but leave the format open enough and the discussions loose enough that you will encourage discussion, not just rote answers to questions. What you are seeking here is the voice and opinions of the customer regarding what their needs are. Delve for real needs. You will find more than a few customers who will want to tell you *how* to meet their needs. That's fine, but what you're *really* after is the underlying need. Then you can decide, based on your knowledge and expertise, how you might best meet that need. Those of you involved in process improvement activities are probably familiar with the process of looking for root cause. Think of your interview with the customer as looking for the "root need" and feel free to probe by asking "why" five times to get to it. Because of the time it can take to explore needs to this depth, it is more effective to conduct these interviews as one-on-one rather than focus group sessions. It is also important to capture that need in the customer's own words. There are always biases in any data collection process, but by capturing customer phrases that express their needs and wants in their own words, we minimize our bias. Attachment 1 is an example of an interview guide that was developed for The San Ramon Valley Unified School District for exploring the wants and needs of customers in the area of communication.

Following the precepts of the Plan-Do-Check-Act cycle, conduct some initial interviews with the interview guide to validate it.

The logistics for conducting the interviews may vary. In the ideal setting, you have professional equipment in a research facility for easy taping (and perhaps video-taping, as well) and interviewing, with the capability for associates to "sit in" on the interview behind a two-way mirror. This enables additional questions or clarification to be picked up by viewers and incorporated into future interviews, and allows viewers to benefit from seeing live customers expressing their needs and wants. This is also the benefit in video-taping the interviews. Excerpts from the interviews can be spliced together to make extremely effective presentations to the organization, enabling everyone to see and hear the voice of the customer.

If you are unable to conduct interviews in a professional research facility, it is still possible to both audio- and video- tape the interviews in a company conference room, or at the customer's location. Interviewing at the customer location increases the time investment, equipment costs, and logistical requirements for the process, but can provide an added benefit of enabling you to ask to see where and how the product is used. Only once have I had a customer refuse to be audio-taped, and that was due to a general policy about the use of recording devices on the premises.

Many research firms advocate the use of focus groups, because of the interaction among the customers and the belief that more needs are stimulated in a group environment. If, however, one is delving for "root needs," there is a concern that the other participants will tune out while the interviewer is focusing on one person, that the participants get less opportunity to speak individually, and that more assertive individuals in a focus group can sway or stifle less assertive members. It has also been shown that two one-hour, one-on-one interviews are about as effective in the number of customer needs identified as one two-hour focus group of six to eight people (Griffin and Hauser 1993). If it is less expensive to conduct two one-on-one interviews than one focus group, then one-on-one interviews are also the less expensive approach. The number of interviews required (per segment) to gather customer needs is another critical question. Using analytical probability, Griffin and Hauser (1993) estimate that thirty customer interviews will provide 89.8% of all the customer needs, and that twenty interviews will provide 90% of the needs identified in the thirty interviews.

Whether by individual interview or focus groups, or your employees just talking to customers on-the-job through sales or customer service calls, talk to your customers, listen to what they're saying, capture their needs, and where you can, capture them in their own words and phrases.

STEP FOUR: Synthesizing the Data

Out of these interviews come a long list of phrases from the customer of their needs, wants, solutions, and problems, perhaps 1,000 or more. To be able to deal with these, it is necessary to analyze them and cull duplicates, solutions, and problems (keeping them for future reference, but removing them from the "needs" data). This will enable a focus on needs and will usually result in a reduction of needs and wants to approximately 90 to 120. A group of this size is workable and can be organized into logical and manageable groups of similar or related ideas. There are two fundamental approaches to accomplishing this. A team from the company can sort and group the needs, or customers can be solicited to do the sorting. Each approach will provide different sorts, and each offers a degree of bias. Ideally, the customers' needs and wants should be sorted by both customers and the company to view and recognize the different perspectives.

The company will tend to organize the data based upon the organizational structure of the company: Marketing needs, Engineering needs, Production needs, and so forth. But customers tend to organize the needs based upon how they will use the product or service. "Customer-sort hierarchy provide(s) a clearer, more-believable, easier-to-work-with representation of customer perceptions than the (corporate) group-consensus charts," (Griffin and Hauser, 1993, p. 15) providing additional insights into customer needs and, thereby, opening the door for creative and breakthrough thinking to derive solutions to those needs, and opening the door to the possibilities beyond the traditional structures and constraints, and to new paradigms.

An additional advantage of having customers sort the data into logical groupings is the ability, at the same time, to have the customers provide their perspectives on the relative importance of those needs and provide valuable feedback on performance by rating the company as to its current performance in meeting each of the needs. With this approach, you are gaining a wealth of information for the planning effort. You are discovering what your customers need, which of those needs have priority, and which you need to focus on to improve in order to be more competitive (Figure 14.6).

Looking at the logistics of this sort process, as in the original selection of customers to interview, it is important to have a representative sample of customer segments involved in the sorting, prioritizing, and ranking process. It is important for a wide spectrum of customers to be involved in this phase. While a relatively small base of customers interviewed can provide the necessary scope of customer needs, and there is little disparity between customer needs in different segments, there can be significant differentiation in the priorities customer segments place on those needs. Therefore, the spectrum of customers engaged in the sort process needs to be much larger than in the interview step. Typically, 50 to 100 or more customers are invited to participate in the sort process. Customers can be solicited by phone, and then provided with an incentive to sort the data and return it to the company.

Decks of cards (approximately 100), each card containing one need, are sent to the customers agreeing to participate in the process, with instructions to group the cards into logical groups (as many or as few as appropriate). They are then asked to select one card from each deck that captures the

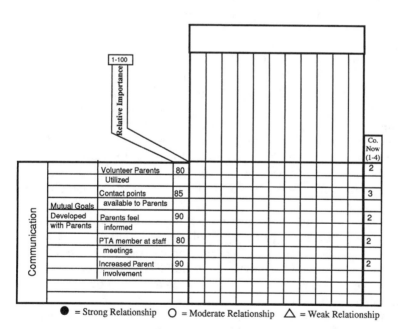

● = Strong Relationship   O = Moderate Relationship   △ = Weak Relationship

Figure 14.6 A first step in using the House of Quality is to identify the customer needs, priorities, and performance. The San Ramon Valley Unified School District identified customer needs for communication, and then had their customers rate the relative importance of those needs and the current performance of the district in meeting them.

essence of the cards in that group, or as an "exemplar" of that group. Once the groups are arranged and "labeled," the customer is asked to prioritize each group and to give the company a grade from A to F on their performance on each group.

Once you have all that data, it needs to be analyzed using cluster analysis to understand the common customer perceptions of priority needs from a strategic and tactical perspective. "Cluster analysis is a statistical procedure that can analyze the patterns of card sorting and produce a hierarchical structure of the customer attributes" (Klein 1990, p. 7). It provides you with primary, secondary, and tertiary needs by which to plan strategies and tactics that are truly customer focused. Cluster analysis looks at the frequency that each card is sorted with each other card, and the number of times a particular card is selected as an exemplar, providing a hierarchy of customer needs. Each need appears in the branch of the hierarchy with the other needs with which it was most frequently sorted. The names of the secondary and primary attributes (needs) are derived based on the frequency of the need being chosen as an exemplar (see Attachment 2, the Hierarchy of Needs—School District Example from the San Ramon Valley Unified School District analysis of customer needs in communication). Finally, the importance values are aggregated across customers to determine the relative importance of each tertiary, secondary, and primary need.

While this would certainly provide the highest level of understanding, prioritization, and assessment of performance, the focus group alternative can be applied where resources are not available for this level of sophistication. In those instances, Focus Group alternatives can be arranged to provide the same basic assessment. Focus groups are provided the decks of cards and asked to group those cards, select an exemplar for each group, and prioritize and grade the company on their performance in each group. The results of these sessions can then be combined by either the market research group or company personnel to reflect the "consensus," or, more accurately, the "average" of the focus groups on the prioritized hierarchy of needs of the customers.

The decision on which approach to use, individual customer sorts or company group sort or focus group sort, will depend on the availability of resources and expertise to analyze the data coming back from the process. There will be a lot more data to analyze if individual customer sorts are used. If you don't have an automated system to analyze the data, you will want to limit the number of alternative sorts.

Is there an easier way? Certainly. It could be most easily managed by hiring someone else to do it for you. This is offered only partly in jest. There are organizations that have the experience, the processes, and the resources to handle the entire process, from interviews to sorting to cluster analysis to translation into strategic and tactical priorities, organizations that are in the business of translating customer needs for other organizations. But this is not an inexpensive alternative, and not every organization can afford such an effort. Those who can't afford to hire someone else, or wish to build the capability in-house, do it themselves. To do this, they will need to have expertise in the areas outlined above: market segmentation, statistical sampling, interviewing, synthesis of the data, cluster analysis, and application of that data to the planning process. An added benefit, though, is that buy-in is likely to be much higher if you do it yourself.

No matter what kind of data analysis you use, you can still listen to your customers. Listen early, listen openly, listen to the voice in their own words, and listen often. Then use what you hear to drive your mission, vision, and planning, so that your products and services meet customer needs, not your perception of customer needs, and not what you want to build and convince customers to buy. Companies today cannot afford to let technology drive their products and services, but must let customer needs stimulate the use of technology to meet or exceed those needs. Neither can they afford to listen once. Listening to the customer is a permanent and year-round job, a job of gathering data on needs and satisfaction.

STEP FIVE: Understanding What the Customer Is Telling You

In our voice of the customer process, we have reached the point where we have gathered the voice and we have reduced and synthesized the data from the interviews and are ready to put it to use. We, or the customers, have grouped that data, the customers have told us the relative importance of the various needs and have evaluated us on how well we currently meet those needs. Now, we must interpret the customers' voice based upon how they expressed, grouped, prioritized, and evaluated these needs. At this point, it is critically important for the organization to understand what the data is really saying, in order to understand that the customers' priorities may not be what the organization thought they were, and that while the performance gaps may be the customer's perception, that perception is a reality for the customer. And everyone in the organization needs to understand this customer data. The market research team, while representative of the various organizations, is not every employee in design, development, or production. Each of these groups needs to see and understand what the customer is saying if the organization is to meet those needs. Understanding will take team discussion, reflection, and perhaps revisiting the original data from the interviews. It will also take an open-mindedness to potentially different perspectives. One way to share this information is in a format that clearly depicts the customers' priorities and assessments (Figure 14.7).

Customers don't always speak the same language. If we look again at the auto manufacturer, and we find one customer need being a quiet ride, what do we interpret this to mean? If customers want a roomier front seat in a car, do they mean leg room, head room, shoulder room, what? If a hospital customer (patient) wants clear, helpful information, what does that mean?

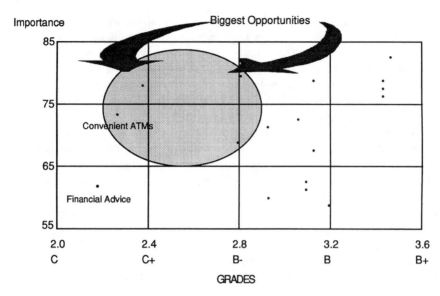

Figure 14.7 Patelco Credit Union looked at where customers placed their importance relative to financial advisors and technology in order to better plan their strategies for the future and customer satisfaction.

Most hospital processes are designed for the convenience of the staff and practitioners. Are they open to a shift to the customer's need for convenience? And what does that mean? These questions can only be answered by thorough review and careful interpretation of the needs specified in the customer's words and, often, additional research into those that have been given the highest priority by the customer. Looking at the secondary attributes that were identified by the cluster analysis, and using the tertiary needs to help expand the definition of that need, is an initial step. Going back to the questions that generated the response is another good source for additional understanding. But it may also mean there is a need for a follow-up survey or discussion with customers to get even further clarification. Keep in mind, though, that at this point in the process, we are trying to understand the underlying need, not come up with a solution.

Before we are ready to look at alternative solutions to meet these customer needs, let's look at how to link them to the planning process.

STEP SIX: Introducing the Voice of the Customer into the Planning Process

Organizations tend to think of quality planning, in which they include customer needs, as separate from business planning. They have a quality plan and they have a business plan. To embed the Voice of the Customer into the planning process, one must have one plan. To do so requires changes in how you operate, measure your performance, and plan for the future. The following steps offer a means for embarking on those changes in a fairly straightforward approach that can then be shared and communicated throughout your organization:

    a. Identifying Core Processes and relating them to customer needs.
    b. Translating customer needs into measures and actions.
    c. Assessing future trends and their impact.

When the Malcolm Baldrige National Quality Award was instituted, tremendous emphasis was placed on an organization's focus on the customer, and the understanding of all members of the organization as to who the customer(s) are and where their job contributed to meeting customer needs. And while some of the weighting has changed over the years, the voice of the customer is still a key to an organization's success, and continues to be heavily weighted in the award criteria. The award has grown each year in the number of organizations requesting the award applications, if not to apply for the award, but to use as a guideline for self-assessment. Category 7 of the award criteria (Customer Focus and Satisfaction) examines the company's systems for customer learning and for building and maintaining customer relationships. It specifically measures such items as: Customer and Market Knowledge, Customer Relationship Management, Commitment to Customers, Customer Satisfaction Determination, Customer Satisfaction Results, and Customer Satisfaction Comparison. In relation to the overall point value for the Malcolm Baldrige Award of 1,000 points, the Customer Focus and Satisfaction category (one of seven categories) represents 250 points, one-fourth of the total points. The questions asked in this category can help organizations focus on their customers and who they are, on how to gather information on them, how to interact with them, and how their organization compares to world class organizations in customer interaction and relationships.

    "The Voice of the Customer," both implicit and explicit, appears throughout the Baldrige Criteria. In the Leadership area, you are asked how your leadership uses customer related performance to assess your performance. In the Information and Analysis area, you are asked how you use information to understand your customers, and how you integrate information on customers and markets to develop or improve products and services, or to prioritize operational changes. The lead question in the Strategic Planning area asks how you consider customer requirements and expectations, and expected changes in customer requirements and expectations, to develop your strategic direction. In the Human Resources Development and Management section, you are asked how training, communication, and reward systems are used to involve everyone in customer-focused improvement. In the Process Management area, you are asked to be explicit about how customer requirements are translated into product and service design requirements and into requirements for improvement. In the Business Results area, you are asked what the current levels and trends are in the key measures of service and product quality. In other words, the Baldrige Criteria has a comprehensive list of questions that guide you in creating a customer-sensitive organization, where strategies, products, services, and operations are all working from customer satisfaction, and toward customer delight (Domb 1995).

Understanding who the customers are and linking them to the mission and vision of your organization, involves understanding not only what the customers' needs are, as we have been exploring here, but also what your core business is—your mission—and relating that to the customer needs you have identified.

a. Identifying Core Processes and relating them to customer needs

A first activity in embedding the voice of the customer in the planning process is to start looking at the core operational processes in the business. A core operational process is one that directly contributes to the provision of the business' products or services—that is, it is aligned to the business' mission.

In this step, the organization examines those *core processes* and assesses how each of these processes supports or affects the specific customer needs identified at the secondary level (Figure 14.8). In so doing, the organization

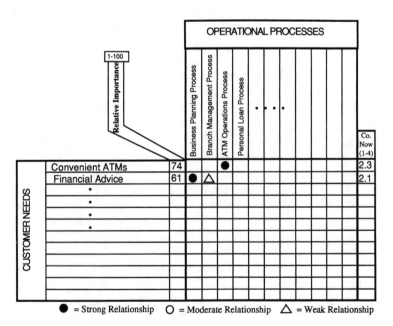

Figure 14.8 Patelco tests their ability to meet customer needs by examining the core processes of the business, including the planning process.

can identify gaps between priority needs of the customers and the strengths and/or gaps in the organization's processes and their ability to meet those customer expectations. Numerical weights can also be assigned to the relative relationships. In including customer priority and current assessment, it also allows the organization to weigh process improvement priorities to meet the greatest improvement need.

Once this has been done, it enables an organization to assess whether the operational processes, those core business processes, are indeed geared to meeting those needs. (Are there any empty rows in the matrix?) It might also identify processes that are not addressing any specified customer needs, in which case one would question why we are doing them. (Are there any empty columns in the matrix?) If there are customer needs that are not being addressed by any of the operational processes, one might question what additional processes need to be put in place to meet those customer needs. Since we've already looked at the customer needs and assessed whether they are in line with what we see to be the mission and vision of the organization, it's assumed that these needs are the needs that you are choosing to address. Therefore, it is important to have the operational processes in place in order to do that. If the needs are not being addressed by current operational processes, and the leadership is unwilling or unable to add new operational processes, then one must look again at one's mission and vision. Is it a case of when we might add processes, or are we looking at a change in the scope of the business? All of these questions are critical to the strategic planning effort.

b.   Translating customer needs into measures and actions

Another piece of the process of embedding the voice of the customer in the planning process is to assess the current internal performance measures that are in place in the organization to assure that those performance measures also support customer needs. It is critically important to take this next step. This step is for the organization to examine carefully the *measurements* by which it currently evaluates its performance, and to assess how each of these measurements reflect the organization's ability or effectiveness in meeting the specific customer needs identified at the secondary level (Figure 14.9). In so doing, the organization can identify gaps in the *measurement process*, determine measurements that are, perhaps, no longer valid, or new measurements that may be required. This is not to say that the only measurements required are those reflective of customer needs, but it does say that the organization cannot know if or how effectively customer needs are being met, unless appropriate measures are in place to delineate this.

These measures need to be SMART measures, as well. That is, they need to be Specific—specific to the customer needs. The customer doesn't care how many tickets were sold to a specific movie, or how many depositors a bank has. But they do care about not having to wait in line, or being safe when

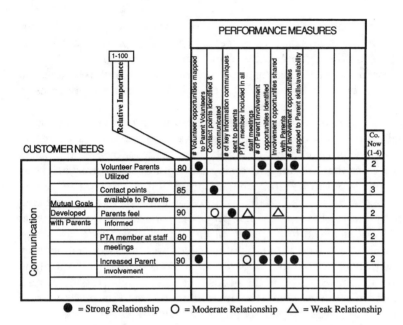

Figure 14.9   The San Ramon Valley Unified School District looks at its capabilities to provide communications to meet customer needs by examining the measures in place to evaluate internally their performance.

going to an ATM. They care about their transactions being handled quickly and accurately, about having convenient ATMs.

The second test of a measure is that it is indeed Measurable; how much, how often, how quickly. It is more than some vague "feeling."

Third, it needs to be Attainable. That is, it is within the control of the organization. In manufacturing, the product can be built to that measurable specification. In a service, the attainment of that measure can be accomplished by the organization. A sewer district, for instance, may not be able to control the river rising during severe rain storms, but they can perhaps control the *safety of the customers' homes* with dams or levees, and measure the effectiveness of those safety devices.

Next, it must be Relevant to the customer need. In addition to relevancy, it should also be predictive of satisfaction. In other words, if the measure is achieved then the need is achieved, and you should be able to predict the level of customer satisfaction.

Finally, the measure should be Time specific. There should be a timeline built into the measurement, or there should be a specified time by which the desired measure will be achieved.

c.   The importance of future trends in planning

Finally, it is necessary for the organization to assess future trends. Without assessment, we may be planning for the business to meet current customer needs, but, by the time we have done that, new needs have surfaced because the environment has changed. In this step, the organization looks to the future, identifying trends that impact the way it does business, future customer needs, and where the organization sees itself in that future. It's a time to assess how each of these trends will support, meet, or somehow impact the specific customer needs identified at the secondary level (Figure 14.10). In so doing, the organization can focus on the future and the impact of technology, regulatory issues, the economy, and so on, as well as how it will enable or alter the organization's ability to meet current and future customer expectations and needs, and how those needs or their priority might change as a result.

This is, perhaps, the most difficult and, by its nature, the most speculative aspect of the planning process. It requires market research, technology research, social or demographic research, and some of the same visionary capabilities that are needed on the part of the leadership in developing a vision. That is not to say that it is not founded on some level of data. One part of strong market research capabilities is based upon the collection and analysis of data, from yesterday as well as today. With this data collection and analysis, we can often see trends appearing and repeating over time.

These future trends also have to be compared with the Strategic Intent of the business—its mission and vision. If the future trends are not ones that align

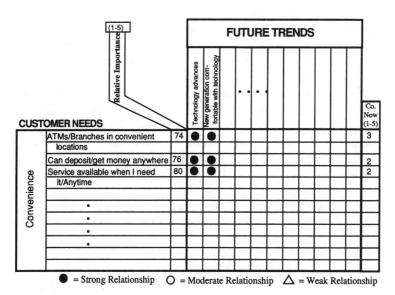

Figure 14.10 Patelco weighs the impact of technology, and the increased comfort level of its future customers with technology, as it plans its investments in capital changes, as well as its focus for the future of the finance industry and its place in that industry.

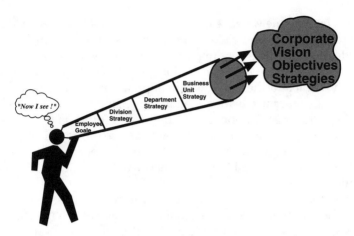

Figure 14.11   With shared information, everyone can see their role in meeting the organization's vision and customer needs.

themselves with the corporate mission and vision, some hard decisions must be made—decisions such as: Are we in the phone business or information transfer? Are we in the business of teaching or information transfer or building learning capability? Are we in the business of banking or financial services?

With these three steps addressed by the organization, it is now in a position to start looking at what the goals are that need to be identified and established in order for the organization to address these three areas—the future trends, the performance measures, and the operational processes that are going to enable the organization to meet and exceed customer needs. Those goals, along with the future trends, performance measures, and operational processes matrices that led to their creation, can then be shared throughout the organization as they are cascaded down and across the organization with specific targets, means, and measurements established to achieve them. Everybody in the organization can then see how his/her goals and targets relate to the overall goals of the organization, which in turn relate to the future trends, the performance measures and the core processes. These in turn support the customer needs, which in turn are an integral part of the organization's mission and vision. Everyone can now see how his/her job fits into the whole of meeting customer needs and making the organization successful (Figure 14.11). Everyone can feel a part of that process.

As was mentioned earlier, gather the voice of the customer first, then measure second, and third, and fourth. As with any planning process, planning with customer needs is only as good as the follow-through with targets, means, actions (Figure 14.12), and the meaningful measures tying them together—to those customer needs, and to the mission and vision for the organization. Otherwise, the individual entities within the organization could find themselves achieving their aims to the detriment of others and the organization as a whole.

STEP SEVEN: Providing the Infrastructure to Use the Plans and Keep It Current

How do you get there? The organization took the first steps with the identification of customer needs. Building the ongoing review of customer satisfaction can now be made part of the day-to-day activity of everyone having contact with customers. The customer service center is a front line that provides great opportunity for continuous feedback, as does the sales force. These avenues can be supplemented with "exit" surveys and mail surveys. Additional customer interviews and focus groups might also be used on a periodic basis to check customer perceptions and changing needs.

To do this, though, requires the commitment of the company to building an infrastructure that supports the customer-focused approach. Not only do measurements have to change to reflect the new focus on customer requirements and the actions to make those happen, but an additional measure for everyone has to be the role they might play in continuously listening to the customer and using that voice to improve their operations, product, and service focus.

A system for constantly renewing that voice must be put in place. In the implementation of any change effort—and planning is a change effort— must be a means to renew the direction and approach based on the ongoing changes that will continue to occur. The "audits" of both the customer's changing needs, and the changes made to improve the ability to meet those needs, enable the potential renewal of both the needs and the goals, targets,

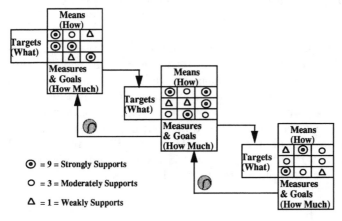

Figure 14.12 The Target-Means Matrix exemplifies how strategic goals at the top of the organization are cascaded down into meaningful action plans at all levels of the organization, with the assurance that they are relevant to those strategic goals.

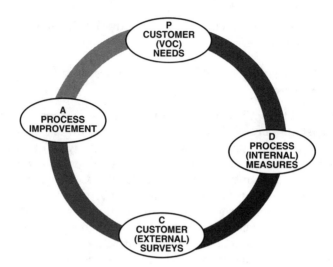

Figure 14.13 The PDCA (Plan-Do-Check-Act) cycle is equally applicable here in the planning process as in any process that needs to be continuously reviewed for improvement opportunity.

and actions to meet them. In an established system, this might be referred to as managing the changes to meet customer needs on a daily basis—or, daily management of customer requirements.

All this emphasizes the need for customer focus to become the focal point of the way in which we plan, operate, and measure our business activities, as well as the need to continuously audit that Voice of the Customer, both formally and informally. As you audit your business, so must you audit your "Voice of the Customer" in your planning process (Figure 14.13).

The voice of the customer provides the foundation for planning. Internal measures enable you to focus on the means to meet those needs through your products and services. External measures, through customer surveys, provide feedback on the value of the products and services in meeting those needs. Where this feedback identifies continued weaknesses, or products and services failing to meet or exceed customer requirements, two alternatives need to be addressed. First, internal measures need to be re-addressed to determine why they failed to assure needs were met. Only then should process improvements be implemented to "fix the processes."

CONCLUSION

Understand who your customers are. *Listen* to their voices, their needs in their own words. Listen openly and often. Listen to customer complaints and praise, but don't stop there. Look for the root cause of the complaint and, yes, of the praise as well, for behind both may lie a customer need that wants to be met, or better met. Heed those words, their priorities, and their perceptions, and incorporate them into your planning process. Measure, measure, and measure. Measure your processes, your measurements, your customer satisfaction. Set in place a system for on-going listening and auditing of not only your measurements and core processes, but of your planning process as well. Standardize your planning process as you would any business process, and then work continuously to improve it based on the future and your customers' needs.

REFERENCES

Albrecht, Karl. *At America's Service*. New York: Warner Books, 1988.

American Productivity and Quality Center. *Measurement Handbook*. Houston: APQC, 1993.

Bemowski, Karen. "The Journey Might Wander a Bit . . ." *Quality Progress*, May 1996, pp. 33–42.

Camp, Robert C. *Benchmarking: The Search for Industry Best Practices that Lead to Superior Performance*. Milwaukee: ASQC Quality Press, 1989.

Day, Ronald G. *Quality Function Deployment: Linking a Company with its Customers*. Milwaukee: ASQC Quality Press, 1993.

Deming, W. Edwards. *Out of the Crisis*. Cambridge, MA: Massachusetts Institute of Technology, 1986.

Domb, Ellen. *The Voice of the Customer*. Windham, NH: Markon Publishers, 1995.

Drucker, Peter F. *Managing in a Time of Great Change*. New York: Dutton, 1995.

Ernst and Young, *Quality Progress*, March 1994, pp. 83–92. Study of Quality Practices in the US, Europe, and Japan. 1994.

Fuld, Leonard M. *Competitor Intelligence: How to Get It, How to Use It*. New York: John Wiley, 1985.

Gale, Bradley T. *Managing Customer Value*. New York: Free Press, 1994.

Griffin, Abbie and Hauser, John R. "The Voice of the Customer." In *Marketing Science* (Winter 1993) 12:1.

Hayes, Bob E. *Measuring Customer Satisfaction: Development and Use of Questionnaires*. Milwaukee: ASQC Quality Press, 1992.

Hronek, Steve. *Vital Signs*. New York: American Management Association, 1993.

International Institute for Benchmarking. Houston: American Productivity and Quality Center, 1996.

Juran, J.M. *A History of Managing for Quality*. Milwaukee: ASQC Quality Press, 1995.

——. *Juran on Leadership for Quality*. New York: Free Press, 1989.

Klein, Robert L. "New Techniques for Listening to the Voice of the Customer." In *Transactions from the Second Symposium on Quality Function Deployment* at Novi, MI. Waltham, MA: Applied Marketing Science, 1990.

Langford, David P. A Teacher's Perspective on TQM: How to Nurture the Spark. In *Quality & Education: Critical Linkages*, ed. Betty L. McCormick. Princeton Junction, NJ: Eye on Education, 1993.

Lawton, Robin L. *Creating a Customer-Centered Culture: Leadership in Quality, Innovation, and Speed*. Milwaukee: ASQC Quality Press, 1993.

Liner, Marilyn, Douglas Daetz, Fredric Laurentine, and Rick Norman. "A Road Map for Gathering Data from Customers: Lessons from Experience." In *Transactions from The Sixth Symposium on Quality Function Deployment* at Novi, MI. Methuen, MA: GOAL/QPC, 1994.

Malcolm Baldrige National Quality Award Criteria. National Institute of Science and Technology (Gathersburg, MD), Department of Commerce, 1996.

Schargel, Franklin P. *Transforming Education Through Total Quality Management: A Practitioner's Guide*. Princeton Junction, NJ: Eye on Education, 1994.

Stack, Jack. *The Great Game of Business*. New York: Doubleday, 1994.

Watson, Gregory H. *The Benchmarking Workbook*. Portland, OR: Productivity Press, 1992.

Zeithaml, Valerie A., A. Parasuranan, and Leonard L. Berry. *Delivering Quality Service: Balancing Customer Perceptions and Expectations*. New York: Free Press, 1990.

Zemke, Ron and Schaaf, Dick. *The Service Edge: 101 Companies that Profit from Customer Care*. New York: Plume Printing, 1990.

ATTACHMENT 1: THE INTERVIEW PROCESS—
SCHOOL DISTRICT EXAMPLE

Recruiting

Here's a potential introduction when you are trying to recruit people to interview: Hello, I'm calling from the San Ramon Valley Unified School District Strategic Planning Communications Action Team. We are conducting a research project with people affiliated in some way with our schools or school system. This is **ABSOLUTELY NOT A SALES CALL, OR A CALL ASKING YOU FOR MONEY**. May I ask you a few questions?

1. First of all, do you, or does any member of your household, work for any of the following types of companies? (**READ ENTIRE LIST AND IF ANY DO APPLY, THANK THEM AND DO NOT USE THEM FOR THE INTERVIEW.**)

    Advertising or public relations agency or department

    Market research or marketing consulting firm or department

    Any school, school district or school board (unless you are looking to interview members of this school system. What you don't want is a *parent* who happens to work for another school district.)

    Have you ever run for a school board position?

2. Which of the following categories includes your age? **READ LIST AND CIRCLE ONE CODE ONLY**.

Under 21	45–54
21–24	55–64
25–34	65 and over
35–44	

Invitation:

We are inviting select individuals to participate in a more detailed interview to talk about how the various components of the school district communicate with you, how you communicate with them, and how they can better meet your needs in the area of communication. It is a great opportunity for people like yourself to express their opinions about our school system's communication process. I assure you that no promotional or political pitch of any kind is involved, and your name will not be released for any promotion, publicity, or political use. Can we count on you to help us?

If Yes, Schedule an Appointment, Record Name, Address, Phone Number, and Appointment Time, as Well as Affiliation and Age Group, on Next Page:

DEMOGRAPHIC INFORMATION

NAME:_____

ADDRESS:_____

CITY:_____   STATE:_____ ZIP:_____

PHONE:_____   INTERVIEWER:_____

APPOINTMENT DATE:_____   TIME:_____

CIRCLE AFFILIATION:

    District Office (business, personnel, instructional, superintendent, service center)

    School Board

    School Sites (principal, teacher, staff, PTA/Boosters, parent (specific site), student, classified, site council)

    Community (general, parents (multiple sites), media, religious, service groups, social services)

    Legislators

    Foundations

    Business Community

CIRCLE GENDER: M F (DON'T ASK, USE VOICE OR NAME TO IDENTIFY.)

Interview Guide

INTRODUCTION

My name is_____. I'm with the San Ramon Valley Unified School District Strategic Planning Communication Action Team that is helping the school district identify some ways they can improve their communications plan. We're conducting a study to find out what people affiliated with the schools/school district want and need from the school system's communication systems. I have some questions I'd like to ask, but feel free to talk about whatever you think is important in the way the school system communicates with you. Any Questions?

No right answers	There are no right or wrong answers. We're here to find out what you think.
Taped	We'd like to record this so we don't miss anything, or spend all of our time scribbling notes.
Lots of probing	We'll probably ask a lot of "Why's." We want to make sure we understand your needs and any problems you're having.
Confidential	These discussions are only for our use, and nobody will ever come back to you and say "I heard what you said about such and such."

THE INTERVIEW
(ONLY ASK THIS QUESTION IF THE PERSON IS *NOT* EMPLOYED IN THE SCHOOL DISTRICT, OTHERWISE ASK THEM TO TELL YOU A LITTLE ABOUT THEIR JOB.) First, please tell me a little about your affiliation with the schools/school district.

Describe the **types of contacts** that you have with the schools/school district/board or anyone else with whom you might have occasion to be in contact.

When do you have contact?

What are these interactions about?

How satisfied are you with these contacts? Why? What could have been better about them?

INFORMATION:

If something important was happening at your_____ (school, school district), how would go about finding out about it?

Why do you use that route?

Where else might you go? Why?

Do you often check more than one source? Why?

Do you get the information you are looking for?

COMMUNICATING:

If you felt strongly about something, or had something important to communicate, how would you communicate it and to whom? Why that route?

What kind of communication do you currently receive?

How do you receive it?

Is some more important? Which is more useful/least useful?

What communications would you like to receive?

How would you like to receive it?

Ideally, how do you think important information should be communicated? Both ways? Why? How would this improve the two-way communication process?

What else should the school district/school do for you or offer you in terms of communication?

CLOSE

ATTACHMENT 2: HIERARCHY OF NEEDS—
SCHOOL DISTRICT EXAMPLE

Strategic/ Primary	*Tactical/ Secondary*	*Detailed/Tertiary*
	Mutual goals developed with Parents	Volunteer parents utilized Contact points available to parents Parents feel informed PTA member at staff meetings Increased parent involvement
	Secretaries have info to answer questions	Secretaries work as team Secretaries participate in office decisions Direct communication from administration Teachers share info on problem students re: attendance Team approach with teachers Info officer for news coverage of good things happening Secretarial/support there to help and answer questions Opportunity to meet with peers and share information
Communication	**Students involved**	Student to student awareness of all that goes on Ask students about new procedures (report cards) Explain what "competent" means Listen to students Make student bulletin information more interesting Students involved in quality control of communications Site administration more in touch with classroom situation Classrooms suited to students asking questions Regular meetings between students and leadership/teachers Ask students, involve students in communication/decision making

Timely pertinent communication	Earlier status on students
	More timely info on student progress
	Quality, cohesive communication from district to site
	Direct communication with those impacted/involved
	Communication of expectations
	Clear messages of what needs to be done
	Consistent communications
	Clear, concise, relevant communication
	Speedy response to parent communication
	Cross grade-level meetings
	More communication from teachers to parents
	More site to site communication
	More site specific, more valuable
	Standards for what needs to be communicated when
	Know what board is doing
	More fluency of communication
	More in-depth communication admin to admin

Index

References to illustrations and tables are printed in **boldface** type.